Policing Sport Mega-Events

CLARENDON STUDIES IN CRIMINOLOGY

Published under the auspices of the Institute of Criminology, University of Cambridge; the Mannheim Centre, London School of Economics; and the Centre for Criminology, University of Oxford.

Recent titles in this series:

Victims and Criminal Justice: A History
Cox, Shoemaker, and Shore

Rethinking Drug Laws: Theory, History, Politics
Seddon

A Precarious Life: Community and Conflict in a Deindustrialized Town
Willis

From Conflict to Modern Slavery: The Drivers and the Deterrents
Heys

Exporting the UK Policing Brand 1989–2021
Sinclair

Penality in the Underground: The IRA's Pursuit of Informers
Dudai

Assessing the Harms of Crime: A New Framework for Criminal Policy
Greenfield and Paoli

Power and Pain in the Modern Prison: The Society of Captives Revisited
Crewe, Goldsmith, and Halsey

Armed Robbers: Identity and Cultural Mythscapes in the Lucky Country
Taylor

Policing Sport Mega-Events

Security, Spectacle, and Camouflage in Rio de Janeiro

Dennis Pauschinger

OXFORD
UNIVERSITY PRESS

OXFORD
UNIVERSITY PRESS

Great Clarendon Street, Oxford, OX2 6DP,
United Kingdom

Oxford University Press is a department of the University of Oxford.
It furthers the University's objective of excellence in research, scholarship,
and education by publishing worldwide. Oxford is a registered trade mark of
Oxford University Press in the UK and in certain other countries

First Edition published in 2024

Published in the United States of America by Oxford University Press
198 Madison Avenue, New York, NY 10016, United States of America

British Library Cataloguing in Publication Data

Data available

Library of Congress Control Number: 2023948079

ISBN 978–0–19–284805–5

DOI: 10.1093/oso/9780192848055.001.0001

Printed and bound by
CPI Group (UK) Ltd, Croydon, CR0 4YY

For my parents

General Editors' Introduction

The Clarendon Studies in Criminology Series aims to provide a forum for outstanding theoretical and empirical work in all aspects of criminology and criminal justice, broadly understood. The Editors welcome submissions from established scholars, as well as manuscripts based on excellent PhD dissertations. The Series was inaugurated in 1994, with Roger Hood as its first General Editor, following discussions between Oxford University Press and Oxford's then Centre for Criminological Research. It is edited under the auspices of three centres: the Centre for Criminology at the University of Oxford, the Institute of Criminology at the University of Cambridge, and the Mannheim Centre for Criminology at the London School of Economics. Each supplies members of the Editorial Board and, in turn, the Series General Editor or Editors.

Much criminological scholarship focuses on crime and justice in the Global North. Similarly, it typically draws on interviews or statistical evidence by way of empirical approach. In *Policing Sport Mega-Events: Security, Spectacle, and Camouflage in Rio de Janeiro*, Dennis Pauschinger takes a different approach, conducting ethnographic research in the Global South.

This engaging monograph begins with a deeply personal, first-hand account of the author arriving in São Paulo in 2002, seeing for the first time both the favelas and high-class apartment blocks as he travelled by bus and being struck by Brazil's stark socio-economic disparities. A few years later, back in Germany, his work exposed the truth about professional sport, that sport is largely about politics, a truth largely unacknowledged by sports' governance bodies. In 2014 and 2016 the World Cup and the Olympics provided the opportunity to investigate how the global security models associated with sport mega-events impact on local security conditions, in this case in Rio de Janeiro, before, during, and after the World Cup and the Olympics. Those who paid attention to the plight of migrant workers in preparation for the FIFA World Cup in the autumn of 2022 will know only too well the fertile ground that Pauschinger would likely tread.

In this study, he considers the impact of policing the poor and how prejudice, and racism in particular, shape police culture and practice, always but particularly when the world's media focuses its attention on a particular city at a particular time. In so doing, Pauschinger does not erase himself from this unsettling picture. Indeed, he reflects sensitively on his own positionality, both his privileges and his oftentimes discomfort, as he accompanies police officers charged with preparing the city for international scrutiny. At times, this makes for difficult reading, broken in places by gentle humour, but always the writing is compelling and authoritative. But if the reader is looking for a simplistic account of brutal policing and disadvantaged victims, they won't find that here. This is, instead, a subtle and nuanced account of how more powerful forces than the police shape behaviour on the streets, with an appreciation of the challenges for those tasked with tidying up.

While rich in empirical data and local colour, this book does not fail in its contribution to scholarship on security governance, particularly in a digital age. It reveals much about the various forms of sovereign power in post-colonial settings, in relation, here, to sport mega-events, a topic about which very little is known in the social sciences. Not surprisingly, Pauschinger finds that security production in this setting follows socio-spatial patterns along lines of class and race and shows how these are historically rooted in the policing (and sometimes killing) of the poor. His work contributes to Foucauldian perspectives by showing that security governance is composed of sovereign power, discipline, and security apparatuses, all working together simultaneously. His other contributions to the development of useful concepts and the theoretical scholarship draw effectively on necropolitics and the relevance of security technologies to that project as he asks the important question for all discussions of security: security for whom?

We are delighted to welcome this new addition to the Clarendon Studies in Criminology.

Mary Bosworth
Carolyn Hoyle
Centre for Criminology, University of Oxford
March 2022

Preface

I remember the day I first came to Brazil in 2002. It was an early morning in late September. I took the shuttle bus from São Paulo's international airport Guarulhos to the city airport Congonhas. I remember when I first stepped out of the airport hall to get my bus ticket how I was hit by the stuffy heat and humidity, completely different from Hamburg in the north of Germany. I remember how I was sitting in a window seat and stared outside while the bus slid into the already heavy traffic jam. The highway ran along the river Tietê. I remember the favelas we passed, half the buildings comprising wooden and stone huts and, not far away, and sometimes right alongside, the skyrocketing high-class apartment blocks. The one-hour trip was a crash course in Brazil's socio-economic disparities and racial divisions. I remember these first hours in Brazil as if it was yesterday.

Brazil, in some ways, had always been around me. By the year of my arrival in 2002, I had spent 13 years with German-Brazilian twins in the same classroom from first grade to our high-school graduation. The twins, and their black mother from São Paulo and their white German father, had always fascinatingly talked about their trips to Brazil. Their apartment in Hamburg was adorned with photographs of their Brazilian family, and the different and tasty food, as much as the parents shouting at them in Portuguese, had impressed me early on. Their aunt and cousin next door today are also friends. I always thought during my childhood and adolescent years how it would be to get to know Brazil, a country that, when they were talking about it, made their eyes sparkle. That morning in late September 2002, I did not know that the flight from Hamburg to São Paulo would be the first of many that would take me to the country I had dreamed of so many times, and that would since that day of my first arrival become an intrinsic part of my life.

When I arrived that day at the domestic airport, it took some more hours until I was picked up with other volunteers who also would work in the social organization Associação Comunitária Monte Azul for a year. My arrival that morning in the community centre changed my life forever. It was composed of a big playground, a sandpit, and trees, and the classrooms, the theatre hall, and offices, all painted colourfully. By then, it was almost noon. The background sounds of singing children who were served lunch in their kindergarten rooms, and of those who streamed out into the centre yard, filled the air. At my first lunch in Monte Azul, I was overwhelmed by the warm welcome from the staff and my fellow volunteers.

I would not be writing these lines without my time in Monte Azul, an experience that shaped me profoundly until today. I met friends for life. What most impressed me was Monte Azul's mantra that says, 'no one knows everything, and everyone has something to give'. And throughout the years I learned how this idea was lived reality in Monte Azul. People from around the world, from different socio-economic and racial backgrounds, would live, work, and have fun together. This is not to suggest that there were no tensions and conflicts. Much to the contrary. Yet, how people as humans with all their imperfections were included in Monte Azul's work and community life was and is something special.

* * *

My entrance to Brazil was through the periphery of São Paulo. The three favelas of Monte Azul, Peinha, and Horizonte Azul, in which the non-governmental organization was working, were my access to Brazilian culture, Brazilian Portuguese, and an incredible life experience. I ate magnificent meals in favela huts that were composed of only one small room. People gave without having a lot. I was made family. I met my spouse in Monte Azul, with whom I have two children today. I gained a new family and experienced the joy of life in the family reunions, the many Sunday gatherings, the epic family parties, and the love of caring for me.

I remember how the first weeks after my arrival passed very smoothly. I learned the language and the codes of living in the periphery and favela. But I also quickly realized that life in these areas is not only joy. Of course not. Right at the beginning we were told that we should take care walking outside after 11pm, when the last students came home from school. One day, people told us to watch out walking home from the nearby bus terminal where someone had been shot dead late at night. For weeks we could see the stains of blood seeping into the ground, only disappearing very slowly. The more I learned the language and made friends, the more I learned about the living conditions in the periphery. The stories of police violence and mistreatment were common; my wife's cousin was shot dead; and when in 2006 I witnessed the attacks of the criminal network Primeiro Commando da Capital (PCC), the First Command of the Capital, that paralysed the city entirely, youth of the favela rebelled against the long-time community leader and shot him one morning beside women and men on their way to work or taking their children to school. The following days shootouts and police raids tortured the neighbourhood and shifted the community power balance in a different direction.

The many accounts of my friends and my family members about their experience and humiliating encounters with the police made it clear how racist and colonial traditions continue unchanged in Brazil. The many funerals I had to attend of young and middle-aged men, or of babies gone too young, made me realize my privilege as a white man from northern Europe. I had lived an adolescence mostly without sudden death; without the experience of discrimination; without the feeling of not having enough to eat; without the lack of good education; without serious money problems; and without police violence.

After the first year in Brazil, I came back to continue my social science studies as a guest student at the University of São Paulo. Beside my studies, I was now fully employed in Monte Azul and coordinated the international volunteer programme, living just a two-minute walk from the community centre. Again, it was a steep learning curve. I transited between the favela and the university. I was shocked by the professor who taught the history of Brazilian thought, walking up and down in front of the class, saying she had pity for the poor kids in the favelas but that her task to improve society was to give classes in this university. It is thus an institution of higher education that is paid for with public money, but that excludes most of those from the peripheries and public schools from studying. I was shocked by all the super-engaged students who were talking about changing the system, but who would not show up to our local social forum in Jardim Ângela, a neighbouring district from Monte Azul, and for them probably a totally different universe. Most telling, however, were my trips from the university back to my neighbourhood, in the fully packed buses that run on one of the city's main streets beside the river Pinheiros back to the periphery. Many people would be standing or sitting asleep, coming back from long working days in the centre. And again, I would stare out of the window and watch the city pass by, calling it a monster that gnashes its teeth at you. And you must gnash back in order to survive and cope with so much beauty and suffering at the same time.

* * *

When the two years in which I could be registered as a guest student had passed, and I failed to fully register by public tender, I had to go back and continue my studies in Hamburg. Although I did not want to go at that time, the decision led to this book. Two years after my return to Germany I had the chance to work as an integration officer in Hamburg's football club. I looked behind the curtain of the football business and was responsible for the integration of the Brazilian players and their families. It was an adventure of two years in which I learned that professional sports are not just sports, but foremost politics. After many political turbulences in the club directory and the decision that they did not want to fully employ me for writing my diploma thesis on the integration of foreign players in the Bundesliga, I decided to return to another topic that had fascinated me since I had left the periphery of São Paulo, namely Brazil's public security and the rise of the PCC, whose paralysation of São Paulo had never left my memories.

After I finished my diploma thesis, I wanted to marry my fascination with how sports are intrinsically political—and the denying of this connection by many sports governance bodies—and the conditions of security governance in Brazilian cities. The opportunity came with my acceptance as a PhD student in an international Erasmus+ programme. The moment could not have been better, with two of the world's most important sport mega-events ahead in Brazil, the 2014 World Cup and the 2016 Olympics. I had formulated a project that aimed at investigating how the global security models associated with sport mega-events impacted upon the local security conditions in Rio de Janeiro before, during, and after the World Cup and the Olympics. During a preliminary research and family visit to São Paulo, I suddenly had the opportunity to travel to Rio and meet with the city's police chief to plumb the possibilities of getting access to security forces to initiate my research. The visit was fully worth it. I was enthusiastic. During the months preceding the start of my fieldwork, I also organized for myself a room in a favela, still fascinated by the bold idea of covering the perceptions of the mega-event security architecture by both community residents and Rio's police members. Soon I would realize that this endeavour was not possible, and that I had to choose one of the sides.

And I did choose the police, but this should not be confused with taking their side. It was strange to me. My image of the police was heavily influenced by what I had lived through in São Paulo, and by what my friends had gone through. And although I was able to distinguish between the individual accounts of humiliating and violent police encounters and every individual police officer that I had to meet without prejudgements, there is no doubt that there is a criminal justice system and long-term project in place that is based upon policing the poor. That is based upon racism and oppression. It is one that polices differently in poor and wealthy areas. One that treats differently people racialized as black and white. And still, I made my choice because I could. Because it was never me who was stopped, frisked, and beaten. Because it was never me who was considered the enemy just because of the colour of my skin or my address. Because I was convinced that this access was rare and exceptional.

There is already a significant and important amount of scholarly work on policing, although access to these institutions is difficult. This is even more so in Brazil, especially if the researcher is racialized as black. I am not suggesting that the access was given to me only because of my whiteness and my European origin. However, this played a fundamental role in securing my entry. For me, then, I took advantage of my privilege to come closer to an understanding of what motivates and drives police officers, police work, and, in the end, the production of what is often rightly analysed as a racist bloody urban war. And my own perspective changed. Better, it became more nuanced. Accompanying the police for my fieldwork has developed my perspective to recognize that it is important to know why the police are doing what they are doing; what the conditions are in which they are doing what they are doing; and what emotions are hidden or openly lived in what they are doing. Only then will we begin to get to the roots of what is driving the urban conflict, the system of oppression, and the racism still so openly present in Brazil and elsewhere.

* * *

I was close to tears the day of the Word Cup finalthat day. I had to leave for a moment. There I stood, emotionally moved. The fresh air did me good. The day had started early. I went with the mobile police station into the security perimeter around the Maracanã stadium. I observed how the surroundings were transformed into what I would later call a 'fortress within a fortress'. An incredible number of police officers, municipality guards, helicopters, and mobile surveillance centres were present. Die Mannschaft had thrown Brazil out of the tournament in a memorable 7–1 victory. Surely this would compensate me for the years-long jokes since the loss in the 2002 final, a game that I watched just before I went to Brazil for the first time, with the two twins from my classroom. The defeat still served for years for people and family in Brazil as a focus for our football talks. Today I have ammunition. 7–1. But now, there was this epic final. In Rio. I was in Rio. Months of fieldwork in. As I had no ticket, I took advantage of the offer to watch how the day was prepared in the security perimeter around the stadium, and from within the command-and-control centre in Rio, the World Cup's security governance heart. When all the heads of states, all the public, and all the other VIPs were in the stadium and the game had kicked off, police officers and I gathered around the TVs and watched. The ambience was in my favour because Germany was playing Argentina. Vibrating, cheering, swearing. Extension. I could not take it. I had to leave. When I was back upstairs, Germany scored. Delirium.

How can one not love this game? Football. Professional sports. The Olympics. And still, I have lost my love. The more I progressed in my fieldwork, the more it became clear how professional sports is in so many ways problematic. One of these problems that came to bother me more and more was how the sport governance bodies and their counterparts in the host cities promoted a discourse that promised heaven on earth. How, through the hosting of a World Cup and Olympics, long-standing difficulties in urban planning, urban mobility, housing, social disparity, violence, and much more would be improved. There were three key moments that made me lose this love for good, and made me perceive sport mega-events as monsters—just as I see the cities of São Paulo and Rio de Janeiro, with which I have a love–hate relationship.

The first one was when I came back to Hamburg from my first longer fieldwork trip after the World Cup. I was immersed in my fieldwork data, reliving the moments in the field at my desk, when the city of Hamburg, supported by an alliance of some key media outlets, some of the city's most powerful companies, famous architect bureaus, and well-known marketing agencies, pushed to bid for hosting the 2024 Olympics. In the runoff for a referendum, the political narrative by a Social-Democratic and Green-led government was built upon putting forth the opportunities for the city instead of also informing people about the risks associated with hosting the most expensive party in the world. With other social scientists I wrote an open letter to the city with the pledge of having an open discourse about the Games, including the risks. They never responded. Luckily, the government lost the referendum. For me, it was the most beautiful political experience of my life, in a David against Goliath moment. But it was the first step in losing the love.

The second moment came when the United Nations Special Adviser on Sport for Development and Peace spoke at an event that I attended, just a few days before the inauguration of the Olympics in Rio de Janeiro. He said that now we should all forget the critique and the protests and just enjoy the Games. The event was held in the port area of Rio, a region rattled by its destruction for the Games, transformed into a sort of theme park for the Olympics. Forget? Forget the suffering of thousands of removed families? Forget the dead? Forget the conditions the city was in? I was speechless.

The third time was when I was standing in the middle of the command-and-control centre in Rio, watching the Olympics closing ceremony. The control room for the event security operations was vividly filled with people working for the smooth delivery of the last hours of the Olympics. On the screen, the International Olympic Committee president in the Maracanã stadium was saying that, 'These Olympic Games are leaving a unique legacy for generations to come. History will talk about a Rio de Janeiro before and a much better Rio de Janeiro after the Olympic Games.' What a punch in the stomach. Days before, I had seen the degraded conditions in the police station. How water had infiltrated the building; how sleeping and locker rooms were in a poor state. Police officers were frustrated and stressed. There were favela incursions with fatal shootings; streams of blood running down the alleys. It is not these words that have killed the passion. It is what they represent and whom they insult.

I had to think about my father-in-law. Ademario came from the north of Brazil to find work and a better life in the city of São Paulo. He found refuge in one of the then still-wooden huts in the favela Monte Azul. He worked as a bricklayer his whole life. He improved his wooden hut and built a three-floor house in the favela. Bit by bit. Brick by brick. One floor after the other. It took years. He raised a family in difficult conditions. Dead bodies would lay in the small favela alleys, stamped upon by one of São Paulo's Special Forces. And still, his children would have only happy memories of a childhood in a special place. He made them feel beloved and protected. Ademario sang and played the triangle with passion for the *Folia dos Reis* songs, the King's Revelry, an Advent Season music parade, that would go from house to house and bless the community huts. When the illness got him, he stayed strong for years. A few weeks before the start of the World Cup, and only two years before the Olympics, he passed away. The public healthcare system had overseen a remaining part of the beast in his body. These were some of the demands of the protestors against the ways in which mega-events were organized in Brazil. Decent public healthcare instead of stadiums and a costly party for the taxpayers. Better cities? Forget?

Now it was too late. Only morphine could do the job. But even this did not work for Ademario sometimes. At night, we occasionally had to bring him to the hospital. In the daytime, too, we sometimes had to bring him to the hospital. The conditions of these places left us in despair. The last one, however, was a beautiful hospice facility, organized by one of the Monte Azul doctors at the other end of the city. The afternoon when he could finally go was heart-breaking. When we were able to put the marathon of getting all the paperwork done behind us, running from one part of the city to the other, I volunteered to sit in the passenger seat of the hearse to bring his body to the São Luis cemetery. Night had fallen. And again, we took the main road along the river. I was staring out of the window. I was unable to gnash back. The monster had won this time.

Acknowledgements

The words and lines in this book are not simply the result of my research. They are the outcome of an incredible experience that started when I first set foot in Brazil and that continues to the present day. This journey would not have been possible without the inspiration, support, and love of so many people in so many places. In many ways, I consider this book as a collective effort, supported and inspired by all of those with whom I have met, discussed, and ranted along the way.

My first and most sincere thanks goes to all my participants from Rio de Janeiro's police forces, mainly the civil police, who have granted me access to their work and life during this research. Without your openness and support, this book could not have been written. I am aware that letting me into your routines and opening your world to me was an enormous leap of faith. We probably do not agree over all my understandings of your reality, but I have tried to do justice to what I saw, heard, and lived, and to what you wanted me to see, hear, and live. This book is and cannot be a holistic picture of all of that; it is merely an interpretation of something in between. Neither is it a just representation of what the police is. Rather, it is an attempt to come to a closer understanding of your work and life. All faults are mine.

All other interview participants outside the security forces, I thank you equally sincerely for your openness, courage, and trust. Without you and your fearless fight for a better Rio de Janeiro, this work would not be the same.

We do not write books without editors and reviewers. Thank you, Kyle Treiber and Loraine Gelsthorpe at the Clarendon Studies in Criminology at Oxford University Press, for accepting my proposal. To the editors, Kate Plunkett and Fiona Briden, thanks so much for your patient and trustful work with me. I am also deeply thankful to the anonymous reviewers and the Series Board for their insightful and helpful commentary on the proposal and manuscript. Nor do I, as a non-native English speaker, write books without proofreaders. Bex Houghton was of tremendous help in proofreading early versions of PhD chapters. I am truly grateful to Majid

Yar who has been a steady companion and hero in proofreading the final PhD version, the later articles, and this manuscript. Thank you for your patience, endurance, and encouragement; it means the world. Many thanks also go to Sally Evans-Darby engaged by OUP to have given this manuscript its final but important language shape. We cannot do research in the same way without research assistants. Rayssa Drumond de Barros Alcantara, you have been an incredible help with the transcriptions of my interviews. This was excellent work, and I express my appreciation. I have received generous funding as a European Commission EACEA Erasmus+ fellow in the Doctorate in Cultural and Global Criminology (DCGC). Thank you.

A very first version of this final product was submitted as a PhD thesis in the DCGC at the University of Kent and the University of Hamburg. It was an honour working with my two PhD supervisors, Keith Hayward in Kent and Susanne Krasmann in Hamburg. I will never forget how I first met Keith in his office in September 2013, when he said to me, 'Great project, now you've got to do it!'. I did it. Keith and Susanne, both your nuanced and severe assessment of the chapters, and your patience and encouragement along the way, have carried me through this at times painful process of writing a PhD thesis. My gratitude.

Thanks to the whole DCGC team in Kent, Hamburg, Utrecht, and Budapest—especially to Bettina Paul in Hamburg, Damian Zaitch in Utrecht, and Phil Carney in Kent. Kudos for all those hours invested and making us candidates believe in this crazy endeavour of writing a PhD thesis in three years, in two different universities, in two different countries. This was interesting! The endless efforts of Kalliopi Glezakou and Sarah Marsh have made me speechless; thanks. To Ulf Beckmann and Marisa Shabaz at the University of Hamburg's Graduate School, thank you for your confidence and patience.

Recognition goes to all my DCGC fellows, especially to Camille Stengel, Laura Naegler, Monika Weissensteiner, Veronica Nagy (the most Brazilian Hungarian I know), and Vitor Stegemann Dieter. To my cohort fellows, Aice Jutahtorn Pravattiyagul, Benedikt Lehmann, Chuan-Fen Chang, Clara Musto, José Maria Cornejo, and Rosa Koenraadt, this voyage would not have been as beautiful without you. Some of you have become close friends, with frequent talks, even if there is physical distance between us. I miss you and think of you. Claudio Altenhain, thanks for the friendship. You are a titan in how you cope with it all. I believe in you, please do too. Stefano Mazzilli-Daechsel, thanks so much for your friendship, ears, and support. Jairo Mattallana Villareal, that special place in my heart. You know it. Gracias! While at the University of Kent, I first shared a house with my colleague Chuan-Fen in Whitstable. What a magical place at the beach. Thank you for all those talks over dinner. Then, the landlords came back from Canada. Susan Turcot, Chris Wilbert, and Quinn, you made my stay in a difficult situation so much easier and made me feel at home. Thank you. PhD offices are a luxury, especially if you have the possibility of sharing them with such wonderful people as Felix Lösing, Clemens Reichhold, Helge Schwiertz, and Eric Bityili bi Nleme. Thanks also especially to Mark Wigley in Kent and Fernando Ribeiro de Almeida in Hamburg. All this would not have been as much fun without your company; thanks.

In Rio de Janeiro, many people have given me support, hosted me, lent their ears, and given me the feeling I could reach out to them when needed. Thanks to David Fischer for the contacts and the joy. Kai Schiller, your company was outstanding. Nicholas Barnes and Sara Koenders, that evening when we first met was decisive for my work in Rio. You showed me how exceptional my access was. Thank you for all the gatherings, talks, and continued support. Ana Beatriz Motta, thank you for showing me the city through your eyes and all the talks. Peer Vorderwülbecke, our late-night conversations after long workdays were essential to mentally survive. Forever grateful to you and *carne seca com aipim*. Christopher Gaffney, thank you for the support in Rio, Hamburg, and beyond. You are the most persistent fighter I know. Remember that night at the kiosk in Botafogo, a day after the closing ceremony? They may have won that time, but you made them stumble. More importantly, you have transformed the moment of defeat into a powerful energy to continue. I am especially grateful to Claudia Sanen and Evgeny Makarov. Claudia, you have so gratefully shared your passion for Rio with me and provided me with so many contacts. Truly thankful. Evgeny, the Gizzle, is there any more faithful, thoughtful, and joyful soul than you? Thank you for being this friend to me! Ilse Block, thanks so much for your unconditional hospitality and for connecting me with my months-long host in town. Tereza Pichniski Araujo, you have made the home a home; thanks for this and your kindness. Silvana Mendes Lima, you have given me so much confidence. Thank you for being there for me. Alessandra Speranza Lacaz and Antônio Pedro Campello Pereira Porto Soares, our conversations, your advice, and living with you, Madalena, and Misha was a moment of peace in these chaotic times. Thank you, Alessandra, for the continued conversations and friendship. Sheena Rossiter and Sandro Augusto Santos Silva, thank you for hosting me when I most needed it. Sandro, we hadn't talked for months and then we were suddenly neighbours in Rio. Our reunion was more than destiny. I admire you and your path! Thanks for this friendship and *vai Cronthians*! Bruno de Vasconcelos Cardoso, your generous sharing of the field, your willingness to provide me with your rich knowledge of our common research topics, and your impressive political analysis have offered incredible guidance. I miss our discussions over lunch and dinner. Thank you from my heart for all your support, *meu amigo*. Regina and César Banhos, you have made all this possible! I thank you for the substantial assistance you have given me, the comfort of a family, and the assurance of having a place to go. This is immeasurable.

I came to Switzerland as a freshly graduated PhD to start a postdoc in the Institute of Geography at the University of Neuchâtel in early 2017. Now, seven years later, I can just say thank you. Gratitude goes to the whole IGG team in Neuchâtel for providing such an extraordinary working environment. Of course, there could have been a few more apéros at the lake. Don't hesitate to invite me to any in the future. Thanks to Noémie Béguelin Caudoux and Floriane Desaules for your endless support and welcome. I am particularly grateful to Ola Söderström for his tireless efforts in discussing ideas and helping me whenever needed. I was chiefly moved by the support of colleagues who have turned into friends during these years. Thanks so much to Evan Blake, who has been such an inspiration and brother in spirit. Isabelle Schoepfer, those runs and talks were great. Sunčana Laketa, you have encouraged me so much. Raoul Kaenzig, your advice and support has meant the world to me. The squad from 2.S.39, Marc Winz, Suzy Blondin, and Loic Bruening—our friendship was essential for this journey. Marc, our talks were of such importance for finding my way. Glad that they continue. To my drone team member Silvana Pedrozo, I have so much admiration for what you have achieved these last years and the decisions you have taken. Thank you so much for our exchanges that endure. I owe much of where I am now to Francisco Klauser. No one else pushed me harder than you to finish (and start) this book. Here it finally is! When you encouraged me more than ten years ago, that evening in Hamburg, to write my PhD thesis, I was not aware of what this meant. The adventure was more than worth it! Your work has been such an inspiration and your unconditional support throughout the years, even before we worked together, so moving. Our professional relationship may have ended; the friendship, however, has just started.

My path into academia was rather uncommon. This book is, for the time being, my last step in this business. The job uncertainty, the obligation to move the family to continue, and the unknown future was not bearable for us anymore. To all of you who are still fighting this fight—do not get drowned. You are so much more than this industry. Your work and effort are worth so much more. Tremendous respect! On my path in academia, I have been invited to workshops and conferences whose audiences have given me feedback that has heavily influenced this book. Thanks go especially to the Gangs, Prisons and Drugs Workshop on the Dynamics of Violence in Brazilian Cities at the University of Cambridge, 2016. Thanks to Graham Denyer Willis for the invitation and all the help. You and your work are an inspiration. Appreciation to the participants for substantial feedback at the Urban Policing and Practices of B/Ordering Workshop at the Dignity Institute against Torture and the DIIS in Copenhagen, 2017 and at the University of Aarhus, 2018. Maya Mynster Christensen and Peter Alexander Albrecht, thanks so much for the invitation and all the support. This was rock 'n' roll. The feedback from the participants at the Gendered and Racialized Urban Transformations in Security Politics Workshop and the special section workshop, both at the Centre for Women's and Gender Research and the Department of Social Anthropology at the University of Bergen in January and October 2018, has made this work better. A special nod to Margit Ystanes and Tomas Salem for their concerted efforts, their invitation, and their encouragement. This was more than just a joint writing project! Also to the brave organizers of the best sports politics conferences, Play the Game, especially Jens Jeser Andersen.

Many people have inspired and helped me with their work and in conversations in and around academia. A special thanks goes to Alessandro Moretti, Anja Vogelpohl, Alex Stevens, Antonia Mischler, Christina Mitmasser, Erika Robb Larkins, Etienne Piguet, Flavia Medeiros Santos, Frank Müller, Giulia Zampini, Ingrid Hapke, Jacinto Cuvi, Jaime Amparo Alves, Joachim Michael, John Lauermann, Jonathan Ilan, Jules Boykoff, Juliana Barbassa, Larry Ray, Luiz Eduardo Soares, Lucas Melgaço, Martin Müller, Martine Rebetez, Matthias Fett, Matthew Richmond, Maximilian Jablonowski, Michel Misse, Niklas Franzen, Paul Mutsaers, Randi Gressgård, Rodrigo Firmino, Stefanie Dodt, Sybille Bauriedl, Ramazan Hakki Öztan (those afternoons at the lake with that water quality), Torin Monahan, and Yvonne Riaño. Sven Daniel Wolfe, we have not known each other very long, but it feels like we have known each other forever. Your support and friendship have carried me these last months. There are no words other than you are the ... of ... and the ... of ...! The future is yours! Pete Fussey, your work has been so important to me; what an inspiration.

Even more impressive and fabulous has been your attitude of helping and including young scholars in academia like I was as a PhD student. Thanks for that advice in Salvador in the taxi to keep pushing for a good publisher. Sebastian Scheerer, if you would not have told me about the DCGC, I would probably not have known. Thank you for the support. Nils Zurawski, you have supported me and opened so many doors. Without you, I would not have known my way to the PhD. Thank you for the endless efforts to push me further, looking at my work, and including me in your projects. The real storms in Aarhus, and the political ones in Hamburg, have just strengthened our ties. Thank you.

On our way, we sometimes come across people from whom we learn so much. I was privileged to have worked with Marinus Bester at Hamburg's professional football club HSV. Thank you for the confidence and support, and for showing me how pragmatism works. Matthias Kreutzer, your support and your generosity have been marvellous. Zé Roberto has been an enormous source of tranquility, wisdom, and friendship. Thank you for the confidence.

It would have been impossible to realize this project without the backing of family and friends in various situations in Germany, Switzerland, Brazil, and elsewhere. I cannot mention everyone here but I thank you from the heart. Thanks especially to Aline Djokic (for opening the door to the world of football), Ana Tereza de Freitas Quintão Américo, Birthe Kalkreuter, Carolin Fischer, Céline Lüthi, Clarissa Cavalheiro Skrepnek, Dagmar Freythaler, Diego Company, Dunja Batarilo, Edda Riedel, Eric Alban (for the long nights in the garden), Fabio Blaser, Friedel Nimax, Henning Drews, Iris Hartmann, Jan Freythaler, Jeremy Mage (for the walks and talks), Julie Kummer, Lena Conradi, Manfred Pauschinger, Marion Farine, Mascha Saß, Maxime Piras, Melf Hinrich Ehlers, Micha Käser, Ole Seidenberg, Oliver Rückner, Stéphan Neri, and Vieira—thank you very much.

I thank the community of Monte Azul which has welcomed me so many times in São Paulo. There are too many people to thank personally, but Cintia Kogeyama, Lindalva Vitorino da Silva, Renate Keller Ignacio, and Ute Craemer have been of special importance to me. Rudolf Völker, you were the first person that I met from the global Monte Azul community. Thanks for all your advice and our conversations. Ronald Stephan, your way of doing things is enthusing. Every talk with you has made me cheer and reflect. Valéria Carrilho Rückner, there are no words to describe the rock of confidence you have been for me. My friend Rogério Vieira, I miss our pasta nights, full of movies, discussions, and music. You have taught me so much about life in the quebrada. Daniel Maldaner, is it really statistics that have bound us together? Of course there is much more. Thanks for everything, especially for your amity.

They might not know how important they were, but Rosa da Silva Wichmann, Karl Wichmann, Sinchi Marcelo da Silva Wichmann, Muna Rodrigo da Silva Wichmann, Miriam da Silva, and Ana Carolina Carvalho da Silva have been essential to sparking my desire to be in Brazil before I was even physically there. Miriam, thanks for the continuous friendship. Ulf Treger, one of the partners in crime against Hamburg's Olympic bid—so happy we have maintained the friendship beyond that. Katharina and Salomon, so good to know you for so long. Salomon, mon Lulu, the late-night black teas and discussions at the Turk have been a source of strength to me. The old Mensa team, also called the Otzen—Evgeny Makarov, Dominik Betz, Maurice Emmerich, and Nils Goede—thank you so much for your support. Nils, you have told me to breathe at the right time. This was essential. To my childhood friends and exclusive members of the Herrenabend, David Kamp, Julien Zazoff, Kester Mayr, Lasse Bagdahn, and Maximilian Wort—it is a privilege to have friends that we consider family. One love. Alain Frund has generously provided me with an office in his spare room to finish this book and became a friend. *Merci infiniment*! Alessandro Covi and Maria Covi-Cosmatu, I am deeply grateful to have you in my life. Alessandro, your amity, moral support, and encouragement have been a guide to me. Our special connection started 20 years ago in Brazil and continues firmly here, now, and in the future. Thank you.

To my Swiss family, who have hosted and supported me whenever I needed—thanks Melaine Laesslé, and Catharina Laesslé, Sophie Laesslé, and Thiery Laesslé. To the La Croix gang, Emma, Margaux, Ambre, Léonis, and Audrey. Melaine your encouragement and friendship mean so much and continue to be a gift. Alain Laesslé and Edwige Ochsenbein, the stay with you when I was 15 has laid much of the ground on which I am walking today. Forever grateful. Edwige, you were like a mother to me then, and such a rock in my life after my stay with you. You have gone too soon, and I miss you terribly.

To my family in Brazil, Ademario Lima, Cenira Pereira, William Pereira, and Sidnei Lima—you welcomed me into your midst from the first day, shared your house, and took me in like a son and brother. The love you gave means so much. I know it is not easy that we are not there. I am deeply sorry for that. Of course, Andrea Sampaio and Rafael Sampaio as well as Cleidiana Lima and Lis, thank you. Ademario, your strength has been that of a titan. We miss you every day. Your story, your smile, and your unbroken optimism lives on in us and we know you are in a better place now, cheering to us.

I am a privileged person to have been born into my family. To my brothers, Robin Pauschinger, Marvin Schmelzer-Pauschinger, and Felix Pauschinger. I could not have imagined having better siblings. Growing up with you has taught me to share, to love, and to fight, all of which has made me the person I am. I would not be myself without you. Thank you to Tina Stalf, Milan and Clea, Hannah Schmelzer, Antonia Restemeier, and Maël for enriching our family. My parents, Carmen and Michael Pauschinger—I can barely put into words how grateful I am for all the support, love, and encouragement you have given me. I have learned to face the world and go out there from you, and still do. Be sure, I will always be there for you. I love you.

Emilio and Luisa Nubia, you both are the joy of my life. You are the best thing that could ever have happened to me. I am humbled by your love and existence. I love you more than you can yet imagine. Finally, to the love of my life, the best mother I could have wished for our children, and the reason for whom I am, Elisangela de Souza Almeida, Lica. You have accompanied, endured, and loved me, no matter what. We have come a long way, and I am so proud of you, for everything you have achieved, and how you carry our family. I learn with you every day, and I would never ever have come so far without you. I thank you from the bottom of my heart and will always be grateful to have had the luck that you found me. I am looking forward to continuing our walk, hand in hand, side by side. I love you so much.

Some parts of this book appeared earlier in *Environment and Planning D: Society and Space*, *Conflict and Society: Advances in Research*, and *Security Dialogue*.

Contents

List of Tables

PART I

SECURITY

Introduction

Security for Whom?

On a sunny day I was standing within the security perimeter around the Maracanã stadium during the 2014 World Cup. I listened to a conversation between a Special Forces member and another regular police officer. The Special Forces officer opined, 'The war came back. You cannot relax. The other day we killed one, injured another, and arrested one of them.' The police officer right next to him objected, 'You didn't kill, it was God who took him.' Nodding approvingly, the Special Forces member replied, 'You are right, we only pulled the trigger.'[1]

The conversation unfolded in the middle of a World Cup surrounded by thousands of officers from diverse police institutions. The military was accompanying the national football delegations, with the stadium totally isolated from the rest of the urban setting, and helicopters were roaring above our heads. Private security officers were checking tickets while municipal guards were bringing young black men to the mobile police station right next to us, young men who, according to the guards, did not fit in this white FIFA[2] consumerist festival. Rio de Janeiro, it seemed, was transformed into a spectacular militarized security fortress.

On my tours around the stadium, I was always struck by the enormous mirrored walls of the Maracanã VIP entrance. In the glass façade's reflection, one can see the traditional and well-known favela Mangueira, located a few hundred metres away. On 30 October 2014, approximately three and a half months after the World Cup, five dead men were found in a car near the favela. The homicides were tied to a fight between rival drug-dealing networks in the community. The Mangueira's reflection in the stadium's VIP entrance is also a symbol of the glittery public discourse from the sport mega-event organizers who try to omit the reality of violence and

[1] All quotes from fieldwork and interviews that were originally in Brazilian Portuguese are my own translations.

[2] Fédération Internationale de Football Association.

Policing Sport Mega-Events. Dennis Pauschinger, Oxford University Press. © Dennis Pauschinger 2024.
DOI: 10.1093/oso/9780192848055.003.0001

death mentioned by my two interlocutors. While the government claimed to have everything under control, the above conversation and the dead in Mangueira speak of a totally different story. These memories are not only emblematic of the public security situation in Rio but also capture many of the problems that were symptomatic of Brazil's mega-event editions, and are representative of the ways in which security at sport mega-events and in urban settings is often organized today.

Since I started my research on sport mega-event security in Rio de Janeiro, I increasingly had the impression that there was something going on that was difficult to grasp at first. There were many moments during the research where that 'difficult-to-grasp feeling', that something was wrong, was popping up. But the longer I accompanied Rio's security forces and civil police officers, the more it became clear what kind of discrepancy had opened up between what happened on the ground and what official sources like the Brazilian security authorities and the sport governance bodies, like FIFA and the International Olympic Committee (IOC), communicated.

As I listened to the two officers on that sunny day, I was struck by this simple question: *security for whom?* Clearly something else was going on other than the *security spectacle* I could observe around me. Now, a few years later, the same question comes back again and again, when one horrific piece of news chases the next in Rio de Janeiro's public security complex: whether it is the cold-blooded assassination of black Brazilian local politician Marielle Franco, the death of children by 'stray' bullets, or the most lethal police raid in the history of the city in 2021 where 27 people and one police officer were killed in the favela complex Jacarezinho.

Security for Whom?

This question lies at the heart of this book. For whom is security organized, in which circumstances, at which costs? What kind of security and with what aims and mechanisms? Centrally, we can ask this question for cities in general; however, it becomes an ever-more urgent issue when we look at urban centres like Rio de Janeiro and others in the so-called Global South where the immediacy of social disparities and the thin line between life and death are everyday realities, where they are daily negotiated in situ.

'Security for whom?' gets even more urgent in times in which Big Data, algorithms, and new technologies are integrated in everyday policing routines in many cities worldwide. Promising greater efficiency, effectiveness, and a reduction in violent conflict, smart and predictive policing strategies, however, co-exist and intermingle with repressive and lethal forms of state violence. This kind of common urban security narrative, which reflects a belief in the ability of smart technologies to resolve our everyday problems of policing and insecurity, is a steady marketing strategy for urban policy-makers and sport mega-event security organizers alike. This book then looks at this global phenomenon of the simultaneity of the implementation of digital security technologies and the continuous police brutality in cities through the example of Rio.

Attempts to come closer to an understanding of 'security for whom?' have a long tradition in the social sciences, both inside and outside Brazil. Yet, the unique moment in history that produced the combination of mega-event security measures and their encounter, adaptation, and implementation in and with the pre-conditions of Rio's public security laid bare the essence of 'security for whom?' and how it is produced by globally standardized security trends, and what effects it provokes locally. Henceforth, this book highlights a global problematic that showed its most dramatic effects locally in Rio, grasps this unique moment, and extends beyond it.

Global Security Going Local

Globalized Urban Security Politics

This book is about so-called urban security politics—security politics that are deeply interlinked with the organization of sport mega-events and general security trends in cities. It is important to state that Olympic security means much more than just organizing safe sporting events. Since the terrorist attacks at the 1972 Munich Olympics, security has become an intrinsic preoccupation for mega-event organizers. However, after the fall of the Twin Towers in New York on 11 September 2001 (hereafter 9/11), sport mega-event securitization dramatically increased.[3] Mega-events are today 'monumental cultural spectacles that pose peculiar and extensive security challenges' and 'security has become an integral part of the Olympic ritual' (Bennett and Haggerty 2011, vii, 5). Yet, security measures at mega-events

[3] The sport mega-event security literature has widely published on these trends. See, for instance, Bennett and Haggarty (2011), Boyle and Haggerty (2009), Coaffee et al. (2011), Giulianotti and Klauser (2011), and Fussey and Klauser (2015). For a more recent study, see, for example, Ludvigsen (2022) on the EURO 2020.

are embedded in general security developments in the post-9/11 era and are both the product and the producer of major security expansions (Klauser 2008, 75).

Urban centres have experienced enormous fortification, militarization, and technologically enabled surveillance of urban space (Coaffee and Wood 2006). Stephen Graham (2010) has helpfully identified these tendencies as a 'New Military Urbanism' within which the military is deployed to police citizens in urban settings, or the police is equipped with military material.[4] Mixed with these provisions, new trends in security and urban management strategies have appeared and introduced new powerful vocabularies like 'smart' and 'resilience' that would make cities appear better prepared to deal with the challenges of the 21st century.[5]

Sport mega-events have increasingly pushed these security measures and their organization is accompanied by a standardization of the militarization of public security, the substantial establishment of camera surveillance, and the de facto isolation of sport venues from the rest of the city, also called 'islands of security'. These mega-event security standards migrate from one host to the next, and are developed further and adapted to the local host conditions. A security-related complex of international corporations uses mega-events to implement, sell, and test new security technologies and establish knowledge networks of mega-event security.[6] In times of the 'war on terror', uncertainty, and incalculable risks, host governments have started to 'plan for the worst'[7] and established 'Olympic spaces of exception' (Coaffee 2015) within which the above-described security measures are being implemented.

Within these trends, security associated with mega-events has currently taken forms that more resemble modern warfare than urban policing (Bennett and Haggerty 2011, 1). The EURO 2016 football tournament in France, for example, was marked by the then recent terror attacks on the surrounds of the Stade de France and at other culturally important venues. The tournament was, therefore, rigorously secured with the help of the

[4] See also Kraska (2007) and Balko (2013).

[5] For more on the use of these 'trendy' vocabularies in urban management and security politics, see Söderström et al. (2014) and Coaffee and Fussey (2015).

[6] For a detailed elaborations for this kind of security measures, see Fussey et al. (2011), Klauser (2013), and Samatas (2014). For the adaptation of specific global security standards to local conditions, see Boyle and Haggerty (2009, 270), and for the knowledge networks, see Boyle (2011).

[7] Boyle and Haggerty's (2012) article on 'planning for the worst' has become an indispensable read for the study of mega-event security.

French military, the police, and private security companies. The London 2012 Olympic Games were probably the contemporary highlight of these trends during the Summer Olympics, where 89,000 police officers were on patrol on important game days (Fussey 2015, 212). Parts of the city were occupied by military forces with surface-to-air missiles on private houses, the British navy stationed a warship on the Thames, and the UK air force launched jet fighters and helicopters over London (Boykoff and Fussey 2014, 261), to name but a few procedures that evoke what Boyle and Haggerty (2009) call Olympic 'spectacular security'. Rio de Janeiro deployed similar numbers of security personnel and types of militaristic strategies, as this book will show.

By hosting the World Cup and the Olympics consecutively, Brazil is an especially interesting site for scientific inquiry, with its highly complex public security scenario. Whereas the main trigger of mega-event securitization has been the 'war on terror', new security challenges have appeared with such events migrating to the Global South. New security and risk scenarios have emerged and been identified, such as 'social divisions' and 'urban crime', that are specific to these national contexts (Giulianotti and Klauser 2009, 51–2).

Times of Unrest

This book is also very much about the politically urgent times in which Brazil's mega-event hosting and its aftermath materialized. It was a special moment for Brazil as much as it was for the Games and its organizing bodies. When the mega-events were awarded to Brazil, the domestically and internationally popular Brazilian President Lula Inácio da Silva from the Workers' Party was in power. A skyrocketing economy had seemed to lift the notorious 'country of the future' out of the shadows of its militaristic and troubled economic past. Millions had been pulled out of poverty and the world looked at Brazil with great awe as the Workers' Party had managed to bring the country closer to mitigating the social divisions that date back to the times of slavery. The World Cup and the Olympics were meant to be the pinnacles of the country's success. Seven years after the end of the 2016 Olympics, next to nothing is left of this enthusiasm.

Much to the contrary, 2016 Brazil's old economic and social elites have impeached Brazil's democratically elected president Dilma

Rousseff on flawed allegations of financial irresponsibility, a major setback for the country's democratic values. This was a clearly politically motivated step to heave political dinosaurs back into office and escape major corruption investigations in relation to the Car Wash scandal concerning the state-owned oil company Petrobras and other construction corporations. Lula has been imprisoned and released as part of this process, based on at least highly questionable evidence. Rio de Janeiro State had to declare a state of financial emergency, the former governor Sérgio Cabral has been jailed over construction contracts for the World Cup, and the country still fights with recession and soaring levels of violence and unemployment.

The global trend that has lifted extreme right-wing politicians into power has not been absent in Brazil. In the State of Rio, an extreme-right populist, Wilson Witzel, was elected governor then removed from office, who has since sparked attention with plans to kill drug traffickers with elite police snipers rather than presenting any real plan for how to solve the political and economic problems. Witzel's successor in office, Governor Cláudio Castro, is similarly relying on the politics of violence and the path of an extreme right-wing populist. The political polarization after Rousseff's impeachment and Lula's imprisonment, mixed with a wave of fake news, elected Jair Bolsonaro president in 2018. An extreme-right populist with 28 years of experience in Congress managed to picture himself and his party as the 'new' politics, free from corruption and with easy solutions to public security issues. Yet, he and his family are tied to racist, homophobic, and sexist commentary and have links to Rio's most violent militias. As president, Bolsonaro damaged Brazil and his people seriously in numerous ways which I am not able to discuss here at large. The most striking one that made world news is surely his continuous inaction regarding and denial of the gravity of the Covid-19 pandemic and ridiculing the death of thousands; he also heaved military generals into political office, incentivized political violence, and threatened not to recognize the election results in his attempt to reach a second term. After he lost the 2022 elections against Lula, who had run to restore his political legacy and free Brazil from the damaging president, Bolsonaro stayed silent for days while his most loyal fans installed chaos on national roads throughout the country. When Bolsonaro finally spoke in front of the press, he did not congratulate his opponent and only asked his supporters half-heartedly to stop the chaos. As a consequence, on 8 January 2023, the National Congress, the governmental palace, and the federal supreme court buildings in Brasília were stormed by pro-Bolsonaro protesters in an unprecedented attack on Brazil's democratic institutions after the end of the military regime.[8]

Brazil's mega-event cycle illustrates, more than ever before, that mega-events have long been more than cheerful sporting celebrations. A year before the World Cup kicked off, the 2013 protests which took millions to the streets during the Confederations Cup showed FIFA and the Brazilian government that many people were not satisfied with the ways in which the football festival was organized. While social inequality, violence, high crime rates, and inadequate public services—such as education, social housing, and public transport—were real problems for millions of Brazilians all over the country, the government decided to build 12 FIFA-standard World Cup stadia.

The Brazilian protests were part of a global trend that saw citizens disagreeing with the manner in which the Games are organized. Cities like Boston, Oslo, Hamburg, and Sion have rejected the idea of hosting the Summer and Winter Olympics. The costs and benefits of hosting mega-events, the negative impacts of the over-sized city development projects that come in tandem with the sport spectacles, the scandal burdening sports federations, and tremendous human rights violations before, during, and after the Games have sparked much criticism among activists, critical journalists, and academics.

Despite protests and public resistance to the ways in which mega-events have been organized in recent years, the prestige of hosting such events still seems to be one of the most desirable endeavours for city governors, as the enduring candidatures and next hosts of Paris and Los Angeles for the 2024 and 2028 Olympics respectively illustrate. Mayors see the possibility of hosting mega-events as a means to hype up their city's marketing and investors see the opportunity for good deals (Ward 2007; Gold and Gold 2017, 10). Mega-events, in the end, serve equally as geopolitical projects for national leaders to reaffirm locally and globally their aspiration to power (Cornelissen 2010; Wolfe 2022). This was no different in Brazil, where the national government thought of mega-events as an example of positioning the country among those who are seen as able to host such major politicized sport events, and the local politicians in Rio thought of the mega-events

[8] For detailed reports on the political turmoil around the impeachment of President Dilma and the Car Wash operation, I recommend the coverage by news sites like BBC Brasil, the Intercept Brasil, and the Agência Pública. Especially helpful was reading Perry Anderson's (2016) piece 'Crisis in Brazil' in the *London Review of Books*. Other important texts that look at Bolsonaro's rise are de Sa e Silva (2020) and Saad-Filho and Boffo (2021).

as an opportunity to boost the city as a tourist hotspot and, more importantly, to achieve this through the improvement of the long-standing urban conflict.

Local (In)Security Unbound

Beside the global trends in urban security politics in cities that are both accelerated and produced by mega-events, this book is about the very consequences these trends have for host cities, especially in the Global South. Rio de Janeiro here serves as an example that illustrates these effects specifically.

The preparations for the Rio Games were accompanied by enormous human rights violations, principally in relation to the mega-event constructions that evicted 20,000 families and a police apparatus that harshly suppressed any public opposition (World Cup and Olympics Popular Committee of Rio de Janeiro 2015, 36).[9] In many ways, the Brazilian mega-event cycle revealed more explicitly than in any host nation before it the real consequences of such events that are organized on the back of the most socially and politically vulnerable in society. The security situation in Rio de Janeiro, paired with the global standards of security preparations associated with sport mega-events, turned the city into an ideal but also very painful case study for the present research.

It was ideal because there has never been any other case in which the host city presented such dire public security circumstances where the global security standards were brought in and adapted to. Within these tendencies of global security adaptations and technological innovations, it becomes increasingly interesting how such measures are implemented and adapted to host cities that already present serious urban security challenges (Giulianotti and Klauser 2009, 53). There has been considerable research on the 2010 South African World Cup, and how sport mega-event security governance was carried out in such a socially polarized country.[10] Yet Brazil's World Cup edition and the Rio Olympics are particularly interesting to analyse because of Brazil's long tradition of an extremely bloody war on drugs and high levels of violence.

[9] The work of the Popular Committee has been key to articulating the protest against the ways in which the Games were organized in Rio and Brazil in general.

[10] For work on the South African World Cup, see Alegi and Bolsmann (2012), Cornelissen (2011a), Eisenhauer et al. (2013), McMichael (2013), and Fonio and Pisapia (2015).

It is also painful because of that 'difficult-to-explain' feeling; because of the question: 'security for whom?'. Between 2011 and 2015, 256,124 lives were lost in the Syrian civil war, while during the same timeframe some 279,592 Brazilians met a violent death (FBSP 2016, 20). In 2014 alone, the year of the World Cup, 58,559 Brazilians died violently, a homicide rate of 28.9 per 100,000 inhabitants. In the same year, the Brazilian police killed 3,022 people, on and off duty, while 398 police officers were killed at work or on their days off (FBSP 2015, 27, 6). While US police institutions killed 11,090 people between 1983 and 2012, the Brazilian police killed 11,197 people between 2009 and 2013 alone (FBSP 2014, 6). Most of the victims of Brazil's homicide epidemic are between 15 and 24 years old and of Afro-Brazilian descent (FBSP 2016, 6). And not much has changed since then. In the first four months of 2019, Rio's police killed 558 people in the state, more than in any similar period previously (Londoño and Andreoni 2019). What happens in Brazilian cities like Rio is, therefore, described by Jaime Amparo Alves (2018, 57–61) as 'police terror' against black bodies.

As the conversation between the two police officers at the beginning of this chapter illustrates, the host city Rio de Janeiro is especially marked by Brazil's public security conditions. Everyday life in Rio is often organized around that violent urban conflict. A plurality of actors such as drug trafficking networks, police officers, militias, and local politicians are engaged in a territorializing fight to gain the upper hand in many neighbourhoods.[11] Characterized by daily shootouts, racialized and violent policing strategies, and discursive acts of othering and fear, violent conflict in Rio establishes symbolic as well as territorial borders within the city. Rio's urban conflict produces everyday physical and emotional experiences for those involved in and affected by the shootings, police invasions, and armed assaults. To live in such circumstances means to be confronted with concrete, desired, and imagined urban borders that are experienced with the constant possibility of being abruptly established or suddenly collapsing (Nielsen 2017, 399). The urban experience becomes one of searching for stability and security in hostile environments characterized by instability and constant tensions.

This is particularly important for this book, as Rio's public security reveals a rationale for securing the mega-events that is both different from

[11] There is an endless list of literature about Rio's urban conflict. Some of the newer writings include the following: Grillo (2013), Machado da Silva (2015), Larkins (2015), Savell (2016), Arias and Barnes (2017), Barnes (2017, 2021), and Lessing (2017).

and similar to other host cities. In London 2012, an unprecedented security spectacle was mainly articulated in relation to the discourse on global terror and youth gangs, and to ensure the tranquil staging of the Games for Olympic sponsors (Armstrong et al. 2016; Fussey et al. 2011). Although risk analysis of global terrorism and the standardized mega-event security models were implemented in Rio, the 'real' threat was considered to be the ongoing violent urban conflict and the supposed dangerous other, the young non-white youth from the favelas.

The traumatic killing of black Brazilian politician and LGBTQIA+ activist Marielle Franco in 2018 has called many out to mourn and protest in the streets. The assassination represents the temporary peak of the mechanisms in a rotten political system within which state agents are responsible for the management of life and death outside of any legal accountability. The killing was symbolic in many ways, mainly because Marielle was a black bisexual woman from a favela who represents a new generation of young people whose voices rise louder and push into activism and politics. Marielle's killing was an attempt to silence these voices that tirelessly denounce the many injustices in Rio. It reveals some of the real Olympic legacies and sparks questions about how to understand the meanings and purposes of Rio's everyday security dynamics before, during, and after the Games.

The specificity in Rio de Janeiro is that the analysis of urban space must consider the heterogeneous distribution of social and racial residential segregation on both a micro and macro level. On the one hand, the micro level is composed of a territorial proximity mixed with social distance between social classes. On the other hand, the macro level is structured by an increasing informal settlement on the outskirts of Rio (Queiroz Ribeiro and Santos Junior 2017, 912). Across these micro and macro scales of urban segregation, there is also a heterogeneous distribution of racial diversity, which makes it difficult to refer to these spaces as uniquely 'black' or 'white', yet in the course of colonial and contemporary Brazilian history these spaces have been racialized as such (Roth-Gordon 2017; Calvo-González and Ventura Santos 2018).

In fact, the segregated space and all the dynamics within it are best understood through the notion of 'porosity', proposed by Bruno Carvalho (2013) in his book *Porous City: A Cultural History of Rio de Janeiro*. Using the example of the inner-city vicinity of Cidade Nova (New City), Carvalho traces back the historical development of the above-mentioned urban segregation, yet argues that instead of referring to Rio as *divided* or described in other dichotomous terms, the city is better perceived as *porous*. Racially and socially unequal individuals, different religions and cultural backgrounds, transit, mix, and overlap throughout everyday interactions in historical and contemporary Rio de Janeiro (Carvalho 2013, 10–13).

Theoretical Foundations

The Triangle of Security Governance

There are many ways of trying to make sense theoretically of the coming together of globalized mega-event security standards and the pre-conditions of Rio de Janeiro's public security as described above; to investigate the coming together of both digital security technologies and lethal forms of policing as a global phenomenon, materializing in Rio de Janeiro; and to grasp the question of 'security for whom?'. This book investigates these antagonistic but at the same time perfectly compatible security strategies by conceptually placing central emphasis upon Foucault's (2007) lectures at the Collège de France between 1977 and 1978, titled *Security, Territory, Population* (see also Pauschinger 2023).

In these lectures, Foucault lays out his interpretation of security governance by advancing the idea of a governmentality triangle, contrasting different sovereign and disciplinary powers and his notion of the mechanisms of security apparatuses. In the mega-event literature, many different security concepts have been used. Much prominence has been given to the Copenhagen School of Security Studies' theory of securitization (e.g. Waever 1996; Buzan et al. 1998) to better comprehend how security has become one of the major narratives in mega-event organization (e.g. Yu et al. 2009; Samatas 2011a; Bernhard and Martin 2011). What I intend to do in this book, however, is to use a Foucauldian approach to security governance during and beyond mega-events.

In recent years, critical security and surveillance scholars have, therefore, revisited Foucault's lectures to thoroughly analyse how security and digital surveillance politics play out in urban security governance (e.g. Fussey 2013, 2015; Klauser 2013, 2017). In particular, Francisco Klauser (2013, 2017) and Pete Fussey (2013, 2015) have powerfully mobilized the Foucault lectures to examine (a) how security is managed in and around mega-event spaces and counterterrorism projects; (b) how at mega-events venues are, on the one hand, heavily protected and, on the other, designed to enable and filter spectator flows; and (c) how surveillance and control mechanisms are deployed for exactly these purposes. Both thus demonstrate how at sport mega-events and other urban security projects discipline and security, enclosure and fixity, as well as openness and flexibility mark securitized spaces altogether (Klauser 2013, 292–6; Fussey 2013, 358; see also Schuilenburg 2015, 63).

In these contributions resonates the common belief that what Foucault theorized as 'sovereign power' has receded into the background, and that discipline and the mechanisms of security apparatuses are much more dominant and helpful to understand security arrangements in contemporary societies. Recently, however, a growing post-colonial body of literature essentially questions whether this shift from spectacular punitive forms of sovereign state power to more subtle practices of discipline, security, and forms of societal control is sufficient to understand the twinning of state violence and digital security technologies in places that are marked by extreme state violence and social discrepancies (e.g. Alves 2018; Pauschinger 2020). Even if Foucault himself never really engaged with the post-colonies conceptually, his writings have heavily impacted upon the analysis in and about so-called Global South contexts. This may hold true for some places, yet in this book I tune into a debate that criticizes these claims, especially when it comes to places like Brazilian urban spatialities where police violence is carried out in spectacular ways.[12] In fact, quite the opposite is the case: sovereign power through spectacle is very much at the centre of both Brazil's routine public security strategies and the Olympic security schemes. I therefore suggest a threefold theoretical analysis of what happened in Rio.

The first one is, indeed, to consider Foucault's triangle of security governance as functioning with its three elements altogether. In the lectures, Foucault introduces the 'apparatus of security' as a new mechanism, one that adds a novel turn to his governmentality studies that further differentiates between sovereignty, discipline, and security. As Foucault says, 'sovereignty is exercised within the borders of a territory, discipline is exercised on the bodies of individuals, and security is exercised over a whole population', yet all three modes must be understood as 'concerned with multiplicities' (Foucault 2007, 11–12). While sovereign power as spectacle was often used to demonstrate to the sovereign's subjects, through military parades

[12] For the spectacular ways of policing and military incursions in Rio, see the work of Erika Robb Larkins (2013, 2015) and Stephanie Savell (2016).

and public killings, that the sovereign decides who lives and who dies, and discipline as an individualizing power was occupied with creating new spaces of control (Foucault 1977), the security apparatus is now concerned with creating a 'milieu' by accepting what reality offers and taking into account the possible, uncertain, and temporal events within these spaces (Foucault 2007, 20). As Foucault has expressed:

> Discipline concentrates, focuses, and encloses ... Now it seems to me that through the obviously very partial phenomena that I have tried to pick out we see the emergence of a completely different problem that is no longer that of fixing and demarcating the territory, but allowing circulations to take place, of controlling them, sifting the good and the bad, ensuring that things are always in movement, constantly moving around, continually going from one point to another, but in such a way that the inherent dangers of this circulation are cancelled out. (2007, 44, 65)

For Foucault, security is no longer a matter of creating new spaces of control, but rather accepting the given spaces and existing territories. Foucault suggests also that disciplinary spaces, built for the purpose of control, work 'in an empty, artificial space', whereas security enables the circulation of what is desired to be in these spaces and tries to minimize any risks; those who are declared as evil by society cannot be erased in full, which means security works with probabilities and planning to predict the future (Foucault 2007, 19–20). Contrary to many security studies approaches, a Foucauldian perspective sees security as the opposite of war and emergency: security is rather connected to normality and liberty (Bigo 2008, 96, 106). Here, security is the direct result of freedom: it pushes boundaries rather than sets them, enabling circulation and refusing discipline and surveillance in disciplinary localities (Bigo 2008, 107). In Bigo's (2008, 97) words, 'discipline is centripetal; the "dispositifs of security" are centrifugal. Discipline concentrates, focuses and encloses'. While discipline differentiates the normal from the abnormal, security enables a monitored coexistence. Security does not replace discipline; disciplinary spaces still continue to exist (Fussey 2013, 358).

To make sense of contemporary security governance in post-colonial settings such as Rio de Janeiro, it is not sufficient to simply mobilize Foucauldian governance modes such as discipline and security apparatuses, as there is a conjoining of overly violent forms of policing and the introduction of digital security technologies at the same time. Scholarly attention has, therefore, been placed upon the question of whether spectacle as a modality of power has really receded in contemporary society. As Foucault writes, 'our society is one not of spectacle but of surveillance' (Foucault 1977, 217). Yet, later he nuances that and suggests that there is not a straightforward displacement of one by the other:

> So we should not see things as the replacement of a society of sovereignty by a society of discipline, and then of a society of discipline by a society, say, of government. In fact, *we have a triangle*: sovereignty, discipline, and governmental management, which has population as its main target and apparatuses of security as its essential mechanisms. (Foucault 2007, 107–8, emphasis added)

In this sense, then, it becomes a matter of what mode of governance in the triangle is predominant or, rather, in what arrangement to each other and in what hierarchical constellations the different modes are settled. Considering the ways in which policing is carried out in Rio de Janeiro, that is the employment of highly mediated and spectacular forms of police interventions (Savell 2016; Larkins 2013, 2015), and how during the mega-events the city was occupied by the Brazilian armed forces invites us to reconsider the importance of sovereign power as spectacle in the ways we read security governance in Rio. Not only is spectacle through military parades present and exercised in the city's everyday life but sovereign power is also exercised through police killings ranging from favelas, to the streets, to the insides of police cars and emergency rooms (Alves 2018, 61).

Whereas spectacle in a Foucauldian sense is rather seen as a way for the state to punish and correct disorder in society, Daniel Goldstein (2004, 25, 182) develops this notion further and demonstrates in his ethnography of lynching in urban Bolivia that spectacular violent performances can configure a mechanism of reclaiming citizenship—making visible what stays unseen in the shadows of a failing democratic rule of law and public services.

Relating this back to Rio, Erika Robb Larkins (2013, 565) has argued how spectacle as a means of 'highly visible performances of state power' plays out in frequent police favela invasions. The police forces promote their actions in mediated spectacles to send a strong message to the public on TV screens outside the favela, but reaffirm their image as ruthless officers within the community. At the same time, drug traffickers use the spectacular to reaffirm their power within the communities and transmit the image of the violent other to the outside (Larkins 2013, 570).

This makes much reference to spectacle as defined by Guy Debord (1992, 13), who understood it as a form of dominant order that exercises social control through mediating late capitalist consumption. Spectacles of violence in favelas normalize war while clouding the fact that realities in these territories are enmeshed with socio-economic, historical, and cultural patterns (Larkins 2015, 13; also Leite 2012). This is indeed helpful in order to appreciate that mega-event security has transformed into a consumerist spectacle in its own right (Boyle and Haggerty 2009).

The latest developments with the far-right former governor Witzel incentivizing Rio's police forces actively to kill and exempting them from any legal accountability, and his public appearances in which he cheers his politics of death, however, require us to think a step further. Sovereign power in a Foucauldian sense is here best understood in the terms of what Achille Mbembe (2003, 27) articulated mainly in his essay 'Necropolitics'. Mbembe lays out the way in which governmental techniques are in essence meant to eradicate the lives of those bodies that are governed in specific spaces of death (Medeiros 2019, 86). Mbembe (2003, 39) expands his concept of 'necropower', in which sovereignty essentially means 'the right to kill', and that entails socio-spatial patterns in which the sovereign decides who lives and who dies, 'who is disposable and who is not' as a form of 'contemporary subjugation of life to the power of death'. What we see in Rio, then, is that contemporary security governance is composed of the three Foucauldian elements of sovereignty (in the very sense of Mbembe's necropower), discipline, and security. Yet, there remains a missing element that is needed to comprehend the functioning of the triangle of security governance in the digital age, very much accelerated by the mega-events in Rio, which leads me to my second argument.

The Government of Things

There is much discussion in the social sciences about how much agency the non-human has in what is largely acknowledged to be the technopolitical (see, for example, Hecht 2011), or, as Frank Müller and Matthew Richmond (2023), the editors of a special issue on technopolitics, have written in earlier versions of their introduction, is 'the desire to pay closer attention, and credit greater agency, to materiality and non-human actors in the formation of the social'. Such increased interest in the agency of the non-human is particularly important for this book, as in the case of Rio de Janeiro we have to find ways in which we might understand the role of digital technology within the politics of security governance before, during, and after the mega-event moment. The Foucauldian security vocabulary introduced in this chapter is interesting as it complements what Foucault (2007, 96) has referred to in the same *Security, Territory, Population* lecture series at the Collège de France as a 'government of things' (Lemke 2015, 2021).

Although there is notable scepticism about Foucault's accounting of non-human agency (e.g. Barad 2007), I here draw upon Thomas Lemke's (2015) article 'New Materialism: Foucault and the "Government of Things"', in which Lemke shows how Foucault actually did account for the non-human. According to Lemke (2015, 9), what Foucault says in his lectures is that governance is not per se something directed solely at humans or departing from humans; rather, 'the qualification "human" or "thing" and the political and moral distinction between them is itself an instrument and effect of the art of government and does not constitute its origin or point of departure'. In other words, what Foucault here advances is that governance—and security governance—can be exercised by both humans and non-humans. As Foucault writes:

> 'Things' are men in their relationships with things like customs, habits, ways of acting and thinking . . . with accidents, misfortunes, famine, epidemics, and death . . . government is concerned with things understood in this way as the interaction of men and things . . . to govern means to govern things. (2007, 96–7).

Foucault here puts forth a deeply relational understanding of subjects and objects. Bringing this back to the apparatus of security here is enlightening. Security, as Foucault (2007, 65) has outlined, sorts and filters what can and what cannot enter predefined territories. This sorting of the good and the bad is carried out equally by both humans and machines and can be referred to objects and subjects in what he conceptualized as the 'milieu', where—as already outlined above—'the specific space of security refers then to a series of possible events; it refers to the temporal and the uncertainty which have to be inserted within given spaces' (Foucault 2007, 20).

Yet, there is another important point that Lemke raises and that helps to shed light on the important difference between the governance modes

Foucault mobilizes. The concept of a 'government of things' reveals a mode of power that is different from that of sovereignty. As Foucault writes:

> it is not a matter of imposing a law on men, but of the disposition of things, that is to say, of employing tactics rather than laws, or, of as far as possible employing laws as tactics; arranging things so that this or that end may be achieved through a certain number of means. (2007, 99)

What we can take from this is that the way in which Foucault advances his idea of a government of things consists of distinguishing it from what he thought was and is sovereign power. The great achievement of Lemke is to expose that there is, effectively, another mode of power that comes much closer to what Foucault (1982, 790) said elsewhere, that power is a mode of action that 'structure[s] the possible field of action of others'. Foucault insists that power in itself does not exist. It is not a substance or property of specific actors but 'exists only when it is put into action' (Foucault 1982, 788).

The key question for Foucault (1982, 786) then becomes how—that is, through what mediating techniques—power is being exercised. Relating this back again to the apparatus of security—which has the filtering of the good and the bad and the enabling of circulation as its core mechanism—it becomes clear that it is the circulation by objects *and* subjects, along with the filtering exercised by humans *and* non-humans as actions upon the actions of others, that is meant here. Said differently, instead of seeing the security apparatus as different from the government of things, I here argue that we have to combine both in order to comprehend the ways in which the human and non-human, the material and non-material, are working together.

My conceptual proposition, then, is twofold: first, to suggest that we can only analyse contemporary security governance with a Foucauldian perspective if the triangle of security governance with its three elements is considered; and, second, that in the digital era, but not exclusively, the three modes of the Foucauldian triangle of security governance are complemented by a fourth dimension, which Foucault named the 'government of things', that grants agency to materiality and, in our contemporary moment, provides greater theoretical understanding of how the exercise of power, discipline, and security is delegated to digital technologies. I now turn to my third theoretical point which is the very interpretation of this Foucauldian analysis that I have named the security of camouflage.

Security of Camouflage

In this book I propose an additional analysis to the consideration of the Foucauldian triangle of security governance and how it is operationalized in Rio. I here discuss the very function, effect, and understanding of the Foucauldian perspective. The following scene can help to make this clear.

I am sitting in the Special Forces' sleeping and locker room in the Cidade da Polícia (Police City), one of the two civil police headquarters in Rio de Janeiro. The police officers, all dressed in black, watch TV, train at the gym, or have just woken up. The room features some simply equipped loft beds where the men rest between their deployments during their 24-hour shifts. We know each other from earlier research visits and engage in a conversation about the mega-event security scheme and the promised Olympic security legacies. It is an early afternoon in August 2016 when the Special Forces member I mentioned at the beginning of this chapter tells me the following:

> They besiege [the city] now so that the world doesn't see Rio de Janeiro's true reality. But after that, everything will turn back to normal: lots of shootouts, lots of dead, and lots of missions ... You see these military forces at the Linha Vermelha [Red Line—route to the international airport]? They cannot move from there. They cannot do anything. They are here for those who come from outside to feel safe. But you know what, that is of no use. Near the military police base there, the drug traffic controls it all.

The statement by the Special Forces officer is comparable to an activity of *camouflage*. The verb 'to camouflage' is defined as to 'hide or disguise the presence of (a person, animal, or object)' or as 'actions or devices intended to disguise or mislead' (*Oxford Dictionaries*, 2019). What takes place in Rio de Janeiro is what I conceptualize in this book as a *security of camouflage* which is grounded in anthropologist Jusionyte's (2015) concept of *States of Camouflage*. Jusionyte (2015, 116) advances the idea that in the three border regions of Argentine, Paraguay, and Brazil, state agents like fire brigades often use their official identities to commit crimes and 'appropriate the imagery of political authority to pursue illicit activities, frequently engage in practices of camouflage'. Camouflage is an act that aims to distract from something else or 'implies the use of one symbolic and material order to protect another from being recognized by blurring the boundaries between the two' (Jusionyte 2015, 116). In Jusionyte's analysis, the state itself as well as agents that use state identities are involved in illicit activities and constantly use the camouflage techniques to actively disguise their own illegal actions:

> Camouflage blurs the arbitrary yet consequential boundary between state and crime. More specifically, this notion enables us to examine how actors other than formal institutions participate in the performance of political authority by assuming its appearance: they deceive the state by indistinguishably blending with it. (2015, 131–2)

For Rio de Janeiro this is not a novel assessment, as state agents are constantly involved in illegal and criminal patterns of behaviour while they are on or off duty (Misse 2006; Cano and Duarte 2012; Grillo 2013). In Rio de Janeiro, camouflage techniques have long been used by the local police when they are involved in 'dangerous connections' (Misse 2006) to sell weapons to drug traffickers or ask for bribes, or when militias, formed by state agents, are extorting whole neighbourhoods (Arias and Barnes 2017). Rio de Janeiro—and this has to be said with the utmost clarity—cannot be comprehended if we do not consider camouflage politics in which state agents enact a performance of statehood to hide their involvement in criminal activities. By approaching the relationship between statecraft and criminality through the concept of camouflage, it allows us to foreground how 'the predatory and brutal' is hidden 'under the just and peaceful' so that techniques of camouflage can be considered as the very 'modus operandi of statecraft' (Jusionyte 2015, 116).

Linking this to Foucauldian spectacle, as something that on the one side can radically direct the spotlight upon specific incidents and simultaneously, on the other side, also render other things invisible (Goldstein 2004, 16), camouflage is a helpful concept for understanding how spectacular mega-event security measures worked in Rio de Janeiro in both putting security operations on display in certain regions, while the very same security apparatus continued to deliver highly spectacular police performances in others. What I essentially argue is that camouflaging best captures how the spectacular fulfils different purposes in different spatialities upon different audiences, yet always works as a reaffirmation of state power that hides, disguises, or puts on display.

For Rio's mega-events, these notions of spectacularly securing the city have blurred with very specific intentions. The notion of a commoditized spectacular security is not a guarantee of security, but rather produces often the very opposite: *insecurity*. Whereas state security is frequently intended to provide security, it means insecurity to those who experience the repressive and arbitrary state apparatus (Goldstein 2012, 16). As Jusionyte and Goldstein (2016, 4) formulate, 'One of the central contradictions of contemporary security making is that, rather than providing assurance and guarantee, practices emanating from the invisibilized security zones often contribute to heightened *insecurity*' (original emphasis). However, *invisible* politics have been in the making in parallel to those that are visible, and represent the real legacy of the mega-event cycle.

Here, 'everyday security arrangements provide security to some while creating insecurity and vulnerability for others' and in its ultimate consequence provides a constant interplay between the logics of security that are based on dichotomized aspects of 'visibility and invisibility' (Jusionyte and Goldstein 2016, 9). Security in this sense has then the double function of representing security for some and insecurity for others. Thus visibility and invisibility are crucial tools that can be connected to the mega-event security in Rio.

In Rio de Janeiro there takes place a twofold process that is deeply rooted within the city's local security conditions, and is nonetheless also valid for Rio de Janeiro's mega-event security operations. This process is the production of a *security of camouflage* that not only features state agents crossing the lines of legality but is also produced to transmit an image and, principally, to omit what happens behind the curtains of the mega-event and the ordinary security spectacle. This book then advances a discussion on urban security provisions and how they are idealized, organized, and implemented in cities like Rio and beyond. To understand the effects and functionalities of the Foucauldian triangle of security governance with its fourth dimension of the government of things in Olympic Rio is to consider the production of a security of camouflage that, so I will argue in this book, is not only considerable as the modus operandi of security making but also the modus operandi of sport mega-event politics, in Rio and elsewhere. Now, embedded in this theoretical perspective, the book also looks at different ways in which we can possibly understand the micro worlds of policing in Rio, which are considered in the next section.

Police Work in Rio de Janeiro

Space, Emotions, and Edgework

Besides these major theoretical ideas, this book looks also at the micro worlds of policing Rio that show the inner dynamics of the camouflage security. This enables me to also shed light upon, and emphasize the importance of, an inside look at the mega-event spectacle and how, in essence, the emotional worlds of police officers contribute to the long-standing urban conflict in Rio. For this reason, a conceptual approach to space and police territoriality is important to note, as only by considering these conceptual entanglements am I able to reveal what happened outside of the spectacular spotlight during the sport tournaments. I therefore combine spatial theory with ethnographic approaches to the police to investigate how emotions contribute to police territoriality. This leads to an understanding of attempts to establish urban order, going beyond the mere physical manifestation of police work. It invokes a sense of the emotional entanglements of police officers that are shaped by and shape the city as a 'bordered space' (Christensen and Albrecht 2020, 387). I do this first theoretically by considering the relationship between the police and the production of urban space, thereby adopting a relational conception of police territoriality (Raffestin 2012), and then by mobilizing an approach to the police using the concept of edgework (Lyng 1990, 1998, 2005a) that originates from cultural criminology (Ferrell et al. 2015) and its phenomenology of emotions (Katz 1988, 1999). I propose two main conceptual contributions both to geography and criminology. The first concerns a comprehension of police territoriality that considers the emotional worlds of police officers that, so I argue, are crucially important for understanding how the production of space and policing are interrelated. The second regards the concept of edgework that most often lacks an important spatial component. Only by taking both together can we better appreciate the ways in which the police shapes and is shaped by space.

From the theoretical and empirical contributions of the 'geographies of police' (Yarwood 2007) in human geography and urban studies, we know that police work and space are mutually related (e.g. Fyfe 1991, 1995). Police officers' spatial tactics influence the maintenance of urban order (Franzén 2001, 214), and as Fyfe (1992, 471) has noted, space is 'directly involved in police work'. A wide range of literature has looked into different spatial police dynamics such as protest policing (Wahlström 2010), private policing (Paasche et al. 2014), hybrid policing (Albrecht 2020), border policing (Reeves 2011), gentrification and policing (Raco 2003; Künkel 2017), policing of certain social groups (Stuart 2014), and the governance of space through policing mega-events (Klauser 2013; Fussey 2015). Yet, there are only a few ethnographic studies that focus on the police officers themselves and how they concretely 'make and mark space' (Herbert 2000, 21).

One exception is Steve Herbert's (1996, 2000, 161) study of officers in the Los Angeles Police Department, showing how police behaviour is defined by territoriality and organized by normative orders that 'provide structure and meaning to police actions'. Herbert uses a behavioural concept of territoriality inspired by Robert Sack (1986, 1), who defines it as 'a spatial strategy to affect, influence, or control resources and people by controlling area'. In this book, however, I adapt a relational conception of territoriality, inspired by francophone geographer Claude Raffestin (2012), to understand the police as 'agents of territoriality' (Christensen and Albrecht 2020, 391). I do this to bring to the fore the emotional worlds of police officers that are rarely considered but are an essential component to better grasp the relationship between the police and space.

Acknowledging the conceptual debates in geography around the different meanings of territoriality (Klauser 2012; Murphy 2012), the reason for my decision lies in a perception of space as a relational scheme inspired by the Lefebvrian 'production of space' (Lefebvre 1991). Raffestin (2012, 129) apprehends relational (and mediated) territoriality as 'a system' within which an exchange and 'flux of all sorts between exteriority (the physical environment) and alterity (the social environment)' continuously takes place. Space in this sense turns into 'territory' when it is produced by the human activity within it (Raffestin 2012, 124). In Raffestin's (2012, 130) theory, the production of territory is comprised and activated by three main elements, '(1) things and material states, (2) states of conscience, emotion, and subjective knowledge, and (3) knowledge taken objectively'. The focus on the emotional side of the production of territory creates the possibility to investigate the emotional world of the police that I argue shapes the territorial practices of the officers in Rio de Janeiro.

To bring spatial thought and the emotions of police officers together, I borrow from cultural criminology's relational framework of crime and *crime control*. Cultural criminology recognizes that emotions play an as important role in understanding the roots of transgression, as the social structures within which they are embedded (Hayward 2004, 151; also Ferrell et al. 2015, 73). An inspirational source for cultural criminology's focus on emotions derives from Jack Katz (1988, 1999), who argues that we have to assess the foreground of social performance in order to make sense of other explaining background structures. Katz (1999, 5–6) differentiates between three distinct emotional states and reactions: (1) emotional outburst, which means to react to and engage with directly and beyond a given situation; (2) the emotional states of a person regarding the reaction and interpretation of others onto these conditions; and (3) how persons move from one emotional state into another that drives the sense of emotions as a bodily experience ('sensual metamorphoses'). This three-dimensional concept orientates us to emotions as 'self-reflective actions and experiences' that are 'corporal metaphors that operate implicitly at the foundations of all of our conduct'.

To apprehend how emotions are an essential part of police territoriality, I consider police officers as edgeworkers (Lyng 1990, 2005a). Embedded in the Katzian conception of emotions and combined with the sociology of risk taking, the notion of edgework focuses on those who perform highly risky endeavours at the verge of legality, criminality, and/or between life and death, and thus assesses the boundaries between 'order and disorder' (Lyng 1990, 585). This is strongly connected to cultural criminology's take on the act of transgression, which in itself 'contains distinct emotions, attractions and compensations' (Ferrell et al. 2015, 73). In late modern living conditions, social inequality, monotonous everyday working routines, and unsuccessful attempts at self-realization are often felt as dull, humiliating, and as losses of identity and control. By engaging in edgework, the protagonists seek to regain a bit of that lost control and to compensate for emotional humiliation by developing specific skills through activities such as skydiving or extreme motorcycling. Edgeworkers try to follow a mechanism that makes them take voluntary risks and push themselves to the edge, in search of a rush of adrenaline through constant exposure to risk and the permanent possibility of sudden death or severe injury (Lyng 1990, 857–9). Many transgressive acts in urban environments can be seen as edgework and attempts at retaking control in ontologically insecure worlds (Hayward 2004, 165). Typically, police officers or combat soldiers, who possess very specific skills, have jobs that carry the possibility of such risk-full moments, where adrenaline rushes can serve as an escape from the humiliating experiences of not being able to do what they are trained to do, or to control what they are supposed to control (Lyng 1990, 857).

To date, however, there has been little research that conceptualizes the police as edgeworkers (e.g. Ilan 2016). For instance, literature on anarchist movements (Ferrell 2005), financial trading (Smith 2005), drug taking (Reith 2005), or doing research in high-risk environments (Lyng 1998; Hamm 2005) sheds light on different facets of edgework. While there are important criticisms of edgework for not acknowledging sufficiently gendered dimensions within the concept (Naegler and Salman 2016, 360–3), I want to highlight that there is also a compelling opportunity to address both how state actors become edgeworkers themselves and how the police as edgeworkers produce territoriality. Appreciating police officers as edgeworkers affords me the opportunity to combine the relational approach on territoriality with the emotional concept of edgework, to show through the empirical work in this book the relationship between policing and space and how police officers' emotions are produced by, and contribute to, the production of Rio de Janeiro's urban conflict.

Ethnography in an Olympic City at War

Methodological Strategies

To illustrate and explore the themes outlined above, the book advances ethnography as its core method. In Glück and Low's (2017) scalar approach to security, they investigate the ways in which security is produced socio-spatially on global, regional, national, urban, local, and bodily levels. They differentiate between 'security as a state of being' (the experiential and emotional domain) and 'states of security' (the configurations of state power and governance of security). Spatial theory is here conjoined with anthropological ethnographic studies to demonstrate how macro levels of security states, and micro levels of everyday practices and subjective and bodily experiences of security, are produced through socio-spatial strategies (Glück and Low 2017, 285–7).

Inspired by this, the book investigates how global security models associated with mega-events are deployed and adapted to local security conditions in Rio de Janeiro. In particular, it gathers knowledge from the ground to situate and challenge the official claims that the implemented security efforts improve the Brazilian public security system. This entails a twofold approach. On the one hand, it necessitates understanding the wider dynamics of the technical implementation of mega-event security from the perspective of policy-makers and senior officers. On the other, it means elucidating the meaning of those parachuted actions on the ground for

Rio's police. In other words, the book uncovers how those efforts were interpreted, adapted, and embraced by street officers—both by those directly involved in mega-event policing and those responsible for the ordinary security affairs in the city.

The ethnography in this book is equally inspired by cultural criminology and its long-standing tradition as an alternative way of making sense of crime and crime control in contrast to rather positivistic criminological theories. Cultural criminology proposes a new approach that 'places criminality and its control in the context of culture; that is, it views crime and the agencies and institutions of crime control as cultural products—as creative constructs' (Hayward 2008, 119). Cultural criminology has built a tradition of working with ethnography to better perceive 'theatres of meaning' so as to understand crime and crime control through and with a phenomenological approach (Ferrell 2013, 258). Cultural criminology defines ethnography not as a single method but as a methodological approach for the study of human agency (Ferrell et al. 2008, 178) and the experience of the everyday (Ferrell 2013, 260).

The core of a cultural criminological art of ethnography is what Jeff Ferrell has conceptualized as *criminological verstehen*. Borrowing from Max Weber, Ferrell (1998, 27) understands *verstehen* as a rather subjective interpretation and compassionate engagement with the research subjects, while embedding this into wider sociological and 'various rational understandings of social action and social meaning'.[13] For the purpose of this research I needed methodological and epistemological tools that were able to help me in bringing to light what mostly stayed unseen under the shadows of mega-event 'security spectacles' (Boyle and Haggerty 2009).

Moreover, I had to face the problematic that the events related to the World Cup and the Olympics were spatially distributed across the whole city and took place simultaneously. Registering the moments of 'chaos and confusion' that can arise suddenly and spontaneously can best be grasped with 'instant ethnography' (Ferrell et al. 2008, 180). Embedded in the cultural criminological concept of 'edgework', which implies the study of extremely risky activities where people seek a *controlled loss of control* in order to compensate for the lack of a fulfilling narrative in their everyday and dull lives, instant ethnography catches these very moments of adrenaline rushes (Lyng 1990, 2005; Ferrell et al. 2008, 72). In my particular case I was able

[13] Ferrell is inspired by the writings of Max Weber: *The Methodology of the Social Sciences* (1949) and *Economy and Society* (1978).

to register fieldwork situations where I could observe the sudden anger, sadness, and disappointment of police officers. In addition, the method granted me the opportunity to register the spontaneous, chaotic, and confusing mix of chanting fans and stressed police officers in Olympic Rio.

This book is then as much about the themes I elaborated above as it is about aiming to advance an approach to ethnography that is not only a deep immersion in a group's everyday life but also an ethnography of a special moment for the city of Rio. And for this it needed alternative means from those traditionally used in ethnographic methodologies. Michel de Certeau (1984, 91–3) has powerfully argued that there are two ways of understanding the city: one that is imagined in the spheres of the planners, which he denoted as the 'concept city' and adopts a view from above, and one that is the city experienced by those who walk the streets. For the aims of this research I needed to use an approach that allowed me to grasp both the official security imagination of those who globally and locally planned and implemented the mega-event security strategies and the lived experience of those at street level. To develop an account of both the concept and the experienced city, I adopted this cultural criminology and socio-spatially inspired ethnographic approach that can make sense of the global security gone local.

Fieldwork: Positionality, Time, and Space

The empirical work of this book is rooted in my ethnographic journey to Brazil and more particularly to Rio de Janeiro between 2013 and 2019. My love for the country, its culture, and its people, however, goes back many years when I first arrived in the city of São Paulo in 2002. In these first years I learned Brazilian Portuguese and was able to grasp a sense of the culture in the huge urban agglomeration in the South Zone, a place in which the beauty of vibrant community life and the warm welcome of people impressed me as much as the high levels of gun violence, police oppression, and social inequality. I immersed myself in the life of the outskirts in the South Zone and I might have learned more about the country in these years than in any of the textbooks and lectures in my Latin American studies in the university. There is no doubt that my understanding about Brazil and its society was heavily marked by my entrance through the favela. With the years in the country, I also realized how deeply enrooted the colonial past still resonates with the racism in Brazil today. Along with being a white

German male came the privilege of transiting at ease between favela huts and wealthy elite gated communities as I was not considered suspicious as many of my black Brazilian friends were.

Taking all this together prepared me for my fieldwork for this book. Speaking Brazilian Portuguese, knowing some of the cultural codes, and having had experiences in different social settings made it possible to immerse myself into the policing and security dynamics of the World Cup and the Olympics in Rio de Janeiro. I here also took advantage of those who were in the field with police officers before me and I drew upon a growing body of anthropologically informed literature that highlights the phenomenological, subjective, and bodily experienced emotions of the police (Fassin 2013b, 2017; Garriott 2013; Karpiak and Garriott 2018). In many visits to the different localities of the security forces headquarters and during month-long stays during day and night shifts in the police station, I was able to record interviews with officers, accompany them during their work inside and outside the station, ride with them in police cars, go for lunches and dinners, and pass long hours waiting with them for something to happen. Learning the language of the field (Van Maanen 2011, 13), my long-term stay with the officers in the most varied circumstances, from tranquil and calm to hectic and stressful, allowed me to assess the structure of the social processes that appeared repeatedly over time and helped to differentiate between normal, enacted, and exceptional emotional states (Duneier 2001, 338). I concur with Beatrice Jauregui (2013, 148), who has powerfully described writing ethnography as an 'ethical process' and as a 'dirty job', but who believes 'that somebody has got to do it'.

The research for this book draws upon five fieldwork trips to Rio de Janeiro and sporadic visits to São Paulo. The first one took place in June 2013 and had purely preparative purposes. The second one happened from April to November 2014 and was the research's core fieldwork trip, before, during, and after the World Cup. The third, from May to June 2015, was intended for follow-up interviews and to examine the preparations for the Olympic Games. The fourth research trip between July and August 2016 was dedicated to experiencing the Olympics and undertaking more interviews and observations within the security installations that had been set up for the World Cup and reutilized for the 2016 Games. Finally, I was able to go back to Rio in 2019 during the Copa América and its final to revisit the surrounds of the Maracanã and other fieldwork sites and to meet and talk with many of my earlier fieldwork protagonists.

The social universe this book shares with the reader is inscribed within four main research localities. First, I spent a significant amount of time in a civil police station where I accompanied the officers in their distinct daily routines. Second, I spent all seven World Cup games in Rio at the mobile civil police station within the public security perimeter around the Maracanã stadium accompanying the police officers' shifts. I also passed some time there before the Olympic inauguration and closing ceremony. In addition, I visited several times the mobile Centro Integrado de Comando e Controle (CICC-M) within the World Cup security cordon. Third, I frequently observed the dynamics within the Centro Integrado de Comando e Controle (CICC) in Rio de Janeiro during the World Cup and the Olympics.[14] Fourth, I spent substantial time in the Cidade da Polícia, the civil police headquarters inaugurated in 2013 and home to most of the specialized police departments. There I carried out a series of ethnographic interviews with the members of the civil police Special Forces and observed wider police activities.

With the above-described instant 'ethnographic sensibility', I understood Rio de Janeiro as one entire fieldwork locality (Ferrell 2013, 365). In order to absorb the mega-event ambience, I opted to walk the city, talk to people in the streets, and *experience* the city from below in the way de Certeau described it: 'the ordinary practitioners of the city live "down below", below the thresholds at which visibility begins' (de Certeau 1984, 93). To furnish my arguments with cultural criminology's 'thoroughgoing consideration and appreciation of the visual' and to make sense of the meanings on display, I used these *strolls* around the Olympic city to photograph the mega-event security spectacle and the routine local security provisions (Hayward 2010, 4).

In total I conducted 62 ethnographic interviews.[15] The participants covered a wide range of different positions within the mega-event security architecture. Among them were ministers and secretaries from high offices, planning staff, and street police officers, as well as FIFA and IOC security officers. To enrich my knowledge and to furnish the content of this work, I also interviewed public security experts such as university professors, security consultants, and activists. This sample gave me the opportunity to

[14] I also visited the integrated command-and-control facilities of the armed forces and local organizing committee. Furthermore, I visited several times Rio's Smart City centre and once the integrated command-and-control centre in São Paulo.

[15] On the specificities of ethnographic interviews and qualitative research methods, see May (2011, 136) and Hollway and Jefferson (2013, 33).

investigate the insights of those who planned, managed, executed, and generally worked with the mega-event security.

Structure of the Book

The rest of the book unfolds as follows. The book is structured in three parts, (I) Security, (II) Spectacle, and (III) Camouflage, which each features ethnographic accounts that elucidate its respective themes. Part I, Security, brings the reader closer to the political importance of a globalized mega-event security and the local conditions in which they have been inscribed. Chapter 1, Securing and Policing Sport Mega-Events, highlights the making of sport mega-event security regimes. It illustrates how in the post-9/11 era, security and its key elements like surveillance and militarization became one of the defining elements of contemporary everyday urban life and how mega-events developed into products and producers of these trends.

Chapter 2, An Olympic City at War, highlights the complex Brazilian public security architecture and Brazil's police history. It likewise investigates the historical roots of Rio's urban conflict and presents the attempted changes in Rio's public security politics in the run-up to the mega-events that greatly echo the vocabulary found in other cities around the globe, mantled around pacification, urban smartness, and resilience.

In Part II, Spectacle, I take the reader with me to the spheres of the imaginations and plans of those who idealized the mega-event security and how these plans materialized. In addition, I take the reader to street level to show how the different modes of the Foucauldian triangle of security governance were operationalized. Chapter 3, Planning and Imagining the Fortress, critically examines the Brazilian mega-event security plans and the imaginations connected to them. The chapter presents how the federal government planned the mega-event security architecture and the ways in which this was reflected in Rio de Janeiro. Global mega-event security standards were adapted to Rio's specific public security circumstances, leading to the establishment of a complex and specific Brazilian mega-event security organization.

In Chapter 4, The Permeable Fortress, I investigate how the mega-event security has been concretely implemented in Rio. The chapter demonstrates how the fortress ambitions were established spatially and illustrate the strategy of occupying Rio with police and military forces, creating a fortress within the fortress. The chapter dives into the immediacy of the security perimeters around the Maracanã stadium and the Olympic Park. It reveals how porous and permeable the fortress was throughout both events, producing novel insecurities.

Chapter 5, Working at the Edge in the Police City, brings the reader into the immediacy of police work in Rio's everyday security operations. The chapter dives into the routine dynamics of a civil police station to assess the defining elements in understanding the police officers' daily frustration in losing control of effectively handling Rio's public security problematics—which ultimately led to acts of violence. Examining the militarized civil police Special Forces shows how daily war-like activities spark distinct everyday emotions such as adrenaline rush, frustration, and pleasure, and upset in practice the rationales of static and technology-based event security models.

Part III, Camouflage, then brings to light the techniques of camouflaging to hide away and put on display the various mechanisms of securing the mega-events.

Chapter 6, Security of Camouflage, develops the notion of the security of camouflage that made specific aspects of security visible and, simultaneously, produced insecurity to make intentionally invisible the city's public security drama. I here advance how the triangle of security governance is best understood when considering the act of camouflaging as the modus operandi of mega-event politics.

Chapter 7, Non/Material Legacies, examines the main official sport mega-event security measures that were meant to become long-lasting security policies in Brazil. Ranging from material (technologies, camera surveillance architectures, and the CICC buildings) to non-material legacies (the cooperation between the different security forces), the ethnography reveals how the technology, the buildings, and the cooperation strategy had only worked in very specific contexts in Rio but failed to provide a long-lasting security strategy, and how in Rio today the triangle of security governance is complemented by a fourth dimension, the government of things, mainly present in the materiality of security.

In the Conclusions, I highlight that sport mega-event security has clearly failed to improve any of the painful realities that are lived in the everyday experiences of those who work within the public security sector and/or are victims of the deadly effects within these insecurity patterns that are best described in Mbembe's terms as necropolitics. These insecurity patterns could not be improved as the mega-event security measures focused on rational technological solutions instead of considering deeply entrenched configurations and the immediacy of the emotional life of police officers that feed the everyday routines of violence and insecurity.

1
Securing and Policing Sport Mega-Events

In the early morning hours of the 2016 Olympics inauguration ceremony in Rio de Janeiro, I tried to access the Maracanã stadium area through one of the nearby metro stations. On the bridge towards the stadium, military police officers stopped me because I did not possess any access credentials. From the position on the access bridge, I can see how a plethora of security forces from all kinds of policing institutions patrol the area. CCTV cameras are installed in different localities and the Brazilian military stands guard. Disappointed, I take the metro back to the next stop and try my luck from the other side. This time, the access to the stadium is controlled by heavily armed soldiers from the Brazilian military and the area is devoid of cars, as the stadium's surroundings have been declared security perimeters to guarantee the security and safety of athletes, spectators, VIP guests, and high-level politicians and representatives of the world's most powerful sports organization, the International Olympic Committee (IOC). While the soldiers do not bother to control me and I can walk freely around the stadium to examine the security measures in place, helicopters are roaring above the stadium and soldiers in two ranked lines march beside me. On my way back to the ramp that finally leads to the metro station Maracanã, smiling and laughing participants of the inauguration ceremony take pictures, TV teams start their reporting, and Olympic volunteers guide the way. Later that day I arrive at the Centro Integrado de Comando e Contole (CICC), the centre in which cutting-edge surveillance technology, communication tools, and house-high video walls are meant to support the many different security agencies to guarantee a secure staging of the Games. The jingles of cracking radios, the flickering of CCTV imagery, and the hectic voices of ministers, high-ranked police officers, and Special Forces coordinators mix together into the sound of the Olympic security operation. I remember how I thought about my impressions of that day, when I took the metro back

Policing Sport Mega-Events. Dennis Pauschinger, Oxford University Press. © Dennis Pauschinger 2024.
DOI: 10.1093/oso/9780192848055.003.0002

home, long after midnight: security has indeed become one of the major narratives of sport mega-events (Bennett and Haggerty 2011, 5).

Much scholarly attention has been placed prominently upon the study of sport mega-events. Whereas there is an overwhelming amount of research dedicated uncritically to mega-events—the ways in which events like the Olympics can have effects upon the host nations, athletes, sports, and society at large—a smaller community of researchers is committed to critically examining the political dimensions. Within this community it goes relatively uncontested that sport mega-events should be defined as what they are: highly political, globalized, symbolically mediated spectacles moved by intrinsic capitalistic motivations which have tremendous effects upon the host nations (e.g. Müller et al. 2021).[1]

For a long time, it was clear that hosting the Games was associated with 'the ultimate accolade that a city can earn on the world stage' (Gold and Gold 2017, 10). This gains even more importance when it comes to countries from non-Western locales that strive for greater recognition within the global community and to gain a greater geopolitical voice (Wolfe 2016, 2022). When former IOC president Jacques Rogge proclaimed Brazil as the host of the 2016 Olympics, then Brazilian president Lula Inácio da Silva said: 'Now, we are going to show the world we can be a great country' (quoted in Boykoff 2016, 211). Lula's statement in itself demonstrates how deeply political the Games are, even though the sports' governing bodies repeatedly insist that world sports should not be misused for political purposes. As Boykoff observes:

> In reality the Olympics are political through and through. The marching, the flags, the national anthems, the alliances with corporate sponsors, the labor exploitation behind the athletic-apparel labels, the treatment of indigenous peoples, the marginalization of the poor and working class, the selection of Olympic host cities—all political. To say the Olympics transcend politics is to conjure fantasy. (2016, 2)

The political projects attached to mega-events arise from a powerful alliance of those who are considered the winners of mega-event organization: the FIFA and IOC members, government officials of the host

[1] I will not join the definition debate in the study of mega-events. The reader who is interested in finding out more about the ways in which mega-events are defined is directed to Müller (2015).

countries, the construction and tourism industry, the sponsors, the broadcasting partners, the national Olympic committees, and the international professional sports associations (Preuss 2017, 148–58). One of the major narratives attached to contemporary sport mega-events is the promise of this political alliance positively transforming the host nations through the Games in many respects: from boosting the tourism industry to triggering urban transformations, helping local industries, heaving the host nation into the global political spotlight, and even promising world peace, as FIFA's former secretary general Fatma Samoura has done in an interview with the German magazine *Der Spiegel* (Pfeil and Wulzinger 2016, 112). The recent and increasing resistance to hosting mega-events by a variety of cities is also tied to the fact that these sustainability promises cannot match the reality in the different host cities (Müller et al. 2021).

Because mega-events are political, symbolically overloaded, and spectacular, one of the major narratives in their organization is security, as both an immediate necessity before and during the events and as a legacy promise to improve public security conditions. To understand how and in which way security has developed into what I have shown in the opening vignette, the aim of this chapter is then to prepare the ground to appreciate how security is organized at sport mega-events so that we can later better comprehend how the global mega-event security measures were orchestrated in and adapted to Brazil's and Rio's specific public security conditions. It proceeds in three major steps. First, the chapter provides an overview of the historical developments of security into an intrinsic feature of sport mega-event organization and considers the main triggers of these developments; second, it explores how security has become highly standardized and highlights the importance of the elements from the above vignette—the total security strategies, electronic surveillance, and militarization processes; and third, it identifies the research lacunas this book wants to address in the literature on sport mega-event security.

History of Sport Mega-Event Security: From Counterterrorism to Resilience

Most scholars refer to two main events which have heavily influenced the security development of sport mega-events. The first is the Palestinian terrorist attack on the Israeli Olympic team during the 1972 Olympic Summer Games in Munich. This incident connected mega-events and wider security discussions for the first time (Coaffee et al. 2011, 3313). In the aftermath of the Munich tragedy, security became a major concern in terms of the safety of the athletes during the Games, as well as for the event itself (Lenskyj 2000, 110).[2] The second event associated with a real push towards the current situation of highly secured sport events is the Al-Qaida attack on 11 September 2001 in New York, as has been pointed out by numerous scholars (e.g. Boyle and Haggerty 2009, 258; Coaffee et al. 2011, 3311; Cornelissen 2011a, 3221; Giulianotti and Klauser 2011, 3157; Samatas 2011, 3347; Taylor and Toohey 2011, 3260; Spaaij 2016, 452).

Since then, counterterrorism has been one of the main triggers for security precautions at sport mega-events and dominates the security planning as such (Taylor and Toohey 2011, 3260; Samatas 2011a, 3349). And indeed, terrorist attacks have been a steady companion of Olympic Games, and have been authored by a wide variety of different groups (Fussey and Coaffee 2011, 37). Two other key incidents contributed to mega-event security becoming a major narrative for the event organizers: the North Korean and Japanese Red Army attacks on the South Korean aviation industry in which the IOC was later involved on a diplomatic level (Fussey et al. 2011, 47) and domestic bomber Eric Rudolph, who attacked a semi-public Olympic site rather than a fortified Olympic venue at the 1996 Games in Atlanta (Hassan 2014, 629). The Atlanta bombing had a direct influence on the planning of London 2012 (Fussey et al. 2011, 50). While the arguments of mega-event organizers are all too often based on the threat of *global* terrorism, the Games' history shows that the real threats stem from local terrorist groups that aim to attack soft targets (Bennett and Haggerty 2011, 2; Fussey et al. 2011, 57).

Returning to the aforementioned discussion on the role of 9/11, the scholarship presents a unified picture. The 9/11 attacks accelerated the general security development at mega-events (Bennett and Haggerty 2011, 4), increased the heavy costs in security material (Giulianotti and Klauser 2011, 3157), and increased the availability of human and financial resources

[2] Nonetheless, the Olympics that followed after the key Munich incident contributed to the mega-event security spiral. Innsbruck (1976), Montreal (1976), and Lake Placid (1980) became the blueprints for future Olympic security programmes. The short period of the 'Cold War Games' in Moscow (1980) and Los Angeles (1984) made it very clear that political issues have an important place at mega-events. Still, organizers had to deal with both their own 'total security' promises and further terrorism threats to future mega-events (Fussey et al. 2011, 41–7).

and new law-enforcement measures (Fussey et al. 2011, 66). These security expansions are embedded within general debates on security.

Klauser understands sport mega-events as much more than simply a catalyst for a broader set of security developments. They are

> both the product and the producer of a general cluster of developments in security politics: the urbanisation, globalisation, technologicalisation and commercialisation of security/surveillance issues. Yet these developments do not enter into antagonism with each other. On the contrary, each development embodies and nourishes the others. For example, the predominantly urban-centred proliferation of high-tech surveillance technologies also highlights current trends in security politics which is becoming increasingly global in scope (addressing globalised social risks and bringing together globalised security partnerships) and commercial in nature. (2008, 75)

In this sense, sport mega-event security is at the same time embedded in general security developments as it is the driver of such. These developments have been shaped since the 1980s by the fear of violence and strategies of militarizing and securing cities (Davis 1990; also Hayward 2004). The fear of crime had raised support for new and harsher policing tactics and zero-tolerance schemes to the extent that the urban landscape became framed by categories of menace (Garland 2001). After 9/11 this was partly replaced by the fear of terrorism (Coaffee 2003, 4) and counterterrorism became the justification for a variety of new strategies to design urban space with the aim of increasing security. Coaffee (2003, 13) argues that militarization has increased dramatically after 9/11 and needs to be understood as the permanent chaperone of privatization. As a consequence, risk management has become the key tool used to promote the aforementioned urban changes.

These approaches of governing security in cities through the lenses of risk and uncertainty have been complemented by what have famously been titled *resilience* concepts, which have risen remarkably after 9/11 and address these uncertainty and risk frames (Coaffee and Rogers 2008; Chandler 2014). As Welsh (2014, 15–16) asserts, resilience is mostly understood as the capacity to prepare and better deal with dangers of catastrophic dimensions and to recover after devastating shocks in rapid ways. Moreover, resilience discourses have been widely used to *govern through resilience* and principally shifted security discourses from a purely state-based security approach towards neoliberal security practices that foster 'society-based conceptions of distributed risk and reaction' (Welsh 2014, 19). The literature on resilience has focused upon many topics: the ways in which resilience has been 'enacted through infrastructure' (Sage et al. 2015); resilience as critical infrastructure (Coaffee and Clarke 2017); how urban planners were urged to include resilience within their projects (Coaffee 2013); and analysing how resilience could become a concept that has often been presented as a 'superhero' to solve security-related problems (Cavelty et al. 2015, 4).

In the realms of urban security and with relevance to mega-event security, Coaffee and Fussey (2015, 91–5) demarcate a three-level logic of security-driven resilience within the UK that fosters electronic surveillance and territorial enclosure, preventative actions of businesses and communities, and resilience embedded in more local everyday life practices, all of which prioritize security and counterterrorism, 'which, in turn, draw security infrastructures, organizations and practices into the delivery of resilience'. In these aforementioned conditions, the late modern world is marked by these forms of uncertainty, risk, and governance through resilience. These tendencies inform and drive mega-event security.

Standardization of Sport Mega-Event Security

Sport mega-event security measures are today highly standardized. The causes of such a standardization are manifold. On the one side, the reasons are to be found in the security politics that arose after 9/11 and introduced the worldwide standards in counterterrorism measures in which sport mega-events are embedded. On the other side, another reason is the drive of the sports organizing bodies themselves. In 1983 the IOC introduced a 'security delegate' who was responsible for the security knowledge transfer from former to future hosts; for conveying the IOC's security expectations; for managing its advisory role with the host country; and for fulfilling a diplomatic role in building a bridge between the IOC, the local organizing committee, and local security agencies (Fussey et al. 2011, 60).

As securing and policing sport mega-events like the Olympics or the football World Cup is such a complex endeavour, the standardized security models are transferred from host city to host city (Coaffee et al. 2011, 3316). More specifically, these standard models are not static and adapt to the local conditions in a more or less malleable form (Bennett and Haggerty 2011,

12). Cultural, social, political, and economic conditions on the ground automatically shape a host nation's approach to how and on what scale they realize the standard mega-event security model (Samatas 2011a, 3359).[3]

We can find an example of this within the setting of the 2012 London Olympics. Overall, the London Games were special because of the local circumstances and approaches to counterterrorism. Although mega-events serve to enable governments to implement long-planned security policies, the London Games relied on pre-existing experiences, as well as surveillance and security measures which were already in existence (Fussey and Coaffee 2011, 43). In other host nations, mega-events clearly acted as a catalyst for a wider set of developments in both security policies and urban development (Giulianotti and Klauser 2011, 3161). During the 2010 South African World Cup, the government understood the World Cup as an opportunity to advance security policies in order to tackle the country's crime problems (Cornelissen 2011a, 3223). Unsurprisingly Brazil's mega-event cycle—starting with the 2007 Pan American Games, then the later World Cup and Olympics—is strongly associated with changes in local crime policies and the introduction of new technologies designed to supplant crime in the city (Gaffney 2010, 17).

The security-related knowledge transfer consists of an interaction between private security firms, insurance companies, and the government (not to forget FIFA or the IOC). These networks operate on state institutional, transnational, and non-state levels within a self-contained circle that uses and reproduces security knowledge (Boyle 2011, 172). In this sense, Boyle (2011, 181) argues that sport mega-events are 'experimental battlegrounds' for new security technologies whose mechanisms often lead to contracts with very much the same transnational, security corporations like IBM, General Electrics, and Science Applications International Corporation (Fussey et al. 2011, 60). Within such a 'mega-event security-development nexus (MESDN)' (Molnar and Snider 2011, 152), companies explore opportunities for new alliances between state- and privately driven security actors at mega-events. Private security corporations interact

[3] Analysing the 2004 Athens and 2008 Beijing Olympics, both of which were carried out in post-authoritarian (Greece) and authoritarian (China) states, Samatas (2011a, 3348) argues that security at SMEs (sport mega-events) can lead to serious democratic problems and an intensification of anti-democratic tendencies. While there was more resistance in Greece to the surveillance strategies that, eventually, would restrict civil liberties due to their authoritarian past, in China the regime took full advantage of the opportunity to fortify their authoritarian style of governance. Nevertheless, Athens 2004 still made use of technological surveillance that remains in place up to the present (Samatas 2014).

with state agencies at mega-events, following their own commercial goals (Yu et al. 2009, 401) in what is also known as 'security beyond the state' (Abrahamsen and Williams 2011).

These sport mega-event security standards make use of a wide range of measures that are summarized in the following list:

1. Pre-planning: control zones around the central venues, evacuation plans, contamination and decontamination, major incident access and technical information to plan everything in advance.
2. 'Island security' and 'locking down strategies' (Fussey et al. 2011, 141): areas of host cities are furnished with large expanses of steel fencing and concrete blocks surrounding the sporting venues. Strong police presence, private security, permanent and temporary CCTV cameras, and airport-style checkpoints to screen spectators. Test-fields for new technologies.
3. Air and ground control: periphery buffer zones with police presence, law-enforcement techniques, helicopters, no-fly zones, 'fleet of mobile CCTV vehicles, road checks and stop and search procedures' (Fussey et al. 2011, 141).
4. Security legacies: the attempt to have long-term benefits for crime reduction is considered a 'stimulus' for the host country to build up a permanent security plan (Fussey et al. 2011, 141).

Principally, the latter came to the fore in the wake of the Brazilian bid for the 2016 Rio de Janeiro Olympics, which was inspired by the London Olympic security preparations (Coaffee et al. 2011, 3323).

Differently and in addition to this account, Bennett and Haggerty list other important points to be included in a standard model of sport mega-event security:

> increased use of video-surveillance at prominent and vulnerable sites; uses of secure perimeter fencing; criminal background checks for employees, volunteers and athletes; vehicle monitoring; the use of radio-frequency identification devices (RFIDs) on passes and tickets; biometric identification measures; satellite monitoring; the designation of special 'fan zones' for collective viewing of events; the regulation of protest and dissent; overhead unmanned aerial vehicles; mobile fingerprinting identification systems; and enhanced controls at land, sea and air borders.

> Each mega-event now exhibits a 'total security' effort akin to planning and deployment in times of war. (2011, 1)

In essence, there is an urbanization, globalization, technologicalization, commercialization, and militarization that composes the sport mega-event security standardization (Yu et al. 2009, 391; Klauser 2008, 75, 2011a, 124). In other words, the globalized and technology-driven standards of sport mega-event security are not only forwarded by the interests of international security corporations but also intrude into urban space. Three of these standards are most important for this book, as the totality of security claims, the surveillance schemes, and the militarization of public security lay at the core of Brazil's mega-event preparations too.

Total Security Strategies: 'Olympic Spaces of Exception'

The total security strategies are similarly carried out together with diverse policing efforts distributed on three differential pillars: exceptional, event-driven policing; private policing; and militarized policing (Fussey et al. 2011, 63). As outlined above, a world that is framed by terrorism threats and high degrees of risk and uncertainty will consequently affect sport mega-event security measures as organizers have to effectuate their 'planning for the worst' (Boyle and Haggerty 2012). Organizers utilize a security discourse to convince the public of the necessity of applying sport mega-event security measures to 'the nature of contemporary risks, the appropriate method of response, and the need to accept such methods in the face of unpredictable risks' (Boyle and Haggerty 2012, 255). The security measures deployed 'at mega-events reinforce the taken for granted sense that such measures are required' to avoid risks (Boyle and Haggerty 2009, 269).

The direct consequences of the post-9/11 context have impacted on the proliferation of standardized total security strategies as

> the threat from terrorism is spatially imprinted in 'total' security ensembles that simultaneously standardised, transferable and mobile, and which risk being disassociated from their host environments. (Coaffee et al. 2011, 3323)

These total security measures at mega-events are known as *islands of security* or *lockdown* measures that isolate the sports venues from the rest of the city. Long before the Covid-19 pandemic, lockdown strategies were experienced in London as counterterrorism measures, also known as 'rings of steel' that are intended to create temporary resilient entities (Coaffee and Wood 2006, 512), were then transformed into 'Olympic rings of steel' (Fussey and Coaffee 2011).

Increasingly, authors have also made reference to Agamben's (2005) 'State of Exception' (Lyon 2007; Neocleous 2008; Hagemann 2010; Graham 2010; Fussey and Coaffee 2011; Fussey et al. 2012) to explain how contemporary security governance is carried out and how the exceptional nature of mega-events shapes the conditions within which event security unfolds in 'Olympic States of Exception' (Fussey and Coaffee 2011; Fussey et al. 2011). Here it is argued that sport mega-event security creates isolated spaces of exception within a city, deploying very specific forms of security and order. Others argue that the prism of a state of exception can bring to the fore 'lockdown' security strategies within host cities which are then absorbed into the normal security schemes present before, during, and after the Games (Coaffee 2015, 200). These spaces function at a different tempo and under different rules to the other parts of the city and are inspired by the lockdown strategies mentioned above (Fussey et al. 2011, 61). Klauser (2011b) showed this through the example of FIFA Fan Zones and Fussey et al. (2011) with the Olympic Park in Newham. After reviewing the total security standard at sport mega-events, I now turn to the other important standard of electronic surveillance in the following section.

Surveillance at Sport Mega-Events

Alongside the total security politics, the literature indicates another central process that underlines sport mega-event security: the surveillance of public space (Klauser 2008, 64), carried out by a variety of actors from the public and private sectors (Fussey et al. 2012, 271; Klauser 2013, 291), often in public–private partnerships (Samatas 2011a, 3354; Klauser 2012, 1046). Some of the studies carried out in the realm of mega-events in relation to surveillance are important guidance for my own work and for the Foucauldian framework of this book.

Electronic surveillance is here defined as the focused, routine, and systematic process of data gathering (Lyon 2007). In the realm of mega-events, surveillance techniques have become one of the most important tools for security agents to control urban space. Since the 2006 World Cup, Fan Zones, originally not managed by FIFA and UEFA, have become a fixed requirement for tournaments (Klauser 2011, 128) which enable the control of social activities in specific small and manageable units. These specific portions of space, separated from their surroundings, were transformed into 'disproportionally commercialized spatial entities' (Klauser 2008, 75). According to Klauser (2013, 280), there are, therefore, three central functions associated with surveillance in the mega-event environment. First, surveillance technologies separate, control, and manage access; second, they manage circulation; and third, they monitor internal organization and specific spatial enclaves. Klauser makes an important argument that surveillance at mega-events can only be understood in full when we consider the mutual relationship between space and surveillance:

> surveillance (in its spatialities) has to be studied simultaneously with regard to fluidity and fixity, flows and presences, circulations and enclosures, external separation and internal organisation, because it is the articulation and reconciliation of precisely these contrapuntal pairs of logics that condition the functioning and implications of urban surveillance today. (2013, 291)

Furthermore, Klauser (2013, 291) stresses the importance of space for surveillance and vice versa, making the important distinction that the secret is not hidden *in* the space itself but rather in the *motivation*, in the aims, and in the intentions that drive surveillance today. Klauser (2013, 296–7) highlights these motivations in three principal findings from EURO 2008 in Austria and Switzerland. Firstly, he found that a variety of complex spatial logics of surveillance entered into conflict, shaped one another, and complemented each other. For example, railway stations at EURO 2008 not only worked as a means to monitor spectators but also were highly secured zones 'in their own right' (Klauser 2013, 295). This is the result of 'intertwined ambitions to channel, filter and follow circulations, to enclose, fix, monitor and organise spatial enclaves, and to create and defend spatially bound atmospheres' (Klauser 2013, 296). Second, Klauser argues that these surveillance measures have a dual function. On the one hand, they enable people to move around, but on the other hand they prevent others gaining access to certain areas. Third, he shows that these surveillance measures serve the purpose not just of one singular actor in the field but rather a variety of actors (Klauser 2013, 297). Klauser (2013, 294) embeds his framework in Foucault's (2007) concept within which the French philosopher describes a 'security apparatus' that does not fix the territory any more but allows circulation, and guarantees that there is a constant flow and movement, which provides the foundation for the analysis of this book for the Rio de Janeiro case study, as shown in the Introduction and as will further appear in Chapter 4.[4]

Fussey (2011, 106–8) connects electronic surveillance measures at mega-events to the use of these devices in general. Crucial issues of surveillance measures at mega-events can be related to the 'scale and reach' of these technologies as they are subject to shortcomings that can affect the event's security (Fussey 2011, 109). More important is to consider ethical issues that are bound to the use of technological surveillance. Fussey (2011, 109) identifies these as 'legacy', 'legitimacy', 'locality', 'listings', and 'legislation'. In other words, surveillance technologies must be questioned for the long-lasting imprints they may leave within host cities once the Games have passed, and what legitimacy is acquired for this long-term use of such measures which will become important for this book looking at the surveillance legacy in Rio de Janeiro. Having outlined the various patterns of surveillance at mega-events, let us now turn to the militarization dynamics that contribute to the standardization of mega-event security.

[4] Another Foucauldian concept that scholars have frequently used to refer to mechanisms of surveillance is the panopticon (Foucault 1994). The literature, however, is rather divided as to whether Foucault's panoptical concept explains the ways in which surveillance materializes in contemporary societies. Klauser's (2013) results shed light on the fact that the Foucauldian concept of the panopticon cannot fully explain contemporary surveillance strategies. It is no longer about 'a delusive pattern of surveillance' (Bennett and Haggerty 2011, 3) but about sophisticated digital networks that grasp vast quantities of data on an everyday basis and shape everyday life in a completely different way. While Baasch (2011) argues that Foucault's disciplinary societies, in combination with Deleuze's (1992) concept of control societies, can give birth to a strong analytical framework, Haggerty and Ericson (2000, 608–9) opt to frame the newest surveillance measures as 'assemblages'. It seems as if the definition by David Lyon (2001, 2) takes these processes into account: '[surveillance] is any collection and processing of personal data, whether identifiable or not, for the purpose of influencing or managing those whose data have been gathered'. This managing is no longer deployed by simply controlling objects and subjects in one particular space but rather, as pointed out by Foucault's (2007) lectures at the Collège de France (1977–8), it enables and controls flux and mobility in space.

Militarization and Militarism at Sport Mega-Events

The total security strategies laid out above refer to militarization processes at mega-events (Giulianotti and Klauser 2011; Coaffee et al. 2011). However, sport mega-events are not only used to militarize public security; increasingly one can observe that the military itself delivers and participates in securing mega-events (Clavel 2013). As indicated, mega-event security patterns cannot be analysed without relying on ongoing trends and tendencies in more general security developments within the host cities, as mega-event-related security is indelibly connected to the militarization of urban space, everyday life, and society as such. Both *militarization* and *militarism* are relevant concepts for understanding mega-event security mechanisms and have to be understood in their difference (Kinsella 2013, 105).

Whereas *militarism* refers to multiple and cross-disciplinary significations and can be understood as an ideology or as military build-up (Stavrianakis and Selby 2013, 11–16), and 'stresses aggressiveness and the use of force and the glorification of military power, weaponry, and technology as the means to solve problems' (Kraska 1998, 102), *militarization* has been mostly used to refer to a process that describes the ways in which military options become relevant in the social field, when power relations shift towards the military sector to the detriment of the non-military sectors in society (Kinsella 2013, 105), and when 'any part of society becomes controlled or dependent on the military or on military values' (Enloe 1980, 132, quoted in Kraska 1998, 102). These tendencies towards a militarization of civil spheres, as much as the use of the military within mega-event security, are discussed and analysed in the mega-event security-related literature, as the following paragraph illustrates.

Minas Samatas (2007, 2011a, 2011b) has analysed the militarizing effects of the 2004 Athens Olympics on the city's public security. Alongside the extreme surveillance that materialized in Athens, the city witnessed one of the largest security operations in peacetime Europe. The 2004 Olympics were the first Summer Games following 9/11 and served to exemplify how sport mega-events have become the testing ground for major surveillance and security operations (also Floridis 2004). Athens was the first city that transformed its Olympic venues into high-security zones and clearly linked the international fear around terrorism and the international security industry to mega-events (Samatas 2007, 221). Furthermore, Athens was the first example of a city that used installed security devices as a security legacy for ambitions of counterterrorism and the combatting of everyday crime in post-Olympic times (Samatas 2007, 221). The 2010 FIFA World Cup and its security governance is the most recent example (Cornelissen 2011a, 3223), and Brazil planned to use the mega-events for the same purposes (Gaffney 2010, 17).

In Athens, the SAIC–Siemens collaboration put the largest ever security and surveillance system, called C4I, in place. It became famous for its tremendous technological problems and its de facto failure during the Olympics (Samatas 2011b, 63). Notably, the system was originally designed for military purposes and its deployment in Athens underlines the militarizing trend in mega-event security. With the C4I failing, the military took over and deployed 15,000 troops to supervise and participate in the Olympic security schemes (Samatas 2007, 229). Similar issues arose in London 2012, where the security corporation tasked with managing the spectator controls failed to provide enough personnel and the military and police were required to step in (Hobbs et al. 2014, 9). London was in many respects the climax of the military participation in, and militarization of, mega-events before the Brazilian Games a few years later. The 2012 Games had a double effect: on the one side, the police were militarized through military equipment and the installation of rapid emergency teams. On the other side, military materials such as 'Rapier and Startreak surface-to-air missiles' were widely deployed in public spaces (Boykoff and Fussey 2014, 261–3).

Reconnecting with the discussions on militarization tendencies at mega-events, we can observe that these are inherent to many societies globally. Militarization of public security is something that has been on the march for a long time, although it accelerated after 9/11 when the US Department of Homeland Security released new fluxes of money to equip local police SWAT teams with new material and expanded these Special Forces to smaller towns (Balko 2013, 242). Notably, the militarization of North American police forces also goes in tandem with the rise of so-called Police Paramilitary Units, which have been observed as being normalized in the United States (Kraska and Kappeler 1997, 2015), thereby continuously blurring the boundaries between the police and the military (Kraska 2007).

Stephen Graham's (2010) theory of a 'New Military Urbanism' can help us to understand both security measures at mega-events and the mega-events as a mirror for further developments in wider security realms. In his book *Cities under Siege*, Graham outlines how new military ideologies break ground in the everyday life of ordinary citizens. Although not all aspects of his theory seem to fit this example, it is worth outlining some key features for the purpose of understanding better the ways in which cities and everyday life have become militarized. Graham (2010, 62) illustrates strategies of urbanizing warfare and stresses the argument that the military, mainly consisting of soldiers from rural environments, is increasingly deployed in urban settings, besieged cities, and troubled neighbourhoods. Cities and their boroughs are invaded by the military to pacify *problematic* neighbourhoods, as seen on different occasions in the United States.

Increasingly, external and internal security have merged, and governments apply the strategy of framing international security as something that has to be defended globally: the war on terror is fought in the Middle East, national police divisions are trained as anti-terror units, and the military is deployed within national territories (Bigo 2006, 389). Central to these developments are the agencies that stand between the police and the military: the private security corporations and the transnational think tanks that have a vision of a catastrophic future (Bigo 2006, 402). More to the point, it is exactly this process that can be witnessed at sport mega-events: armies exercise policing roles, global and national intelligence agencies work together, the police engage in restoring democracy on a global scale, and all agencies focus on both global and local threats.

Within the new military urbanism, military technologies merge with civilian use as technologies which were meant to work in military spheres, such as surveillance mechanisms, communication, and simulation, and are now transmitted into everyday urban life and for the governmental control of ordinary citizens (Graham 2010, 65). The new military urbanism

> uses the power of the state to violent [*sic*] reconfigure or erase urban space, as a means to allay purported threats, to clear new space for the exigencies of global-city formation, neoliberal production, or the creation of an urban tabula rasa capable of generating maximally profitable bubbles of real-estate speculation. (Graham 2010, 83)

Taking Brazil as an example, the occupation of the favelas, the slum clearances, and the real-estate speculations in the years prior to the World Cup and the Olympics bear a strong resemblance to the claims made by Graham. Although in Rio de Janeiro the use of military troops is nothing new, it is breathtaking how similar to the above description of a new military urbanism were the mega-events organized in the city (Saborio 2014; Savell 2016), as I will show in this book.

Research Lacunas

The literature on security at mega-events puts forward two arguments, both of which indicate the niches in which serious and substantial research has yet to be conducted. First, Yu et al. (2009, 401) point out that there should be a clearer focus on the ways in which mega-events can provide information about the various relationships between security-related issues on a variety of levels: the local, the regional, and the global. Furthermore, they raise the question of how global security partnerships between different stakeholders from private and public agents intervene in very specific local circumstances, both on a short-term but even more so on a long-term basis. Second, different authors repeatedly direct their focus to the lack of research on security legacies in general: the security policies, security and surveillance technologies, and security-related legislation that remain in place in a country, region, or host city long after the mega-event has finished and moved on to play out its spectacle elsewhere (Klauser 2008; Giulianotti and Klauser 2009; Klauser 2015).

Diverse studies have addressed these lacunas and looked at the ways in which the specific security measures for mega-events have turned into permanent models of local security governance in host cities. One of these studies is put forth in Mina Samatas' (2014) most recent monograph, *The 'Super-Panopticon' Scandal of the Athens 2004 Olympics and Its Legacy*, within which the author demonstrates that the 2004 Athens security operation still prevails in the city more than ten years after the Olympics. The study of the 2000 Sydney Games by Toohey and Taylor (2012) shows similar Olympic security effects that extended far beyond the Games and led to securitization and enhanced surveillance measures in Australian sporting arenas. Other studies expose the electronic camera surveillance-related legacies deriving from the 2006 World Cup (Eick 2011a), the militarization legacy for the Olympic Winter Games 2010 in Vancouver (Molnar 2015), and how the policing practices for London 2012 left a legacy within the everyday police work in London post-Olympics that also impacted on social exclusion patterns (Armstrong et al. 2016).

However, how we frame legacy is also important. Coaffee (2015, 205–8) has shown that if we look at 'transnational legacies', the 2012 London security preparations had an influence on the 2014 Sochi Games and on the host city of Rio de Janeiro. This gives insights into the already-mentioned security knowledge transfer that will reach an important level when looking at the concrete security preparations in Rio de Janeiro. In addition, a paper by Boykoff and Fussey (2014) sheds light on the fact that there are, on the one hand, visible security legacies and ongoing conflicts resulting from the Olympic Games, and on the other hand, rather shadowy legacies such as a knowledge transfer and new standards for military operations: 'In sum, the London 2012 Summer Games anted up a legacy not touched in bid materials: a repression-ready security state' (266; also Lindsay 2013).

Giulianotti and Klauser (2009, 51) make a strong case for more research to be conducted in the Global South where sport mega-events took place more recently, as there is still a lack of research on and about mega-events' globalized security patterns and how they impact on established local security dynamics within a Global South setting. This book attends to this need. With Brazil as the host for the 2014 World Cup and the 2016 Olympics, there appeared a unique research opportunity to investigate how mega-event security impacts in a Global South setting.

As stated in the Introduction to this book, one of the rare exceptions offering research in a Global South setting are the studies by Cornelissen (2010, 2011a, 2011b). Other works on South Africa have been conducted by a variety of authors to illustrate how FIFA and other stakeholders had an interest in deploying surveillance at very specific spaces that are of strategic interest to the mega-event organizers, owners, and sponsors (Eisenhauer et al. 2013), as well as how specific policing tactics shifted from reactive to proactive during the 2010 tournament (Fonio and Pisapia 2015). Further research in South Africa has investigated how police and military forces have contributed to the maintenance and enforcement of their own power and have helped to secure wealth accumulation (McMichael 2013). A series of academic writings have addressed the cultural significance of the World Cup and urban renewal at the South African World Cup edition with no focus on questions of security (see Alegi 2008; Cottle 2011; Steinbrink et al. 2011; Alegi and Bolsmann 2012; see also Brogden and Shearings (1993) for a more holistic view of police work in South Africa).

When it comes to research about Brazil's mega-event cycle and the host city of Rio de Janeiro, many studies concentrate on the urban transformations (Gaffney 2010; Silvestre and de Oliveira 2012; Brownill et al. 2013; Alves dos Santos Junior 2015), gentrification processes (Gaffney 2016c), how the city aimed to lift up its image (Steinbrink 2014), and what it means for mega-events to take place in such socially divided cities as Rio (Curi et al. 2011). A whole volume sheds light on the various urban and social impacts of the 2014 World Cup, as well as the conflict relationships during preparation and delivery in the tournament's various host cities (Alves dos

Santos Junior et al. 2015; also Kassens-Noor et al. 2016). However, there is only a small amount of research that concentrates on the specific mega-event security of the World Cup and the Olympic Games in Brazil.

The limited scholarship on security-related topics regarding the Brazilian mega-events is often an analysis of the plans and possible outcomes of the mega-event security (McRoskey 2010; Gaffney 2015), or the various dynamics of smart technologies that are analysed as being part of the mega-event security preparations in Rio de Janeiro (Gaffney and Robertson 2016). Further scientific inquiry has focused on the discourses of the pacifying police programme in Rio (Prouse 2012). An exception is the research by Bruno Vasconcelos Cardoso (2012, 2013a, 2013b, 2014, 2016, 2019), whose analysis of the surveillance patterns and the technologization of Rio de Janeiro's public security within the CICCs sheds light on the history, impacts, and functions of surveillance patterns in Rio independently from but influenced by—and influential for—the mega-events in Brazil. Nonetheless, research rarely looks at the specific conditions within the immediacy of the state security apparatus before, during, and after the mega-events, which is a shortcoming to be addressed within the present work. There is a lack of studies that explicitly look at the local security conditions from within the security forces at mega-events in a Global South setting, a setting in which state violence and serious public security issues are an everyday reality. This book investigates, therefore, the different layers of hierarchies of *those who plan*, *those who manage*, and *those who realize* the mega-event security operations.

Giulianotti and Klauser (2009, 57) clearly illustrate that 'the social dimensions of SME [sport mega-event] securitisation have been rather underplayed'. In a bid to address this and the other research gaps, this book aims to cover the identified shortcomings by investigating how global sport mega-event security may impact on local and established cultural and social implications of security conditions. However, *social implications* may be understood not only as social consequences for the urban poor but also—and for this work more importantly—for members of the police forces involved. Therefore, this book also investigates 'the resonances and dissonances between globally established exemplars and locally anchored traditions and practices as they are negotiated in situ' (Klauser 2015, 223).

This work is concerned with the various effects of globalized mega-event security standards and how these adapted to the local Brazilian security conditions, and thus continues the research tradition of sport mega-event security scholarship on the standards of mega-event security. In addition, it seeks to fill the research lacunas of studies that look at Global South settings and presents a particular challenging security scenario in the case of Rio de Janeiro. The Brazilian authorities have consistently framed the adapted global security models within the local security strategies as able to both leave a legacy and improve the local Brazilian public security. This will be contested in the course of this book.

The scene is now set to switch to Brazil and look at the pre-security conditions at the time of the FIFA World Cup 2014 and the Olympic Games 2016.

2
An Olympic City at War

In October 2009 Rio de Janeiro made worldwide news for an incredible incident after the World Cup and the Olympics had been awarded to Brazil. A police helicopter was shot down by drug traffickers in the city's North Zone, in a favela called Morro dos Macacos (Monkey Mountain) around ten kilometres away from the wider favela complex Alemão (German Complex). Two officers died and two were seriously injured (Jornal Hoje 2009). The incident marked the temporary climax of the urban conflict that has shattered Rio de Janeiro since the 1980s. The shootout also happened a year after José Mariano Beltrame, Rio de Janeiro's State Secretary of Public Security at that time, announced that he wanted to reduce the day-to-day gunfights between the police and the drug traffickers.

In his autobiography published in 2014 Beltrame says that when he took office in 2007, he wished to stop the vicious circle of a police force that kills and dies too much (Beltrame 2014, 78). For many years that vicious circle of violence in the city had cost too many victims in too many boroughs. In particular, the racialized police operations in the many favelas and at the outskirts of the city terrorized the everyday life of ordinary citizens who were caught in the gunfights between the drug-trafficking groups and the police. Although these circumstances were ongoing for many years, Beltrame only pursued the idea of the famous peacekeeping military police units (Unidade de Polícia Pacificadora, UPPs) after a series of incidents in the same year that spread horror among Rio's population also outside of the favelas. The drug-trafficking network Commando Vermelho (CV) (Red Command) set fire to a public bus on the populous Avenida Brasil within which seven passengers died. In the same year, the death of the six-year-old boy João Hélio was equally shocking. After an assault on the car in which he was travelling with his mother, João was dragged along outside the vehicle, trapped in his seatbelt, for seven kilometres. Another incident marked the government when two military police officers were assassinated and their weapons stolen. With only two months to go until the 2007 Pan-American

Policing Sport Mega-Events. Dennis Pauschinger, Oxford University Press. © Dennis Pauschinger 2024.
DOI: 10.1093/oso/9780192848055.003.0003

Games, Beltrame, as he says in his book, decided to give the drug traffickers a hard time and 'attack' them by occupying their major refuge, the favela complexes Alemão and Penha (Beltrame 2014, 98). As Alves and Evanson (2011, 1) record, 'Governor Sérgio Cabral, who had recently taken office, described the operation as a declaration of war.'

What Beltrame and Cabral talk less about is that for many residents in Rio's favelas life under the rule of drug traffickers, militias, and constant invasions by the police have long had a war-like scenario in the making. The war allegory, also chosen as the title for this chapter, therefore holds much truth as the siege of Rio's communities would become the normal conditions for the hosting of future mega-events in the city. And indeed, speaking to members of the Special Forces or favela residents, the experience of a war-like quotidian routine is something that had been present for many years before 2007. Following Beltrame (2014, 100), the above scenery turned the wheel of the urban conflict: 'The occupation of the two complexes at that time has been an inflection in the carioca security.'[1] Both complexes were occupied by police forces and gave ideological contributions to the birth of the idea of the UPP project that has, without doubt, heavily marked both the debate about, and the organization of, public security in Rio de Janeiro in recent years (Cano et al. 2012, 3).

The occupation of the city by military forces was nothing new to Rio. Already at the beginning of the 1990s this happened when Rio de Janeiro became a global stage for the United Nations Conference on Environment and Development (NCED), or ECO 1992 for short. After that, the road to hosting the World Cup and the Olympics was marked by a series of experiences with other major events such as the aforementioned 2007 Pan-American Games, the 2011 Conseil International du Sport Militaire (CISM) (Military World Games), the 2013 Jornada Munidal da Juventude (Catholic World Youth Day), and the 2013 FIFA Confederations Cup. Clearly, none of those previous events had the global importance of what lay in the future, and Beltrame and his team knew that they had to do something to diminish the urban conflict.

In addition, devastating levels of violence rattled the whole country. Looking at the data for the periods of the mega-events, the 2014 'Map of Violence' in the year of the World Cup, a government report on homicide and crime numbers, revealed that murder was the single most likely cause

[1] *Carioca* is the name that is given to people living in or who are from Rio de Janeiro. One can also say that when you speak about security in Rio, it is *carioca* security.

of death for young black male adults between 15 and 29. The Map showed that 56,337 homicides were committed in Brazil in 2012 alone, the highest number ever. This represents a homicide rate of 29 per 100,000 inhabitants (Waiselfisz 2014a, 35). The United Nations consider a rate higher than ten to be evidence of an epidemic. In Brazil, between 2008 and 2011, 206,005 homicide victims were registered; between 2004 and 2007, the 62 global armed conflicts—among them Iraq and Afghanistan—claimed 208,349 lives (Waiselfisz 2014b, 33). These numbers are also reflected in police killings, as the Brazilian police are one key factor in the insecurity dilemma faced by Brazilian society.

Between 1983 and 2012, North American police killed 11,090 people, while in Brazil, the police killed 17,688 between 2009 and 2015. In other words, the Brazilian police killed more people in a period of seven years than the US police did in 30. The victims here are the same as those most represented in the general homicide rates: young black men between 15 and 29, from the favelas or peripheries, and with very low-income backgrounds (FBSP 2016, 6–7). No other police force in the world kills as many people as the Brazilian police. The rate of people killed by the police per 100,000 inhabitants in Brazil (1.6) exceeds that in South Africa, although in the African country the homicide rate is higher (34.0). On the other hand, it must be said that Brazil has one of the highest rates of mortality among police officers: 393 died in total in 2015, 103 on duty and 290 off duty (FBSP 2016, 6–7). Looking at current data and new releases by the Brazilian Forum of Public Security, these numbers have even grown, as 6,357 people were killed following police interventions in 2019 (FBSP 2020, 12). To comprehend better the conditions of these devastating numbers, a look into the mechanisms of Brazil's public security organization and Rio de Janeiro's foundation of the urban conflict is necessary.

This chapter aims to analyse the historical development of the conditions that shape the security landscape of Rio de Janeiro today, and attempts to investigate how it came to be that the city presents such an urban conflict that is hardly comparable to any other city. Therefore, the chapter concentrates on the development of the violence and what I call the *urban conflict* that has put the city on the entrenched frontlines between drug-trafficking networks, militias, and the many different police agencies. Furthermore, the chapter illustrates the new phase of the conflict with its public security policies that are based upon the implementation of the UPPs and technological solutions for complex urban security challenges. But first, the chapter sheds brief light upon Brazil's public security sector to understand the ways in which the police forces in Brazil are organized, and to comprehend the many turns of Rio's urban conflict.

Violence in Urban Brazil

Many Brazilian scholars have written extensively about Brazil's and Rio's public security dynamics, and this book cannot do justice to all those who merit acknowledgement here (e.g. Cavalcanti 2020). What stands out in these works, however, is that it is not by accident that most of the victims of the city's daily shootouts are black, young, poor, and from favelas and the city's outskirts. The racial and class spatialization of the conflict is powerfully described by the phenomenon of the 'social accumulation of violence' (Misse 1999, 81) in which very early forms of state violence are directly linked to the labelling by political and economic elites of criminal behaviour upon non-white and poor populations and their territories in the city (Fischer 2008, 155), upon which I will further elaborate later in this chapter.

The story of state and public violence in urban Brazil is strongly connected to the ways in which cities grew between the 1950s and the 1980s (Caldeira 2006, 105). Driven by droughts and hopes for a better life, thousands left the Brazilian north-east region for the cities of São Paulo and Rio de Janeiro. People arriving in the urban centres could not afford to live in formal housing. In the big cities, thousands found refuge in favelas and peripheral neighbourhoods where urban development took place under disordered conditions. Barred from the minimum of public services, people in these areas needed to cope with the absence of water supply, healthcare, sanitation, social security provisions, and public services (Cardia 2000, 11–12).

Violence in these intensively disorientated urban areas increased especially in the late 1980s. Fast and uncoordinated urban growth (Cardia 2000, 5–12), and the *lost decade* of the 1980s, are some of the reasons for the high violence rates. As in so many post-colonies, neoliberalism has also hit Brazil with its full force (Comaroff and Comaroff 2006, 19–20), and an insufficient number of formal jobs forced the urban poor to work in the informal job market (Caldeira 2006, 114). As Caldeira (2006, 114) puts it: 'As a result of the economic crisis and related changes, the distribution of wealth—already bad—worsened, and perspectives of social mobility shrank considerably.'

When Rio de Janeiro became a crucial transit city for drugs smuggled from the Andes countries to Europe, drug trafficking began to play an important role in the Brazilian context and for the increasing violence (Coelho 2007, 351). In both Rio de Janeiro and São Paulo drug dealers recognized the youth as cheap labour, where mostly young men could earn more than in any of the other jobs available to them (Cardia 2000, 9). Linked to the drug-trafficking trade, the appearance of small arms ensured that conflicts and social disputes made the business incredibly deadly (Peres and Santos 2005, 59).

Contributing to the unbound violence in Brazil is the desolate condition of its prison system—a state-run system that follows the politics of 'killing and letting die' (Dal Santo 2022). At a public event in 2015, Rio's Ministério Público (Ministry of Public Prosecution) stressed that Brazilian prisons are 'houses of torture' and perpetuate inhuman conditions (Recording, Public Event Ministry of Public Prosecution Rio de Janeiro, 18 May 2015). While 49% of the prisoners are serving sentences for property crimes, 26% are in jail for drug-related crimes, and only 12% for homicides in the year of the World Cup (FBSP 2014, 7). The inhuman conditions in Brazilian prisons have served to encourage the formation of criminal networks within their walls.

The criminal organization Primeiro Comando da Capital (First Command of the Capital) is said to control 90% of the São Paulo state prisons, as well as prisons in several other states, and has the monopoly of the Brazilian drug- and arm—trafficking trade (Biondi 2010, 2018; Denyer Willis 2015). In 2021, 759,518 people were imprisoned (in Federal and state prisons, and police incarcerations), with 76.1% of these in closed regimes, still waiting for sentencing and being held under remand conditions (FBSP 2021, 15). In contrast, the prison system had in 2020 a deficit of 242,561 vacancies (FBSP 2021, 193). The major struggles of the system are, therefore, overcrowding that leads to inhuman conditions in the cells and an aggressive atmosphere among inmates. Institutional violence, the lack of legal and medical support, torture, no rehabilitation measures, regular escapes and rebellions, and too many homicides are just some of the tremendous problems (Salla 2003, 421; Adorno and Salla 2007, 18). Notably, the prison system reproduces the same population profiles as seen in the homicide rates: black, poor males from the favelas or peripheries, making it a racist system of the 'punishment of the poor' (Wacquant 2009). Of note, 66.3% of the Brazilian prison population about which ethnic information is available (599,932) are considered black (FBSP 2021, 203).

The Brazilian Police: Continuation of the Militaristic and Colonial Past

Writing about security and violence in Brazil, we have to look closer at the police, its organization, and its history.[2] I start doing so by examining the transition from military dictatorship to democracy, and the new 1988 constitution that was a very important landmark for Brazilian democracy, and will later also look at the police origins in the times of slavery. Indeed, the 1988 constitution asserts rights that are crucial for the democratic experience and it is one of the most extensive constitutions in the world (Zaverucha 2010, 45). The text established central civil rights and guaranteed the protection of minorities such as indigenous populations, criminalized torture and racism, and ensured the right to life of every citizen (Pinheiro 1990, 43).

Nonetheless, the 1988 constitution has been criticized extensively. The core critique of aspects focusing on security mainly implies that the military has not forfeited any of its power. Although the constitution introduced democratic structures and free elections, this did not change the problems which existed prior to the military dictatorship such as the racist and colonially infused past (Fausto 2002, 290). During the military dictatorship, torture, death squads, arbitrary detainments, and political persecution were part of the governance strategy. As the military were able to modulate the transition from their regime to democracy at their own will (Koonings 1999, 207), this led to the maintenance of certain privileges for the military such as the extended amnesty law that would make it impossible to legally prosecute military members for any crimes committed during the dictatorship (Schwarcz and Starling 2015, 470).

Even today, Brazilian society is divided in its view on how to judge this chapter of its history. Did the military help to maintain national integrity and security, or did it harm the country? The military itself is still convinced that it saved the nation from communism and persecuted the political enemy for the sake of the country (Koonings 1999, 215–16). The election of Jair Bolsonaro, without doubt, helped a revitalization of glorifying the military dictatorship and the defence of using violence against groups that should be protected by the Brazilian constitution (Salem and Larkins 2021, 77).

[2] A detailed history of the Brazilian police and reform efforts is analysed in the edited volume by Riccio and Skogan (2018).

Most importantly, the transition embedded the militarization of the public sphere into the 1988 constitution. It is to a large extent the organization of the security sector as regulated in the document that makes reforms so difficult even today, also because the term 'public security' was chosen over the term mostly used in other Latin American countries, that of 'citizen security'. Looking at the ways the Brazilian state construes the term, it is the security of the state, not that of citizens, that is emphasized (Mesquita Neto 2011). The critique of the constitution stems from exactly this authoritarian definition of public security.

By way of example, it is worth consulting the constitution's article 144, 'On Public Security'. The article defines exactly who the Brazilian state understands to be responsible for internal security: the federal police, the federal highway police, the federal railroad police, the civil police, the military police, and the municipal guards. Most interesting is the fact that the military police and the firefighters are not subject to any civil law, but respond exclusively to military courts and are designated as the reserve of the armed forces. Strikingly, article 142 designates the military as being responsible not only for defending the homeland against external threats but also protecting constitutional power and the law, and maintaining public order. To put it another way, Brazilian public security is not limited to but is strongly dominated by military forces. Zaverucha helpfully summarizes:

> The militarization of public space in Brazil did not happen by chance. It was constitutionally protected, and it has been occurring with increasing frequency at the federal and state levels, in governments both the right and the left. (2000, 9)

Even though the public security sector is marked by the military police, the different police institutions, by constitution, have different tasks. As stipulated in article 144, the federal police, military police, and civil police principally shape the Brazilian policing landscape. The federal police force is responsible for crimes that have dimensions which pass across the frontiers of the state units. Their speciality is investigating cases of organized crime, corruption, and drug trafficking. In each state capital, the federal police have a regional office. In addition to these investigations, they are the organization that regulates immigration at the Brazilian borders. Related institutions are the federal road and the federal environmental police. In the year of the World Cup, the federal police forces operated with a comparably small number of approximately 11,000 officers nationwide (Souza and Battibugli 2014, 297). Nonetheless, the federal police had a crucial role within the mega-event security plans, as will be shown later.

The constitution demands that each of the union's states has a military and a civil police force, both of which have very different functionalities. The military and civil police institutions are clearly crucial for understanding the security sector in urban Brazil. To date, these two police forces have the most important tasks in the Brazilian security sector, which is to prevent and to resolve crimes. Because of this constitutional obligation, the Brazilian federation has 54 different police institutions, each of which has its own organization, culture, and tradition. As stated above, Brazilian municipalities can create the office of municipality guards, who oversee the security of public places, public buildings, and public property in general (Brazilian constitution, art. 144, §8). In some states such as São Paulo, the municipality guards are allowed to carry firearms, while in Rio de Janeiro this is not permitted. Although the constitution regulates the tasks of each police force, cooperation is often impaired; they regularly investigate the same crimes and do not share any of their data (Rolim 2007, 12–13). Furthermore, the civil and military police forces do not have shared and integrated software, which would enable them to build up common databases. Confidence between the two police forces is also lacking, which gives leeway to failures and ineffectiveness (Silva Filho 2006, 131). During the World Cup's opening match in São Paulo, these differences threatened to ruin the tournament on the first day, when a personal conflict between members of the policing institutions almost led to a sniper killing another policeman approaching the Brazilian president during the Brazil–Croatia game (interview, public security specialist, 25 September 2014).

Institutional conflicts between the different police forces have historical roots. Prior to the armed forces taking over in 1969, the civil police was a relatively prestigious institution. However, the military decided to take them off the streets and allocated the patrolling function exclusively to the military police (Battibugli 2009, 39). In the course of Brazilian history, the organization of the security sector has passed through a series of changes and the Brazilian police trajectory is tightly connected to the city of Rio de Janeiro. The city was the former capital of the Portuguese crown and the capital of the Brazilian republic. The reforms of the policing institutions have been a steady adaptation to changes in the Brazilian political system, clearly demonstrating the relationship of mutual influence that police, politics, and power are involved in.

Rio de Janeiro's police forces have changed during the different epochs, from the 1809 proclamation of the Republic to the Vargas era between 1930 and 1945. The military regime then exacerbated the situation by once again changing the ways in which the police forces were configured and giving them the form that they have retained up to today. The division into one military and one civil force had already been established in 1831, and was not touched by the military regime. However, as noted above, the generals took away the prestige of the civil police, granting the 'privilege' of patrolling the streets to the military police (Caldeira 2000a, 143).

In Brazilian history the police have generally had wide autonomy to fulfil several duties: to maintain public order, to investigate crimes, and to punish whomever they arrested—independently of any judicial legislator. Instead of bringing people to court, the police could establish their own rules and imprison, beat up, and even torture suspected perpetrators (Fischer 2008, 154). This autonomy dates back to the times of slavery where the police could arbitrarily enforce their power on slaves (Holloway 1993, 52). Later they expanded these racist practices to the urban poor. This led to the complicated relationship between the police and the population, who experience the institutions as arbitrary and repressive. Put in a different way, the tasks of the Brazilian police have traditionally been both those of resolving and preventing crimes, but also of controlling the poor (Caldeira 2000a, 144) and targeting especially the populations of African descent (Alves 2014, 2016, 2018).

The Brazilian police forces today are in many ways a relic of the military dictatorship which applies to the military police in the most concrete ways. Violent practices were deeply entrenched during the military regime and continued in the democratic era. In his famous book, *Meu depoimento Sobre o Esquadrão da Morte* (*My Testimony about the Death Squad*), Helio Pereira Bicudo (1977) gives an account of a death squad that was formed by police officers and widely supported by politicians and justice system officials. Scheper-Hughes' (2006) research on death squads in the north-east of Brazil shows that these phenomena continue regardless into the democratic present. Another example is the police unit ROTA (Rondas Ostensivas Tobias de Aguiar) from São Paulo. The unit was founded in 1969 to combat terrorist activity and act against groups of bank robbers, and continued to be used during the democratic regime (Mingardi 1992, 73–4; Caldeira 2000a, 169; also Barcellos 2008). It becomes apparent that state violence, in both its physical and social forms, represents two sides of the same coin. The policing institutions have had a mandate to fulfil their tasks in their own ways and had the support of those ruling the country, regions, and municipalities. The generals institutionalized violence in such a way that, after the transition, the civil government was unable to simply switch to a different policing system. These kinds of transitional problems with police forces from an authoritarian regime to democracy are not limited to Brazil or other Latin American countries. Brogden and Shearing (1993) have powerfully laid out how in South Africa this transition faced enormous challenges. Much as in South Africa (Shearing 1986), Brazil also has a large private security sector in which official state police officers work on their free days (Larkins 2023). In Brazil the militaristic path has continued in the democratic presence and transformed into the current policing model.

Several incidents that happened in the early 1990s illustrate how the police, often supported by large groups of the population, killed suspects, cleansed the streets of the unwanted, or took revenge for any kind of social dispute. The famous massacre of 111 prisoners in the Casa de Detenção de São Paulo, popularly known as Carandiru prison, exemplifies how police killings were presented as the appropriate method for societal conflict resolution. Although the rebellion in the prison was already over, the ROTA was sent in with bloody results (Caldeira 2000a, 174). In 1993 military policemen were accused of killing eight sleeping street children in Candelária Square in Rio on the night of 23 July. That same year, on 30 August an invasion of 40 police officers, disguised as civilians, killed 21 inhabitants without any prior criminal records in the favela of Vigário Geral. Yet another invasion in 1994 in the favela of Nova Brasília cost 21 civilians their lives (Caldeira and Holston 1998, 266–7). In 2000, one of the survivors of the Candelária massacre, Sandro do Nascimento, took hostages in a public bus in Rio, an incident that became famous as the Bus 174 drama, for its live nationwide TV broadcasting, and for the tremendous police failure (Pinheiro Ramos and Aparecida Nova 2003). After many hours the police tried to capture the kidnapper while he came out of the bus with one of the hostages. The police killed the hostage and later Sandro do Nascimento in their car, who they first had to save from lynching by a furious crowd of spectators (Padilha 2002).

These events expose the complicated relationship between the tradition of police violence, the state, and the population who often demands these actions. Although many years have passed, the ROTA still cruise the streets of São Paulo and tough-on-crime policies are still popular. The former ROTA commander Paulo Telhado won the majority of votes in the 2012 state elections when represented the Partido Social Democrata do Brasil

(PSDB) (Social Democratic Party of Brazil) in São Paulo state, the same party of former sociologist and Brazilian president Fernando Henrique Cardoso. Telhado sees no shame in publicly bragging about the number of criminals he has already killed (Denyer Willis 2015, 37).

However, it is not just the military past that marks the functioning of Brazilian police today. Roberto Kant de Lima's (1995, 140) ethnographic study on Rio's civil police paints a picture of a police that is a mirror of the judiciary system, a system that reproduces the inequalities of Brazilian society, which is hierarchically classified by attributing different degrees of citizenship and civilization to different sectors of the society. This happens despite the 1988 constitution that awards all Brazilians at least theoretically with equal rights. As Zaluar points out:

> Even after the enactment of the new constitution in 1988, which guaranteed civil rights to all, the poor continued to suffer grave violations of these rights at the hands of the police. (2007, 40)

Often the police decide to whom they attribute these rights. They continuously apply their own ethical codes that are only defined and known by the police themselves (Kant de Lima 1995, 141). These ethical codes agglomerate a set of rules and practices that are rooted in an autonomous interpretation of the Brazilian law (Kant de Lima 1995, 65). In other words, the police use both the official legal system and a set of unofficial codes that are inherent to the police tradition (Kant de Lima 1995, 134).

One of the more complicated aspects within the Brazilian criminal justice system stems from the fact that the civil police is the first juridical instance someone faces after an arrest. This turns the police station into a legal registry or notary office. Stated differently, what is written in official police reports is officially recognized as the truth as it was approved by a legal instance (interview, Roberto Kant de Lima, 18 September 2014). Almost never is it questioned how the results of a police report, the confession of a perpetrator, or the testimonial of a victim came into existence. Common police practice is to 'discover the truth through confession' (Kant de Lima 1995, 84). Following Kant de Lima (1995, 84), this contributes to the use of torture within the civil police as a tool to advance police investigations. The Brazilian police, therefore, is confronted with a paradox as they seem to be both an agency of surveillance and an auxiliary branch of the Brazilian judiciary (Kant de Lima 1995, 85). As Kant de Lima (1995, 85) summarizes, 'The consequence in practice is that the police turn into a non-official agency of judgement and punishment of [those who are] right and [those who are] criminals.'[3]

Yet, we know relatively little about how police officers themselves deal with doing police work in a city like Rio.[4] Only a few studies have focused on the civil police officers themselves, including Mingardi's (1992) ethnography with civil police officers, Denyer Willis' (2015) ethnographic account of homicide detectives in São Paulo, and Kant de Lima's (1995), Husain's (2007), and Medeiros' (2018) brilliant work with Rio's civil police. Being a police officer in Rio also means to be entangled with, to participate in, and to suffer physically and mentally from the working conditions in a hierarchical organization and a most deadly police routine (Cano and Magaloni 2016). This book will contribute to these studies by shedding light upon the police officers and their work during the mega-events.

When I once asked a Brazilian police officer why the police forces are so violent—mainly against black and poor people—she defended herself by answering that the police are just a mirror of Brazilian society. And indeed, what is engrained in the ways in which policing is carried out in Rio today reflects how 'colonial and racist legacies' are embedded 'in the Brazilian social order', as Ystanes and Salem (2020) write, referring to post-colonial and feminist Brazilian literature. In particular, the inspiring works of Abdias do Nascimento (1990) and Léila Gonzalez (1988) have promoted a much-needed critical analysis of how a modern Brazilian state-building project consistently erases the black heritage in both popular culture as a project of whitening and of death politics. This persistence of racial and social othering reflects directly in the ways in which urban life is structured by and through the constant controls and killings of black populations (Alves 2018). Following Jaime Amparo Alves' (2018, 57–61) urgent analysis of policing in São Paulo, the police produce a racially informed social order by waging war against black bodies in spatially distributed territories (favelas and urban peripheries) through killings, so that 'police terror, then, becomes a tool for the spatial arrangement of racial difference' (also Medeiros 2019). In this sense, police work in this way is exactly how it is wanted in modern Brazil. The relic of the past has become a reality of today. And this is reflected directly in the roots of Rio de Janeiro's urban conflict.

[3] My own translation from Brazilian Portuguese.
[4] An exception, for example, is Roxana Pessoa Cavalcanti's (2020) book.

Rio de Janeiro's Urban Conflict

Rio's current security dynamics are strongly connected to the general public security history of Brazil. Whereas much has been written about the composition and the becoming of Rio as a city rattled by an urban conflict, a standout is the work of sociologist Michel Misse, who analysed Rio de Janeiro's criminological landscape intensively in a series of publications (e.g. Misse 1999, 2006). Misse (1999, 81) describes the phenomenon of violent urban conflict in Rio de Janeiro as the 'social accumulation of violence'. In other words, he puts forth a series of historical events that have contributed intensively to the level of complexity that Rio de Janeiro presents to date.

During an interview I conducted with Misse in September 2014, he stated that to understand the Rio de Janeiro of today, one must start looking at the city from 1960 (interview, Misse, 9 September 2014). During that epoch the city of Rio de Janeiro stopped serving as the capital of Brazil and the federal government was transferred to the newly built Brasília, inaugurated by President Jusceline Kubitschek on 21 April 1960 (Schwarcz and Starling 2015, 422). The transference of the federal government left a political vacuum in Rio de Janeiro. Further complications arose from the fact that the city of Rio was transformed into a proper state (the state of Guanabara) for a short period of time, and then was reintegrated as the capital of Rio de Janeiro state. The merger of the two states also signified the unification of two different police forces. As already seen, at the beginning of the military regime the generals allocated the ostensive policing to the military police, which was the starting point for the conflict between the civil and military police forces (interview, Misse, 9 September 2014).

Following Misse (1999, 2006), Rio's urban conflict did not start with the end of the military regime. All too often the arming of criminal groups is attributed to the 1980s. However, it actually dates back to the 1950s as a reaction to the police who started to kill criminals who could have been captured alive. The formation of very early forms of death squads and extra-legal killing commandos in Rio de Janeiro drove common criminals to invest in weapons to resist when the police approached. The episode of politician and gubernatorial candidate Tenorio Cavalcante, who was famous for walking around with a machine gun, exemplifies that vigilantism and extra-legal killings were popular in Rio de Janeiro and embedded in the political reality at that time (interview, Misse, 9 September 2014). It was during the 1950s that property crimes and robberies increased and death squads appeared in Rio de Janeiro city and in its outskirts (Misse 1999, 172).

An integral part of tracking back the roots of urban conflict in Rio de Janeiro is the highly popular game Jogo do Bicho (Animal Game) and all its components that have so heavily influenced both the city at the Guanabara Bay and Brazil as a whole. The Animal Game is an illegal lottery where money is bet on animal signs that represent a certain combination of numbers. If these numbers (usually a combination of four) appear in the draw, the fortunate can win a significant amount of money. Starting in the late 19th century, the Animal Game became an attraction for power and money and was fragmented within territories with a structure of a powerful chief (called a banker), a sale point manager, sellers, and kids who wanted to earn some money watching out for the police. The managers could also have gunmen and lawyers at hand. Despite its popularity, the game has been illegal since the 1940s and is, therefore, occasionally repressed by the civil police.

In the early 1980s the manifold bankers united under the command of Castro de Andrade, who later founded the league of the Samba Schools in Rio de Janeiro. This process, to some extent, legalized Animal Game activities and furnished clean money. Until then, and foremost between the 1940s and the late 1970s, the conflict between different selling points of the Animal Game represented an important factor behind the violence that sparked in Rio de Janeiro. More importantly, however, has been the involvement of the police within the Animal Game who constantly worked for or protected the main leaderships. This spread a wide system of illegal markets and networks that have characterized Rio de Janeiro in ways that influenced the further course of the city's criminal landscape (Misse 2007, 142–4).

Interwoven with these networks, another crucial phenomenon adds to these dynamics. Misse (2007, 139–40) notes that different illicit markets are treated completely differently in Rio de Janeiro. While the illegal CD/DVD market, for example, had been widely accepted, the drug trade was not. There seems to be a difference between the conceptual criminalization by the penal code, social representation, and real incrimination. These differences in judging as well as perceiving illicit activities add to the advent of the death squads and demarcate the starting point of what Misse has described as the criminal subjection:

> The criminal subjection is the process through which identities are constructed and attributed. These identities are meant to fit what is

> represented as a 'world apart' or the 'world of crime'. The criminal subjection takes place therefore when certain social types such as criminals or potential criminals are reproduced. (1999, 70)[5]

This quote exemplifies how in Rio de Janeiro authorities, and society in general, construct a criminal other. The *carioca* society produces a criminal subject to represent the evil criminal that is associated with their fears (Misse 1999, 72).

The Rise of the Commandos, 'Dangerous Connections', and 'Political Merchandise'

Just a few yards from the FIFA Fan Shop on Copacabana beach, one afternoon in June 2014, I am on a photographic stroll to record the ambience a few days prior to the World Cup's kick-off. Later that year when I was looking over my pictures, I realized that I had taken a photo of a metal rod, protruding from the famous sidewalk. The metal's white colours were already worn from the weather conditions. Two letters, tagged on the metal, caught my attention: CV. This stands for Comando Vermelho, the Red Command, one of Rio de Janeiro's most powerful and traditional drug-trafficking networks. The scene was a reminder of Rio's most particular contradictions. The proximity of poverty and wealth; thin alleys within favelas and posh high-class apartments; high society and exclusion; FIFA World Cup festivities and heavily armed drug traffickers.

The rise of the CV dates back to the military regime. The military dictatorship envisioned cracking down on armed political opposition movements considered a threat to the state. The Lei de Segurança Nacional (LSN) (National Security Law) from the end of the 1960s served the generals as a juridical tool to imprison opponents, and therefore many members of the communist movement ended up in jail. The Cândido Mendes prison on the Ilha Grande island in Rio de Janeiro state served as the fortress within which these political enemies met with common criminals (Amorim 2010, 64). Although the LSN prisoners tried to distinguish themselves from the common inmates, the latter learned from and adapted to the political organization (Lessing 2012, 68).

[5] My own translation from Brazilian Portuguese.

The founding members of the CV, originally known as the Falange Vermelho (Red Phalange), were all inmates of the LSN prison wing. In this sense the military regime contributed to the foundation of the CV. Quickly the network spread within the prisons and consolidated their power by introducing a system of membership, solidarity, and cruelty. The CV's business within the prisons was to control and consolidate power, while outside of the penitentiary system the task resumed to commit armed assaults and abductions. It is in 1984 that the commando takes a turn into the direction it works today, when the leadership decided to fully embark on a leading role in the drug trade. This initiated the deadly routine in the fight for Rio de Janeiro's favelas (Amorim 2010, 213). Rio's favela population has since then lived continuously in the 'cross fire' (Misse et al. 2013, 12; also Alves and Evanson 2011) between the police and a variety of different drug-trafficking networks.

However, as Misse narrates in the interview, the CV's expansion coincides with two important facts: the mistrust and misunderstanding between the military and civil police and the political rise of governor Leonel de Moura Brizola in 1982. Brizola's political history is highly connected to the military regime as he was exiled and then returned under the amnesty law in 1979 to run for office (McCann 2014, 68). Brizola's policies of public security may be one of the most important changes that occurred under the military regime. The governor searched for a way to control the military police that was still run by the military command. Brizola had in mind to change the relationship between the military police and the population. He intended to change the repressive police into a force that would respect human rights. His solution to bring the military police under the control of the governor was to create two secretaries: one for the military police and one for the civil police. Brizola empowered Carlos Magno Nazareth Cerqueira who assumed both the role of the public security secretary and the general commander of the military police. From that moment, the military police leadership could only be chosen by the governor and no longer by the armed forces.

Brizola's approach to the police was somewhat revolutionary at that time. The simple fact of selecting a black working-class military policeman to be both the commander-in-chief of the institution and the secretary of military police was a symbolic earthquake. Cerqueira has been an important figure for public security policies as he had graduated in philosophy and psychology. He was a vivid writer and student of post-Lombrosian criminological thinking who had contributed extensively to the creation of the

Instituto Carioca de Criminologia (Carioca Institute of Criminology) (Leal et al. 2010, 21, 33). Cerqueira was advocating for a police that should stop randomly incriminating favela residents and accept them as full citizens, which led his opponents to say that he was granting civil rights to bandits (McCann 2014, 102). Whereas important outcomes were achieved by the unusual duo, such as the creation of the Council of Justice, Public Security and Human Rights which replaced the secretary of public security in which the governor awarded representatives from favelas and social movements permanent seats within this council (Soares and Sento Sé 2000, 7), the police blamed Brizola for the rise of the drug-dealing networks in Rio de Janeiro, as if he had forbidden the police from doing their work (Misse 2007, 139–40).[6]

Different from other cities, Rio de Janeiro's drug traffic represents a series of unusual scenarios. The drug trade, concentrated on packaging the drugs for sale and selling them mostly within the favelas, is mainly dominated by commandos whose leadership is in jail and yet they still have strong ties to their home boroughs. In addition, the drug traffic has been able to oppose state forces for years, although the state, at least since the 1980s, has steadily enforced its strategy to fight the commandos (Lessing 2012, 63). The status quo prior to the UPP programme in Rio de Janeiro's security landscape consisted of a dynamic within which different drug-trafficking networks, the many subdivisions of the military and civil police, the militias formed by former or active police members, and the armed forces fought a heavily armed conflict. At least three major drug-trafficking groups, the CV, the Amigos dos Amigos (AdA) (Friends of Friends), and the Terceiro Commando (TC) (Third Command), try to keep the upper hand in Rio's drug-trafficking trade.[7] Besides the conflict between the police and the commandos, the drug-trafficking networks dispute territories to pack and sell drugs within the many favelas.

The militias represent a competitive balance to the drug traffic. As said above, the militias are formed by active or former (often dismissed) police officers from the military and civil police, penitentiary officers, public security employees, members of the armed forces, and civilians (often

[6] For the detailed story of these developments, see the outstanding book *Hard Times in the Marvelous City: From Dictatorship to Democracy in the Favelas of Rio de Janeiro* by Bryan McCann (2014).

[7] There have also been other factions such as the youth section of the Red Command. For more details, see the work of Arias (2006). Primeiro Commando da Capital (PCC) also operates in Rio de Janeiro. See Nunes Dias and Paes Manso (2018).

inhabitants of the controlled communities) (CPI das Milícias 2008, 45). First, they emerged as neighbourhood-watch-like groups that wanted to free their own and other boroughs from the drug dealers. Once this had been put into practice, the militias started to build up a sophisticated system of charging for providing public services such as selling gas and operating local transportation systems. Far from being a welfare organization, the militias enforced their own rules with the use of lethal force. With strong connections in politics and support within the city council and state parliament, they were for a long time exempted from any legal investigations. Through their rule in the communities they could guarantee political candidates many votes (Arias 2014, 150). Although a parliamentary investigation, initiated by the then member of Rio de Janeiro's state parliament Marcelo Freixo, had put many of the *milicianos* (militants) in jail in 2008, the militias still operate in Rio de Janeiro (Cano and Duarte 2012). Their territories have been widely ignored by the UPP system.

Today, the militias are stronger than ever before. The killing of councilwoman and black LGBTQIA+ activist and favela resident Marielle Franco, who worked with Freixo in the parliamentary investigation back at the beginning of the 2000s, by militia members speaks volumes for their ongoing power and strong connections to the police and politics. The killers of Marielle and her driver, who also died in the attack, have possibly strong connections to the presidential family of Jair Bolsonaro. Although the killers have been arrested, those who ordered the crime have not yet been located, and the case remains unsolved (Paes Manso 2020; also Garmany and Pereira 2019).

In order to understand why and how violent urban conflict has proliferated to this extent, it is essential not only to look at the political reform backlog and institutionalized violence (Misse 2006, 88). It was exactly during Brizola's second mandate (1991–4) that violence ignited throughout the city. As Brizola left the government to run for president, Nilo Batista took over the state of Rio de Janeiro. The following 1994 elections saw social democrat candidate Marcello Alencar make use of the public security crisis, playing this card very skilfully. Rio's population still remembered the federal troops that were deployed to secure the United Nations conference ECO 1992. The people now asked for a return of the armed forces that was offered to governor Batista by the federal government to give support to the opposition candidate Alencar. Batista was pressured to accept the troops and Alencar won the elections. The governor from the PSDB party completely opposed Brizola's public security policies and nominated as public security secretary a general who had actively participated during the military dictatorship and who reintroduced the secretary of public security. General Nilton Cerqueira took a tough-on-crime approach and even went a step further. He paid financial rewards to police officers who killed criminals, also known as the 'far-west gratification policy'. These tendencies strengthened significantly the war logic that had already started to develop in Rio and would not vanish (Soares and Sento Sé 2000, 20).

Another key element is to understand that the drug trafficking itself would not work without the involvement of state actors. While Brizola has been held responsible for the spread and empowerment of the drug trade at the end of the 1980s, the story has another side too. It is widely acknowledged that the drug trade in Rio de Janeiro is organized through criminal networks that have multiple sources of income and distribute these to multiple actors such as residents, state officials, and civic actors (Arias 2006, 190).

To explain such phenomena, Misse (1999, 2006) talks about two different illegal markets that shape the city. In the first market different parties exchange illicit goods such as drugs, arms, and stolen commodities. However, in the second market public employees and police officers exchange public goods such as security, protection, and other favours. Misse (2006, 208) analyses these goods as 'political merchandise'. These contain a political resource which is expropriated by state officials and in consequence privatized for their own purposes, producing a political or economic exchange value. The controlling elements of the networks depend heavily on supporting the main political actors within the two illegal markets (Misse 2006, 225). These networks cannot constitute themselves without the help of state agents, often from the military or civil police. Here, Misse (2006, 198) conceptualizes these relationships as '*ligações perigosas*' (dangerous connections) that principally trade '*mercadoria política*' (political merchandise) in the illegal markets such as political favours, protection, and security. These dangerous connections lead the way to a vicious circle within which the political merchandise feeds itself from the criminalizing practices that are exercised by the police and other state agents (Misse 2006, 206). Inevitably, the drug traffickers have to cooperate and bribe police officers. They even negotiate deals for protection and weapons. At the same time, these deals help many police officers to have a less dangerous life on Rio's streets and supplement their humble salary (Misse 2006, 198).

The most recent and one of the most compelling works on Rio de Janeiro's drug-trafficking trade in CV territory is an ethnographic study by Carolina

Grillo (2013).[8] In her work it once again became clear that the police have an active role within Rio de Janeiro's drug trade. The drug-trafficking trade has never been under the control of a generalized and meta-commando as in the case of the Animal Game. However, the localized structure of the drug trade presents similarities to the localized organization of the game between the 1950s and 1970s and its territorial control system (Misse 2006, 191). In other words, the drug-trafficking trade consists of a structure that is a mixture of the old Animal Game, the prison hierarchies, and the strategies of the drug lords to take a quick path to economic prosperity (Misse 2006, 190–5).

Brizola's successors at the head of Rio de Janeiro's state government did not bring much change to the incursive urban conflict. Governor Anthony Garotinho started by promising reforms, principally because he made social scientist Luiz Eduardo Soares sub-secretary of citizenship and research within Rio's public security secretariat. Soares, however, was dismissed after he encountered resistance to his reform agenda and had political disputes with the governor as well as with the secretary of public security (Soares 2000, 467–8). He even had to flee the country due to death threats from the militias. Nonetheless, the civil police reforms and the Delegacia Legal (Model Police Station) project and the creation of the official statistics institute Instituto de Segurança Pública (ISP) (Institute of Public Security) were important, despite the limited advances they brought with them (also see Paes 2006; Pereira 2008; Misse 2010). Furthermore, Garotinho established the Grupamento de Policiamento em Áreas Especiais (GPAE) (Special Areas Policing Group) that fostered a community policing approach (Husain 2007, 139) which later also served as an orientation for the UPP programme. However, independent of who commanded the police forces during Garotinho's government and during the terms of his successors,[9] the policies did not change the war logic of the conflict between the police and the drug traffickers.

That said, the police are themselves a main contributor to the development and enforcement of urban conflict in Rio de Janeiro in terms of raiding favelas with their Special Forces and thus contributing to the heavy shootouts, or by actively trading weapons and, more importantly, political

[8] For more work on the drug trade in Rio de Janeiro, see Zaluar (1985, 1996, 2004a); Barbosa (2005); Feffermann (2006); Neri (2009); and Lyra (2010). For life under criminal governance, see Nicholas Barnes' (2021) work.

[9] Benedita da Silva (2002–3) and Anthony Garotinho's wife Rosinha Garotinho (2003–7).

merchandise. The many weapons that circulate and the public policies of confrontation have made the city of Rio de Janeiro one that lives with daily gunfights and a normalized conflict that has claimed many victims. It is in this scenario that the World Cup and the Olympic Games were awarded to Rio de Janeiro, and which will be the subject of the next section.

Smart, Secure, Resilient: Welcome to 'A New World'

Arriving in the Olympic city in July 2016, it was clear that the city was certainly a different one compared to when the mega-event cycle was initiated with the Pan-American Games of 2007. Most striking was the official slogan of the International Olympic Committee (IOC) that announced 'A New World' from every other Olympic banner.[10] By the year 2008, Governor Sérgio Cabral and mayor Eduardo Paes constructed the vision of a city that would compete globally for new markets and transform the old image of a beautiful, but violent and decadent, city into an image of a global and smart metropolis.[11] What they imagined was to create a 'New World'. This strategy was tightly connected to Rio's Olympic project that envisioned opening the city for global capital and real estate speculation (Gaffney 2010). As Boykoff puts it:

> In a way, the use-value of militarized spectacle was moot. The wider significance of the ostentatious policing power in the lead-up to Rio 2016 is its exchange-value: the symbolic transformation of Rio into a business-friendly metropolis smack in the center of the circuit board capital. (2016, 226)

Within this frame, the city's public security needed to be shaped in a way that would not only convince the IOC to award Rio de Janeiro the Olympics but more importantly deliver a safe FIFA World Cup and Olympics. Mainly, Rio de Janeiro's public security and city actors tried to do this by implementing two strategies that will be the subject of this last part of the

[10] For a nice take on the 2016 Olympics slogan, see the blog post of critical geographer Christopher Gaffney (2016b): http://geostadia.blogspot.de/2016/08/what-kind-of-new-world-for-whom.html.

[11] Both politicians were at that time from the Partido do Movimento Democrático do Brasil (PMDB) (Democratic Movement Party of Brazil).

chapter: first, the UPP programme and second, technology-based solutions for the security sector.

At all costs Rio de Janeiro needed to break out of the deadly routine that had claimed too many victims in too many vicinities. The UPP strategy was one that envisioned community policing at its core. The strategy promised to bring peace to the most violent communities and introduce a new type of police officer who would not be trapped within the old mechanisms of corruption and repressive violence. In a pilot project, a first UPP was installed in the Santa Marta community in the South Zone of Rio de Janeiro and was then expanded to another 38 units. The implementation of the strategy involved visible joint operations run by Rio's police and sometimes even military forces. They aimed to expel the drug traffickers, implement permanent UPP units, and provide publicly funded social projects to improve the living conditions within the communities. As Freeman (2014, 9) asserts, the UPPs, among other state programmes, aimed to incorporate the favela inhabitants into the 'formal city' and award them citizenship and inclusion, as both are basic rights that are difficult to achieve while living in urban areas that lack basic infrastructure and state services. However, the achievement of such highly ambitious goals is widely contested.[12]

Analysing the urban conflict in Rio de Janeiro, one cannot neglect the fact that something needed to be done to let the city breathe again. With a violent death rate of 54.3 of 100,000 inhabitants in the city of Rio de Janeiro in 2007 and a police that produced a killing rate of 14.6 per 100,000 that year (ISP 2015)—a number never before seen—the conflict in Rio de Janeiro had reached a climax that was not compatible with the planned mega-events. State officials, therefore, tried to assure the national audience that the UPP project, as well as other investments in the public security sector, did not have *any* connection with the mega-event cycle in Rio de Janeiro. When I asked Beltrame if the UPP programme was connected to the World Cup and the Olympics, he said: 'No, there is no connection ... It's for a very simple detail ... Rio de Janeiro cannot afford the luxury to receiving all these events and not keeping any legacy.' Nonetheless, looking at

[12] This book cannot provide a thorough analysis of the outcomes and effects on and within the 38 communities with UPPs, as this would go beyond the scope of the study. There is a variety of studies that examine the UPPs in detail. From a police perspective, see Cano et al. (2012); Saborio (2014). From a resident/community perspective, see The World Bank (2012); Rodrigues et al. (2012); da Cunha (2014); Ganem Misse (2014); World Cup and Olympics Popular Committee of Rio de Janeiro (2015); Machado da Silva (2015); Araujo Silva and Carvalho (2015); Teixeira Pinheiro (2015); Richmond (2015).

the strategies adopted within the state secretary of public security and the mayor's office, it is noticeable that it was a project to prepare the city for the mega-event cycle that aimed to

> be an opportunity to deliver the broader aspirations for the long-term future of the city, region and country—an opportunity to hasten the transformation of Rio de Janeiro into an even greater global city. (Rio 2016 2009, 16)

Although the official public security protagonists do not connect the UPP programme to the mega-events, it seems still to have a tight connection to the main World Cup and Olympic areas. Take the UPP in the famous Mangueira favela, which is located only a few hundred metres from the Maracanã stadium and which has been a natural site for urban conflict as local drug-trafficking groups dominate it. A map produced by the Exclusion Games campaign, a consortium of movements who opposed the ways in which the Games were organized in Rio, illustrates how the UPPs are introduced at very strategic spots in the city that are associated with two main facts: these areas are famous wealthy and touristic hotspots or they are key localities for Rio's sport mega-events (World Cup and Olympics Popular Committee of Rio de Janeiro 2016).

Beside the heavy investments in the UPP programme, Beltrame's office pushed through new approaches for public security in Rio de Janeiro. Further focus was laid upon technological advancements within the public security sector. The investment in technology aimed to *integrate* the many different security institutions that have often had a rather problematic relationship with each other (Cardoso 2013, 120). Beltrame and his team had planned to implement an integrated command-and-control structure and to build a physical space where the different policing and emergency services could be grouped together (Cardoso 2016, 5). A so-called Centro Integrado de Comando e Controle (CICC) (Integrated Command and Control Centre) was already in the planning when the federal government pushed through the Sistema Integrado de Comando e Controle (SICC) (Integrated Command and Control System) as the main mega-event security strategy. This strategy will be analysed in Chapter 3 which features a detailed description and analysis of the World Cup and Olympics security planning. As Cardoso (2014) illustrates in his book *Todos os Olhos* (*All Eyes*), Rio's CICC is the follow-up structure of an already-existing surveillance centre in Rio.

Paired with the technological initiatives of the state of Rio de Janeiro within the security sector, the city of Rio has embraced the global concept of smart cities and has also invested into an algorithm-driven model of urban management (Coaffee 2015; Gaffney and Robertson 2016). These smart governance ambitions for all kind of urban complexities have increasingly been mantled within resilience discourses. Many definitions range around the smart city term (Willis and Augiri 2019). In essence it is meant as a way in which a city 'smartly' prepares to confront the complexities of ever more competitive and globalized markets. The *smart* describes how a city can optimize its everyday challenges in terms of the economy, urban mobility, and living quality of its citizens. Corporations like IBM and Cisco provide the technological solutions to attribute the smart label to a city. In other words, the more technology is applied, the smarter a city gets. Söderström et al. (2014) emphasize that it is 'corporate storytelling' that furnishes the smart city concepts, and cities frequently use smart as their branding and marketing strategies instead of effectively improving their urbanity.

In the run-up to the mega-events, Rio de Janeiro transformed its urban governance structure and adopted principles of 'entrepreneurial management, city marketing, privatization and technologization of urban systems' (Gaffney and Robertson 2016, 7). In many of my interviews it came to the fore that Brazil in general, but Rio de Janeiro more specifically, needed to adopt strategies to re-brand their image as a violent and chaotic city, and that the mega-events were *the* opportunity to do so. Therefore, the municipality of Rio de Janeiro under the mayor Eduardo Paes started to plan and execute the smart city centre and to adopt a resilience strategy. Rio de Janeiro's smart city centre was inaugurated at the end of December 2010 and, according to its own representation, it fulfils the task of 'integrating' more than 30 different institutions at the municipal and state level that overlook the key everyday activities within the city 24 hours a day. The Centro de Operações Rio (COR) (Operation Centre Rio) has become a 10.6-million-dollar infrastructure where more than 560 cameras from different institutions send images to the 80 square-metre video wall to enable them to anticipate, manage, and process eventual crises. Inspired by the control centre in New York City, Rio's mayor implemented the COR for image and promotion reasons (Gaffney and Robertson 2016, 9) and nourished the narrative for the implementation that the city had to be *smartened* as a response to landslides that had cost many lives and to prevent such natural catastrophes in the future. The centre features a First Responder Coordination and Emergency Alter Notification System, monitors bus lines, and tracks the weather so as to be able to react much more quickly than in the past (interview, COR resilience officer, 7 June 2014).

Cities that adopted smart urban governance strategies connect within a global smart city network, in which Rio was elected the smartest city in the world 2013, a title which is more than contested. In an interview, one of Rio's smart city staff members emphasized that the daily data collected within the COR could be useful to develop the city and actually *re*-direct the city's urban planning in a more effective way. However, the data is only gathered but not used for such purposes (interview, COR staff member, 24 July 2014). This being said, the COR has developed into something that regulates traffic, informs about the weather, or signals urban and natural incidents, but has not relieved the excessive number of cars and traffic in general.[13]

Often, the smart city projects are linked to urban resilience strategies. Resilience discourses have promoted ideas of how cities may better prepare and develop abilities to resist and cope with sudden shocks and chronic crisis. As Marc Welsh (2014, 19) points out, governments promote forms of governance through resilience in order to 'reproduce, broader, neoliberal practices of security that shift from state-based to society-based conceptions of distributed risk and reaction'. Beside many urban governance purposes, resilience practices in general have also turned 'towards the priorities of security and counter-terrorism, which in turn, draw security infrastructures, organizations and practices into the delivery of resilience' (Coaffee and Fussey 2015, 95).

Unsurprisingly, in the attempt to transform Rio de Janeiro from a city haunted by a most violent conflict into a global metropolis famous for its effective urban management, the city government under Eduardo Paes introduced a resilience strategy and was embedded within an international framework of resilient cities sponsored by the Rockefeller Foundation. In my interview, Rio's resilience officer told me that they understand resilience as being

> the capacity of a city to resist abrupt shocks and chronic stress and to return to normality as quickly as possible and to learn from the crisis

[13] For an analysis of the COR as a specific form of urban governance of infrastructural flows, see Luque-Ayala and Marvin (2016).

> in order to prepare the city to be less vulnerable to these impacts. (interview, 7 June 2015)

Following the officer's elaborations, the ultimate goal is to learn from the mega-event cycle to even 'become an example. We want to be the next Sydney and Barcelona' (interview, 7 June 2015). During the talk with the resilience officer, a Dutch consultant from Accenture interrupted our interview several times to add details or contribute her version of how Rio de Janeiro had embraced the new path towards a *smart*, *secure*, and *resilient* city. One of her most astonishing comments was that the time that state forces are responsible for *everything* should be over and that initiatives to improve the city must come from the residents. As an example, she referred to a community with a UPP unit that called a meeting with the police officers after a deadly shootout. It was astonishing to see how a consultant from a globally operating corporation could be so ignorant about the history of violence in Rio de Janeiro. More shocking was, however, that the corporation was so present in the city's governance structure. In a thorough analysis of different resilience approaches, Welsh asserts that urban policy is frequently shaped by resilience strategies which

> operate on the normative assumption that communities can and should self-organise to deal with uncertainty, that uncertainty is a given not something with a political dimension, and the role of government is limited to enabling, shaping and supporting, but specifically not to direct or to fund those processes. This locates the responsibility of 'communities' as needing to organise themselves, primarily in the context of sustaining economic growth. As a consequence, there is little sign of a profound engagement with a politics of resilience as a means for conceiving of change; of revolution through resilience. (2014, 20)

As seen, this sense of delegating responsibility from the state to communities is deeply embedded in Rio's resilience discourse. Moreover, the statement of the Dutch Accenture consultant demonstrates how this discourse lies at the centre of the concept that started to be shaped by Mayor Paes, and which focuses on an abstract city that disconnects from its citizens instead of including them. Using favelas as an example of good resilience, the Accenture consultant lays bare the flawed concept as these spaces have experienced the absence of the state since their creation.

The contrasts could not be more visible. While many neighbourhoods of the city live with a daily urban conflict that features victims of gunfights between factions that want to regain or defend territories, the state and the city government have invested heavily in technology-based governance instruments or the militarization of public security. The mega-event cycle has served as a catalyst for these investments and shaped a discourse that these solutions could make life in Rio de Janeiro better. As stated in the Introduction to this book, this research attempts to critically assess these claims.

This chapter has shown Rio de Janeiro's particular security conditions. Within a historical perspective the chapter illustrated the roots of Rio's ongoing conflict. In many ways Rio is embedded within the violent pluralism and the paradox that has shaped Brazil before and since the transition from military dictatorship to democracy. Only the interwoven relations between the police, the drug traffickers, and politicians have made it possible for Rio's security crisis to reach such devastating levels. In order to prepare the city for the mega-events and to improve the city's image, new strategies such as the UPP programme and technologically based public security policies were implemented. This is what lays bare the mega-event mechanisms and makes Rio de Janeiro such an interesting place in which to analyse how global mega-event security measures were adopted, and how they impacted on established security conditions in the city.

When the Olympics were over, the IOC president said that the Games were

> iconic Games, but it is also a Games in the middle of reality. It has not been organised in a bubble but in a city where there are social problems and social divides, where real life continued ... This was very good for everybody, to be close to reality and not in a bubble for 16 days and isolated from society.[14]

Herewith the IOC president addresses his critics who accused him and the IOC of organizing the Olympics within bubbles far removed from reality. In his statement, he did not mention the price that was paid by the Brazilian taxpayers, the many victims of human rights abuses, and the policemen and women who were involved in an Olympic security operation while their daily struggles were not improved. He says it was 'very good for everybody'. These Olympic bubbles will be burst in the following chapters.

[14] See https://olympics.com/ioc/news/ioc-president-hails-rio-2016-as-iconic-games.

PART II
SPECTACLE

3
Planning and Imagining the Fortress

I am standing on the third floor of the Integrated Command and Control Centre (CICC) in Rio de Janeiro. I am looking down into the main hall with a video wall that is 17 metres high and 5 metres wide and composed of 98 flatscreens, and is the core element of the World Cup security strategy, the regional CICC, or CICC-R, as the Brazilian authorities call it. My glance goes from the video wall to the rows of desks that are reminiscent of a NASA command room furnished with flatscreens. Military police officers in marine-blue uniforms are staring at their monitors.

Behind me, the room of the World Cup security operations centre features another, smaller video wall. The room is set up with desktop niches, three major offices, and a conference room. Here, Brazil's most important security institutions are working together to manage the World Cup security plan. I am still amazed that I am standing here, in the middle of the storm, with a researcher pass proudly hanging around my neck. The World Cup starts and the long-expected street protests are flickering across the video wall, directly from São Paulo to the commando room in Rio de Janeiro.

I am concentrated on watching the scenario when I suddenly feel a tapping on my right shoulder. I turn around slowly and look at the face of the military police colonel who is one of the directors of the command centre and had given me the pass.

'Can I speak to you a moment please?'
'Of course.'
'Please follow me into my office.'

In the colonel's office, one of the two civil police representatives in the central command is waiting. He looks at me with worry-filled eyes. The colonel mumbles:

Policing Sport Mega-Events. Dennis Pauschinger, Oxford University Press. © Dennis Pauschinger 2024.
DOI: 10.1093/oso/9780192848055.003.0004

> 'You know, we didn't expect that you would be here during the whole World Cup. Today the hot phase of the security operation starts. I already asked the civil police, how did you get here and what your plans are?'

His words pound loud in my head. I am standing in the middle of the most important security organization of the World Cup and I am about to lose this opportunity. With hope their decision could be reversed, I confront both with the fact that I see the fusion centre as the most important piece of the security structure in Rio.

> 'I can understand this, but I need you to understand our concerns. We would like you to leave.'

No chance; just the vague offer to come back early the following week to see how future visits to the building might be possible. On my way out, the secretary at the reception desk asks me to return my researcher pass that gave me unlimited access to the building.

Game over.

The disappointment at that moment was strong, but the very same day I managed to get access to other World Cup security operations within the stadium security perimeters. Continuously I go back to the centre and accompany the press briefings, and, on the day of the World Cup final, I get my access back. Two years later, I can stay in the centre for many days during the Olympics. The nervousness of the authorities in these first days of the World Cup is down to very long preparation periods and the fear of scenarios all too well known from the previous year during the Confederations Cup final, when the players could hear the protests and smell the tear gas from the riot police on the pitch. To avoid a repetition of such circumstances, the Extraordinary Secretary for Mega-Event Security said in an interview for this research: 'In no other World Cup has a structure like this one been installed. This is, without doubt, the biggest security operation ever built for a World Cup' (interview, 10 June 2014).

This chapter sheds light on this mega-event security operation planning. The scenes above and the statement are a reminder of one of the core purposes of this book: to shed light on the ways in which how the global and standardized security models associated with mega-events unfolded in Brazil and Rio de Janeiro. And more than that, it aims to uncover how the mega-event organizers adapted the global security standards to the very specific pre-security conditions in a country like Brazil, and in a city like Rio de Janeiro, in which the public security landscape is shaped by its long-lasting violent urban conflict. In a more global perspective, exploring these issues will bring us closer to a broader understanding how globalized security patterns are negotiated, adapted, and influenced in the digital era. Michel de Certeau (1984, 94) has distinguished between the *concept city* that is imagined by those who plan it and the city that is experienced by those who actually live in it. In a different but comparable way, Jonathan Raban (1974, 2) has argued that there is a *hard city*, which is one of maps and plans, and a *soft city*, which represents what cannot be grasped by the corresponding projections of architects. This chapter sets out to shed light on the planning side of such a duality. It explores how those in charge of the mega-event security, at both federal and Rio de Janeiro's local level, have worked out the plans to secure the World Cup and the Olympics.

Legal Preparations and Anticipating Risk Scenarios

As shown in Chapter 2, when Brazil was awarded the World Cup and the Olympics, local public security had been in a very bad shape. In 2006, the year before Brazil was given the World Cup, the criminal network Primeiro Commando da Capital (PCC) staged a riot in the majority of the state's prisons simultaneously, and launched direct attacks on police officers and the public transportation systems (Adorno and Salla 2007; Biondi 2010; Denyer Willis 2015; Feltran 2018; Paes Manso and Nunes Dias 2018). In the year of the Pan-American Games, and only two years before Rio would be elected host of the 2016 Olympics, Rio also experienced the provisional climax of its long-lasting public security crisis. Drug-trafficking networks set ablaze public transport buses, and the urban conflict between the police and the drug trade continuously rushed from one devastating tragedy to the next. These events dramatically laid bare the poor conditions of Brazil's public security sector and one of the most striking complexities, the structural architectures of the binary state police system and the conflict of interests and communication between the police forces in general. With these structural problems and the crisis of those times, the security organizers for the tournaments needed to both take care of the consistent internal security matters and adopt the globally standardized but adaptable mega-event security measures.

The tensions between the many policing units could jeopardize the mega-event security plan in various ways. As a high-ranking civil police officer stated: 'The intersections [between the different police institutions] cause a great number of difficulties' (interview, 12 August 2014). Consequentially, the Brazilian government tried to separate the day-to-day security planning and arrangements for the mega-event by creating an agency for the unique purpose of planning the security for the tournaments, one that had a clear mission to bring the many forces for the events together.

The guarantee of the security arrangements given to FIFA, for example, induced the government to create the federal Secretaria Extraordinária de Segurança para Grandes Eventos (SESGE) (Extraordinary Secretary for Mega-Event Security) by way of Decree No. 7,538 of 1 August 2011 as a continuation of the first organizational commission for the World Cup (Grupo de Trabalho da Copa 2014, Olimpíadas 2016, Paraolimpíadas 2016 e Eventos Afins—GTCOPA) (Working Group for the 2014 World Cup, the 2016 Olympics, and Paralympics and Associated Events).[1] As a sub-secretary of the federal Ministry of Justice, it had responsibilities 'to plan, define, coordinate, implement, and evaluate the actions of the public security [sector] for the mega-events'[2] (SESGE 2012, 7). Thus, the SESGE was the organ that coordinated the security effort for the federal government in all the host cities during the World Cup, and in Rio de Janeiro during the Olympics.

Moreover, the Brazilian government was obliged to sign several contracts with FIFA within which the country guaranteed to fulfil certain demands that the private football organization imposes on World Cup hosts. The most important one was Guarantee No. 5, which states that the Brazilian federation guarantees the safety and protection of all visitors and participants in the tournament. The same guarantee is given to the IOC in the law number 12.035 from 1 October 2009, called the Olympic Act, where in article 12 the federal government accepts the responsibility to assure the security of the event 'without any cost for the organising committee'.[3] There were no formalized demands that would go beyond this guarantee; however, it encompasses the crucial elements that held the Brazilian government responsible for the overall security of the tournament.

[1] GTCOPA was established on 14 January 2010 via presidential decree.

[2] My own translation from Brazilian Portuguese.

[3] The entire Olympic Law is available at www.planalto.gov.br/ccivil_03/_ato2007-2010/2009/lei/l12035.htm. Also, its amendment is at www.planalto.gov.br/CCIVIL_03/_Ato2015-2018/2016/Lei/L13284.htm.

Consequently, informal demands were articulated with reference to the formal guarantees, and many other regulations also played an important role. Take only the FIFA stadium regulations, wherein the organization clarifies demands such as the installation of CCTV devices within the stadium (see also Eick 2011a). The security guarantees were granted to FIFA with a number of other promises that materialized in the so-called World Cup law number 12,663 from 5 June 2012.[4] One of the most important sections may be article 22, where the Brazilian federation legally promises FIFA to be liable for any compensation in case the World Cup ends up in financial or organizational disaster. This is the usual business model of the Swiss-based organization. FIFA would not award the tournament to a country that refuses to burden these responsibilities at that time.[5] Automatically, these guarantees have a direct influence on the World Cup security, as the host country does not want to risk anything that could jeopardize the event. In other words, the host secures the sport venues and the city to the maximum level possible. Previous mega-events have shown how FIFA and the IOC have successfully imposed pre-conditions in the security area to host the Games—principally when it comes to technology-based security devices (Eick 2011a, 3334).

In the endeavour to shed light on the ways in which the Brazilian government has envisioned the mega-event security, it is worth looking at the manifold risk scenarios that have occupied and influenced the authorities and for which the legal preparations were introduced. Risk anticipation and major threat scenarios are an intrinsic feature within mega-event planning. A particular set of common dilemmas has been identified for mega-event security planners and comes to the fore within the detailed preparations: the planning is marked by the attempts to identify high risks and unknown scenarios, which are often the reason for running over-budget and the deployment of too many security-related mechanisms (Bennett and Haggerty 2011, 5). In many ways, the Brazilian planning authorities applied these kinds of mechanisms in order to tranquilize both the Brazilian people and foremost FIFA, the IOC, and the expected global audience.

Following the General Coordinator of the CICC in Rio, it was a long process of developing numerous security protocols as an attempt to try to anticipate all possible security risks (interview, general coordinator CICC-R, 1

[4] The entire World Cup Law is available at www.planalto.gov.br/ccivil_03/_ato2011-2014/2012/Lei/L12663.htm.

[5] For more on FIFA's business model and history, see Tomlinson (2014).

September 2014). Within the Strategic Planning Report for the World Cup, the Agência Brasileira de Inteligência (ABIN) (Brazilian Intelligence Agency) prioritized distinct risk scenarios for criminal activities during the mega-events. Beside other pressing topics, organized crime, civil disturbance, and terrorism are those that are most important (SESGE 2012, 28–30).

For instance, the report features a section on the evaluation of incidents and points out that there are four situational risk levels. The first one comprises incidents that are inherent to the city routine and would put the event in danger, but would not threaten its continuation; the second one highlights incidents that would present a clear correlation to the event as they may happen within the areas of interest for the event, but would not put the event in danger; the third risk level comprises incidents that may interrupt the event, but would not endanger its continuation, such as social movements of any kind; and the fourth describes incidents like terrorist attacks that are likely to put an abrupt end to the event itself (SESGE 2012, 23–4). Clearly, the worrying scenarios for mega-event security organizers are incidents which could provoke a sudden end or ruin the tournament.

When sport mega-events are hosted by nations with such unstable public security conditions as in Brazil, the internal threat scenarios are far more likely considered as existential than normal (Giulianotti and Klauser 2009, 53). Therefore, Rio de Janeiro had started efforts to contain the drug-related violence for years prior to the start of the Unidade de Polícia Pacificadora (UPP) programme (see Chapter 2). When the World Cup approached, the security scenario in Rio had improved and the internal threat scenarios dwindled slightly into the background. For the 2016 Olympics, the situation had changed as the decline of the UPP programme had advanced significantly, and in 2015 the violence between the drug trade and the police increased and the number of people killed by the police skyrocketed (ISP 2016, 10).

The risk scenario that has accompanied and determined mega-event security planning in the past is the fear of terrorism (see Giulianotti and Klauser 2012). In Brazil this preoccupation was considered by the risk analysts; however, it had not sparked too much of a concern for the World Cup. In contrast, the scenario for the Olympic Games was different. The increasing strength of the Islamic State of Iraq and Al-Sham (ISIS),[6] and even more their latest attacks in Europe, had sparked fears that the 2016 Olympics could become a target. Differently to the World Cup documents, the Brazilian government released an information sheet about

[6] Also known as Islamic State (IS), Islamic State of Iraq and the Levant (ISIL), or Daesh (Cottee 2017, 440).

Olympic security within which terrorism suddenly played a more prominent role. The risks of civil unrest and the public security conditions in Rio de Janeiro decreased, featuring as only number two and three on the list respectively (Presidential Social Communication Secretariat 2016, 6). That said, for the World Cup the government focused in their planning on the internal public security situation within the host cities and did what was necessary to satisfy international worries about possible terrorist attacks.

But this scenario changed suddenly in 2013. A year after the publication of the strategic planning document, another internal threat had surprised the mega-event security planners, one that certainly had the potential to stop the World Cup and the Olympics from taking place. The countrywide protests during the FIFA Confederations Cup in June 2013 heavily influenced the mega-event security preparations thereafter. The protest movement surprised both FIFA and the Brazilian authorities. During the 2013 Play the Games conference in Aarhus Denmark, Walter de Gregorio, FIFA's spokesman at that time, expressed serious concerns about the ways in which Brazil was going to handle the situation. FIFA feared having its most valuable marketing tool—the World Cup—damaged by images of rioting youth during the games. In the words of the Extraordinary Sub-Secretary for Mega-Events in Rio de Janeiro: 'no one expected the intensity and duration of what happened last year in terms of the protests' (interview, 13 August 2014). The sub-secretary was not the only one to cite the 2013 protest scenarios as key worries prior to the World Cup. The military police colonel and general coordinator of the CICC in Rio de Janeiro confirmed that the protests presented a scenario that none of the host cities were prepared to confront (interview, 2 June 2014).

Furthermore, the worries expanded significantly during the Confederations Cup. As one of the Local Organizing Committee (LOC) security officers explained in an interview, protestors cut TV transmission cables in Belo Horizonte and Salvador. An equally worrying incident was the protestors' attack on the minivan with the Johnson & Johnson chief executive officer on board (interview, 14 August 2016). As a consequence, Brazil's intelligence agency and the LOC, as well as the civil police, started to monitor online social networks in order to anticipate planned protests and concentrated more on the risk scenarios of the possible partial interruption or even the cessation of the tournament. Therefore, the Brazilian states started to equip their riot police forces with the famous Robocop armour which was unprecedented in Brazil.

Concerns about civil unrest were added to the major security worries that the Brazilian government had prior to the World Cup, which consisted primarily of the local security conditions as well as of traditional mega-event preoccupations such as terrorism and major crowd incidents. Stated differently, the 2013 protests massively contributed to the ways in which security was organized for the mega-events. Paired with international pressure and internal worries, the protests induced the adoption of a discourse of total security which has become such a well-known global standard at previous World Cups and Olympics (Coaffee 2012, 7). The legal preparations and the anticipating risk scenarios culminated in an unforeseen joint effort of Brazilian security forces.

Militarized Total Security and 'Integration, Command, and Control'

On 10 June 2014, the international press centre of the federal government in the Open Media Centre (OMC) announced a briefing on the World Cup security plans and hosted a wide variety of participants, including the following representatives: the Chief of Joint Staff of the Armed Forces General José Carlos de Nardi; the head of the Extraordinary Mega-Event Security Secretary (SESGE), Andrei Rodrigues; the Assistant General-Director of the Brazilian Intelligence Agency (ABIN), Ronaldo Belham; the General-Manager for Security of the LOC, Hilário Medeiros; and FIFA's World Cup Security Advisor André Pruis, former South African deputy national police commissioner who was involved in the security scheme for the 2010 South African World Cup. The list of prominent participants discloses the structure of the World Cup security plan and highlights the importance of a joint effort to secure the tournament. Their main philosophy would be repeated at press conferences and in many interviews for this research, as if it were a mantra: the many different institutions would work together in an *integrated* fashion. In the following paragraphs this integration concept will be analysed in depth.

The press conference provides an initial inside view of all the aspects cited above that are essential for shedding light on the ways in which the World Cup security scheme was organized. Examining the statement by the SESGE secretary Rodrigues at the Media Centre provides more clarity:

> Good morning everybody ... I am responding for the Extraordinary Secretary for Mega-Event Security of the Ministry of Justice, which is an organ created in 2011 to coordinate all the security activity, security planning and the *integration*, which is *the great asset* of this whole process. The integration of the security forces comprises all the state police forces, all the federal police forces, and the municipal agents [not audible] and the areas of defence and intelligence. (10 June 2014)

Rodrigues' elaboration trains attention upon the complex public security structure outlined in Chapter 2 on Brazil's public security organization. The conflicting police institutions in the Brazilian states have led to rather complicated relationships among the many different agencies. The integration approach is by and large presented as the solution to these problems, and as the necessary tool for getting the mega-event security right. Accordingly, efforts were made to set up an infrastructure which would support the integration of the ministries and the security forces, as Andrei Rodrigues continued narrating at the press conference:

> For the infrastructure we created the Integrated Command and Control System [SICC] which is composed of the regional centres [CICC-Rs] ... These centres received representatives from all institutions, not only from the public security area but also [from institutions that are] partners in this whole process of the event security. Here I name Anvisa [National Sanitary Agency], Receita [National Revenue Agency], Itamaraty [Ministry of Foreign Affairs], as well as, and this is clear, institutions such as the Defence and Intelligence agencies, and the LOC-FIFA [Local Organizing Committee] ... There is not one single World Cup event that is realized by one single institution in an isolated manner. No, we always work in an integrated fashion, in coordination, in partnership for the purpose of the event's security. (Press conference, 10 June 2014)

In this statement what comes to light is how the complex security infrastructure was addressed for the event security planning. It is apparent how the special secretary emphasizes the integration efforts and wants to transmit the total preparedness of the authorities, and even enthuses about their own *excellence* in the planning. The core element of the Integrated

Command and Control System (SICC) is the physical environment of the CICCs.[7]

The Ministry of Justice released a glossy portfolio explaining the SICC as follows:

> The Integrated System of Command and Control (SICC) centers its attention on nationwide public security and civil defense in major events. SICC is organized as follow [*sic*]:
>
> - Integrated Center of Nationwide Command and Control—CICCN: located in Brasília and accountable for strategic management of public security and civil defense actions, overseeing and supporting actions for the host cities, keeping updated and available information for the federal government top management.
> - Alternative Integrated Center of Command and Control—CICCNA: located in Rio de Janeiro and that works as back up; o Center for International Police Cooperation, located in Brasília.
> - Twelve Regional Integrated Centers of Command and Control—CICCR: located in twelve cities that will host World Cup, Olympic, and Paralympic Games.
> - Twenty-seven Mobile Integrated Command and Control Centers of Command and Control: CICCL: placed in the event surroundings.
> - Twelve Local Integrated Centers of Command and Control—CICCL: placed in the arenas.
> - Twenty-two High Observation Platforms—POE: positioned closer to the sites of the events. (Ministério da Justica 2014, 2)

Furthermore, the snazzy World Cup brochure ensures that, in each host city, the integrative working concept is accompanied by representatives of the Comissão Estadual/Distrital de Segurança Pública e Defesa Civil (COESGE) (State and Municipality Committee for Public Security and Civil Defence) and involves members from all three governmental levels. Table 3.1 illustrates the ways in which the Ministry of Justice pictured the tasks assigned to the many security forces involved in the integrated

[7] The Brazilian Intelligence Agency's (ABIN's) representative Mr Belham explained that the agency would also operate a national coordination centre in Brasília to dovetail with the regional host cities' hubs. In addition, ABIN would run an international intelligence service cooperation centre in the Brazilian capital with members from 42 international intelligence agencies. Clearly, ABIN also had an important role in the mega-event security scheme.

Table 3.1 Copy of graphic in information kit of the Ministry of Justice

Federal Police	Borders, immigration, federal and transnational crimes, dignitaries, terrorism	**Federal Road Police**	Federal roads, special operations, and escorting
National Public Security Force	Complementary actions	**Defence force**	Airspace and maritime area, border defence, safety of critical infrastructure, CBRN attacks and counterterrorism
GSI/ABIN	Intelligence/risk analysis	**Revenue services**	Transit of goods, vehicles, and people
Military Police	Intensive law enforcement, civil disturbance, special tactical groups	**Investigative State Police Forces**	Investigations, forensic
Fire Fighters (Civil Defence)	Fire, natural disasters, health related incidents or accidents	**Municipal Guard**	Additional security
Traffic department/ Engineering	Traffic and displacements	**Human Rights Agency**	Promotion and protection of Human Rights; occurrences with children and adolescents.

Source: Ministério da Justiça (2014, 3)

system, and mirrors the three government levels of the Brazilian security architecture that have been mobilized to secure the mega-events. The deployment of the National Force, a troop that recruits its members from all security forces of the country and which is normally deployed in emergency situations, showcases the importance of the mega-events for the Brazilian authorities.

In addition, two important committees were founded to distribute federal and local responsibilities: the first included the federal Executive

Committee for the Integrated Security (Cesi), composed of the presidential chief of staff and the Ministries of Justice and Defence; and the second, on a local level, featured the Regional Committee for Integrated Security (Cesir), composed of the commander-in-chief of the armed forces in the states, the state's federal police chief, and the state's security secretary (Ministério da Defesa 2014, 7).

As apparent within the SICC, the structure built for the World Cup involved a plethora of different centres, and therefore many communication flows. For the 2016 Olympics this system had been adapted to the fact that most events would take place in Rio de Janeiro. While during the Olympics there was still the general coordination in Brasília, the CICC in Rio de Janeiro took over the direct coordination of a diversity of minor CICCs. These were distributed over the four main Olympic sites. Within these areas local control centres had to coordinate the security locally. The structure during the World Cup worked mainly with the national (Brasília), regional (Rio), mobile (security perimeters), and local (stadiums) CICCs. The Olympics featured a national and regional CICC for the main coordination, the sector CICCs within the main four Olympic sites, and the Integrated Security Venue Centres.[8]

It is notable that there is an intensive knowledge transfer from one mega-event host country to the next that induces the use of similar systems in different host countries. This is no different with the command-and-control strategies found in Rio. As Fussey and Coaffee remark:

> What is clear though is that many sporting mega-event security operations repeatedly seek to orientate their strategies around a few core principles. These are normally grouped under the broad headings of 'command', 'control', 'co-ordination', 'communications' and 'intelligence'. (2012, 274)

Whereas Athens 2004 adopted the C4I strategy, in London 2012 a similar structure was named C3. As outlined in the quote, all comprised the *command* and *control* elements. According to the 2010 GTCOPA report, Brazilian delegations had visited the command-and-control centres in New York, Washington, DC, and El Paso (SENASP 2010, 16).[9] This offers

[8] During the mega-events, international police coordination centres and an integrated anti-terrorism centre were also installed.

[9] SENASP = Secretaria Nacional de Segurança Pública (National Public Security Secretary).

insights in the normalized transnational knowledge transfer in the globalized security planning at mega-events and beyond. Moreover, several respondents confirmed that they had visited previous mega-events such as the 2012 London Olympics (interview, civil police officer, 12 August 2014). Unsurprisingly, the Extraordinary Secretary for Mega-Event Security Rodrigues also confirmed at the 10 June press conference:

> These centres are environments that have been created with the global experience of our specialists who visited Command and Control Centres in North America and Europe, to finally build a proper Brazilian system. (Press conference, 10 June 2014)

The statement is a reminder of the ways in which global security models associated with mega-events shape local security practices but adapt to local conditions (Fussey et al. 2011). Stated differently, this illustrates that certain globalized security standards such as the knowledge transfer between both private and state officials across previous and future mega-event hosts materialized within the Brazilian planning (see also Boyle 2011).

The Armed Forces: Militarization of Brazil's Sport Mega-Events

In the case of Brazil, it is a particular mix that has contributed to the creation of these command-and-control infrastructures. On the one side, the strategy has been the inspiration of international examples for the distinct Brazilian mega-event security planners. On the other side, the strategy had already found its way into Brazil's Defence Ministry in 2006. It derived from a particular military management strategy to establish the 'military doctrine of command and control' that has been expanded to the Ministry of Justice for the wider treatment of public security policies and, finally, the creation of the CICCs (Cardoso 2013, 131–3). This means that the militarization of Brazilian public security is not only traditionally anchored within the constitution as a relic of the authoritarian past (Zaverucha 2000, 2010a); it has also materialized within the democratic present.

The integration concept points to the desire to overcome the manifold institutional problems that disturb the smooth flow of public security organization in the states. Too many institutions are at work in the public security sector: different ministries, at least two different police forces, and municipal guards, as well as occasionally federal troops who are all in dispute over responsibilities, investigatory powers, and funds. It therefore cannot be emphasized enough that the integration efforts put forth by the federal government for the mega-events were one of the core strategies for the security planners for both the events as such and beyond the tournaments as a security legacy.

Military participation in mega-event security is nothing new (Clavel 2013). A variety of authors have shown that the use of armed forces in mega-event securitization has long since become an essential part of security delivery (Giulianotti and Klauser 2011; Clavel 2013; Fussey and Klauser 2015). In London 2012, for example, the UK's armed forces placed missiles on rooftops and prepared for 'mass troop deployment' (Fussey 2015, 213). At Germany's 2006 World Cup, NATO Airborne Warning and Control (AWAC) fighters contributed to controlling air space (Klauser 2008, 67). These developments are embedded within the militarization of urban space and the merging of internal and external security that have long been a subject of discussion in the social sciences (e.g. Bigo 2006). Contemporary police forces often behave as if they were going to war rather than carrying out community policing (Graham 2009, 2010; Balko 2013) and urban public space has undergone extended security fortification (Davis 2007; Coaffee 2003). While these developments may be rather new in some places, in Brazil and particularly in Rio de Janeiro, they go back to a tradition of a militarized public security in which the armed forces are deployed to eventually take over public security tasks (Zaverucha 2010a; Harig 2020).

The Brazilian armed forces have established their own, but similar, security architecture to that established by the SESGE to implement their World Cup security tasks. 'The Ministry of Defence at the 2014 FIFA World Cup' is the name of the military press kit, printed on dark-green card with three vivid action pictures, representing each of the three branches of the Brazilian armed forces: the marines, the army, and the air force. On 19 glossy pages, the military illustrates the ways in which they are safeguarding the World Cup. General Jamil Megid pronounces in the kit:

> We are ready to deliver security for the foreign tourists, football delegations and heads of state present at the World Cup ... Within the mandate attributed to the Ministry of Defence we have a special focus on three areas: the defence of strategic infrastructure, contingency forces and prevention, and combatting terrorism. We are activating 12 regional commands that will act in the host cities and the training centres of

the national teams, and all of them are in contact with the permanent operation centre of the Ministry of Defence in Brasília. (Ministério da Defesa 2014, 18)[10]

The marketing brochure features a series of statements like the one above. It transcends a demonstration of how the Brazilian security forces were ready to face whatever risk scenario materialized. It is a perfect example of the management of uncertainty, such as setting out demonstrative and visible security measures and 'fantasy documents' (Boyle and Haggerty 2012, 252). In the above statement it comes to the fore that the Ministry of Defence established a Centro de Coordenaçã de Defesa de Área (CCDA) (Coordination Centre of Area Defence) in each host city.[11] According to the Strategic Planning Report, the armed forces had the mission to deliver the spatial protection in a joint effort with the public security forces. In addition, the military was deployed to protect 'critical infrastructure' hubs such as electric power stations (SESGE 2012, 26). General De Nardi emphasized at the press conference on 10 June from the beginning of this section that at least 170 strategic infrastructure facilities had been identified in the 12 host cities that were essential for the stadiums' energy and telecommunication supply.

Respectively, the military had ten main tasks, which constituted their security package.[12] Most relevant were two areas: airspace defence and counterterrorism. Drawing on the exposition of security measures associated with mega-events in Chapter 1, airspace restrictions through the deployment of no-fly zones are a standard World Cup and Olympic security measure (Bennett and Haggerty 2011). During the World Cup, the airspace was restricted for civil and public aviation at least three hours prior to kick-off and four hours after the matches ended. An additional mega-event security standard that has materialized here is the strong focus of the military forces on counterterrorism activities (Giulianotti and Klauser 2011). During the World Cup the military accompanied some player delegations and occupied strategic spots in the city, but mainly stayed out of the main

[10] My own translation from Brazilian Portuguese.

[11] As there were World Cup team camps in the non-host cities Vitória (ES), Aracaju (SE), and Maceió (AL), the military operated three additional CCDAs in these cities (Ministério da Defesa 2014, 7).

[12] 1. Air defence and control; 2. Protection of strategic infrastructure; 3. Maritime and river defence; 4. Border cooperation; 5. Explosive analysis; 6. Cybernet security and defence; 7. CBRN defence; 8. Prevention and combat of terrorism; 9. Use of helicopters; 10. Contingency troops (Ministério da Defesa 2014, 3–6).

tourist areas. During the Olympics the scenario was different—soldiers patrolled Rio de Janeiro's streets in specific neighbourhoods relevant for the Olympics, as well as occupying certain strategic favelas, and they were visibly more present on Rio's streets.

The security artifice built to secure the events had very specific and localized effects in the host states and cities, which makes it of crucial importance to look closer at the city of Rio de Janeiro, where the federal investments and security structures came into play and where the research for this book was carried out.

Rio de Janeiro's Mega-Event Security Plan: Integration, Technologies, and Lockdown

The national mega-event security plans were adopted on local levels but featured very specific elements. The SICC was realized within the different host cities and, as set out in the first part of the chapter, these strategies materialized in the CICCs. More than just buildings, the CICCs have also been equipped with the newest technological communication, information, and camera surveillance systems. Rio de Janeiro has by far the largest CICC building created to serve the mega-events. However, as Cardoso (2013, 120) points out, the CICC is a logical continuation of Rio de Janeiro State's Command and Control Centre (CCC),[13] which merely contained the military police and firefighters. The CICC, as it stands in Rio today, was planned independently and has reached its current scale due to the federal investments for the World Cup and the Olympics. As seen in Chapter 2 on Rio de Janeiro's urban conflict, under the mandate of Rio's Security Secretary Beltrame, numerous initiatives to technologically modernize Rio de Janeiro's security sector have been on the increase. According to Rio de Janeiro's Sub-Secretary of Command and Control, the CICC is one of the first outcomes of these initiatives (interview, Sub-Secretary of Command and Control, 2 September 2014). As Cardoso (2019, 53) writes in one of his ground-breaking articles, 'the creation of the Integrated Center of Command and Control (CICC) is analysed as a strategy to produce and stabilize relations among agents and institutions that ended up gathering

[13] For more on the CCC, see Cardoso (2014).

elements of a new military urbanism, a New Public Management, and benchmarking strategies'.

Drawing upon the Sub-Secretary's explanations, the CICC in Rio has the functions shown in Table 3.2.

For instance, the Sub-Secretary illustrates that the second and third function within the CICC structure could also be located in completely different buildings. Thus, the first function of the CICC is to serve the daily routines of the city, and the other two levels have been created to serve in special circumstances such as the mega-events, elections, carnival, or New Year's Eve. None of my interviewees denied that the CICC would never have reached its current size without the mega-events and the financial help of the federal government, which paid for 75% of the building (interview, Sub-Secretary of Command and Control, 2 September 2014).

Importantly, the planning, ideas, and idealization of the CICC do not stem from Brazilian sources alone. Rather, they are embedded in a globalized knowledge transfer among security corporations and cities that take place independently of mega-event circulation (see also Bigo 2006). For the CICC, it is a mix between security policies that have been long planned but have gained a major boost through the mega-event security plans. The premise in Rio de Janeiro has been to invest in programmes and security material that would play a role for the city anyway, and serve its quotidian needs after the Games. In another statement, the Special Sub-Secretary for

Table 3.2 Functions of the Integrated Command and Control Centre (CICC) Rio de Janeiro

CICC Rio de Janeiro
1. **Integrated Centre for Civil and Social Defence** • 24h Emergency Call-Centre (Military Police, Ambulances, Firefighters) • Military Police, Civil Police, Firefighters, Federal Road Police, Emergency Services, Municipal Guards, Rio de Janeiro Traffic Agency, Civil Defence Agency
2. **Crisis Management Room** • Room within which the local security authorities can gather to discuss and manage acute security crises (e.g. riots)
3. **Integrated Centre for Coordinated Operations** • This is the centre within which, during the World Cup and the Olympics, security management took place.

Source: Own reproduction from interviews

Mega-Events in Rio lays out the kind of philosophy that served as the organizational lens for Rio's security authorities:

> We worked with two premises: first, the event had to serve the city and the police and not the other way around ... and the other premise was that, if we improve the security ambience of the city ... [by making it a] secure city, [we will have a] secure event. (Interview, 13 August 2014)

The essence in this quote lies within the premise that the mega-event security architecture should at first improve the already existent security infrastructure within the city. The other important thought in the quote, however, contradicts the first one. The Secretary says that if the city would be secure, the event automatically would proceed safely as well. What stands out here is the deep conviction that the investments in the CICC will bring substantial improvements to the public security sector in Rio. It is noteworthy, however, that if the authorities followed these premises, it would also mean that all the efforts to make the city secure were, to some extent at least, directed to ensure the security for the event. Stated differently, it is important to further ask *for whom* a city has been made secure, which is a question that will be addressed throughout this book. These premises also anticipate an imaginary of security at play that mirrors the *hard city* approach, one which seems to ignore the *soft city* which is full of magic and experience rather than being a static and inflexible entity (Raban 1974, 154).

As stated above, the CICCs are the physical spaces within which the SICC was implemented. The buildings were replete with information and communication systems, as well as with camera surveillance software to support the integration efforts and to foster the total control ambitions. The Strategic Planning Report refers to the establishment of a National Information System (Sistema Nacional de Informação—SNI), which projects the integration of pre-existing information and communication systems. Among these are the Interpol I24/7, the INFOSEG,[14] the federal data banks, the OCR[15] systems, and data about who is allowed to access the

[14] The Infoseg system is a data bank that unites information from the federal Secretary of Public Security, the Ministry of Justice, and the inspection organs to gather data about pending prison mandates, drivers' licences, and data from previous police investigations, and that gives authorized people access within all federal states.

[15] Optical Character Recognition.

sport venues and who has actually purchased tickets for the tournament (SESGE 2012, 33).

As a CICC technician emphasized, 'electronic surveillance is the core element of the CICC' (interview, 2 September 2014). The Sub-Secretary of Command and Control equally confirmed that CCTV is the anchor of the security strategies within the buildings (interview, 2 September 2016). To put it another way, the CICCs have been planned not just to serve as localities to unite the different security forces and enable further cooperation but also to operate high-tech surveillance and communication systems. As part of the already-installed surveillance structure in Rio de Janeiro that has been used by the mega-event security infrastructure, Rio de Janeiro's military police had installed video cameras in their police vehicles. From within the CICC, the police can see the officers within the cars and watch images from outside the vehicle. The traffic images from Rio's main roads and tourist hot spots, the stadium videos, and images from the infrared technology-equipped helicopters from the corporation FLIR[16] are also convened in the CICC (interview, CICC technician, 2 September 2014).

Likewise, the CICC is equipped with software that has been developed by the Brazilian technology corporation Comtex,[17] named 'Smart4Cities (S4C)'. This tool enables the CICC officials to track the GPS-equipped police cars on digital Google Earth maps in real time. Another key technological element has been the 'Tide' software, developed by the Brazilian firm Geocontrol,[18] that enables the management of emergency calls within the CICC. An additional technology that was important for the communication between the many security forces was the 'Mutualink'[19] software which can be used to transmit the many different radio frequencies from the various policing institutions into a unique channel (interview, CICC technician, 2 September 2016).

Technological camera surveillance has also played an important role for the LOCs of the tournaments. The following record of my visit on 5 May 2014 to the LOC headquarters in Rio's West Zone is a look behind the scenes of the security environment of the football association:

[16] See www.flir.com.
[17] See www.comtex.com.br.
[18] See www.geocontrol.com.br.
[19] See www.mutualink.net.

> The LOC security officer enables my entry with his work badge and I pass the security checks without any problems. The rain outside gets heavier, which was the reason why my trip to the West Zones took me way over an hour. We walk through long hallways and offices. We arrive at a door with big letters: *SECURITY* (all signs are in the World Cup emblem letters). Entering the room, I see a big screen at the back with two rows of chairs and tables. There might be around ten desks furnished with flatscreens. On the big video wall, I can see the aerial view of the Maracanã stadium. On the right, there is a digital graphic simulation of emergency scenes. Little manikins simulate a fan rescue, or how they regulate the entrances to the stadiums. Only a few technicians are working. On the left, an office with at least ten working spots. On the other end the same. And in the back, a hidden room for the general coordinator. Right after the entrance, on the middle right of the room, a conference space with a huge table hosts a white man in his 60s, whom I identified as André Pruis, the former South African deputy police commissioner and FIFA's security advisor. The room seems clinically clean. It still smells a bit of new carpet and electronic smog. My guide shows me where to leave my things and starts explaining the functions of the room. FIFA can control and monitor all stadiums from this room. They can also monitor all stadium entrances; they have contact with all local security control rooms in all of the 12 host cities. The room will feature a representative from the military police, the civil police, the fire brigade, and the armed forces. But they are just contact persons to the CICC in the city centre. The LOC, he explains, is only responsible in the stadium and in some hotels. All other areas are controlled by the public security, and it is the state, the city, and the federal government who are responsible. 'We need to rely on them', he says.

These words of the LOC security official warrant attention because camera surveillance is an integral part of the World Cup security for both the public and private security actors. In this sense, the standard of CCTV for mega-event security has dominantly materialized in Rio. More interestingly, though, the LOC security officer has repeatedly talked about the public security personnel in a rather patronizing and dismissive way, which is an attitude that had led to tensions between the state forces and the private football association.

During the 2016 Olympics in Rio de Janeiro, the Rio 2016 organizing committee also operated with such surveillance centres. In addition to the

CICCs (of both the public security and the private security), the armed forces operated such command-and-control centres independently of the CICCs. The military had parallel access to video surveillance technologies in the city and the stadiums. In other words, the command-and-control structures operated in three different spheres: the public security forces, the military forces, and the private company responsible for the organization of the tournament. Therefore, multiple CCTV architectures—fixed and mobile—were in place to monitor and operate in different environments of the mega-events. It transcends the goal of total readiness that proliferated among the authorities.

Building the Imaginary of Total Security

As Bennett and Haggerty (2011, 1) have said: 'Each mega-event now exhibits a "total security" effort akin to planning and deployment in times of war.' In Rio de Janeiro, for both the World Cup and the Olympics, such strategies had been planned. Martial police units and the armed forces were prepared to saturate the event city. The military police, however, was the most important institution for the mega-event policing during the World Cup, while the armed forces were also omnipresent at the Olympics. The World Cup operation concentrated clearly on a few important areas: the tourist hot spots in the South Zone of the city with its major attention on the FIFA Fan Fest in Copacabana, the city centre with the bohemian neighbourhood Lapa, and the Maracanã borough with the stadium.

The military police had to make an enormous effort to be able to police the mega-events. The major challenge was to maintain routine policing and to control the different strategic sites. Therefore, the military police forbade its personnel to take vacations during the mega-event months. During the World Cup the military police operated with its Special Forces Batalhão de Operações Especiais (BOPE) (Special Operations Battalion), the Shock Troops, and specially created World Cup units. Two extra battalions with 2,000 members were deployed to patrol the city. The military police academy provided 3,000 police trainees who were in the process of training or had recently finished their apprenticeships. Another 500 men and women came from the special battalion for mega-events (interview, military police colonel, 30 June 2014).

During another press conference in the CICC, Military Police Colonel Beltrami specified that starting from 2 June 2014, extra police troops would patrol the city: first, 1,600 additional forces and then by the final, the day-to-day patrols would be reinforced by 4,900 extra officers (press conference, 30 May 2014). On the day of the final, 25,000 military police were deployed, although the entire state of Rio de Janeiro has only a total capacity of 48,318 officers (FBSP 2016, 113). During the Olympics alone, 13,917 military police patrolled the streets of Rio de Janeiro every day. For the Olympic Games in general, more than 88,000 security personnel were deployed to secure the Games, 41,000 alone from the military (press conference, military police, 1 August 2016). It was not the military police alone who policed Rio during the tournaments. A plurality of public and private policing institutions was deployed. The LOCs trained 20,000 private security guards for the World Cup to provide security in the stadiums (press conference, Medeiros, 10 June 2014). During the Olympics, the security within the arenas was allocated to the national force which was also active during the World Cup. The municipality guards were equally used to police the variety of Olympic and World Cup areas (SESGE 2012, 53).

The installation of *island security* and fortified security cordons in urban spaces in and around mega-event boroughs has become one of the main security measures during mega-events (Baasch 2011; Fussey and Coaffee 2011; Fussey 2015). Brazilian ambitions towards this approach materialized in the planning not only in Rio de Janeiro but also in each host city at both events. Other than the afore-mentioned video surveillance and technological control mechanisms, very classic crowd-control techniques and lockdown strategies were planned. Public roads were blocked hours prior to the World Cup games around the Maracanã stadium. Three different control and security perimeters applied: one inner circle controlled by private security forces in the stadium; an outer security circle that had a mixed approach with airport-like checkpoints with metal detectors, controlled by private and public security forces; and a third external perimeter within which public security forces made their rounds (interview, LOC security officer, 14 August 2014). Close-meshed military police checkpoints and ticket controls furnished the total security vision. At the Olympics, similar mechanisms played out and the sport venues were patrolled by a plethora of security forces.

Beside these concrete and materialized efforts, the security preparations were equally accompanied by total security discourses. It seems as if these statements, full of accurate and well-formulated words, mirror an imagination of something perfect and illusionary, *ideal* for those visiting the events as well as those who are living in the Brazilian host cities. This idealization also flows through the following statements of the planners. Rio de Janeiro's Extraordinary Sub-Secretary for Mega-Events stated this clearly during the interview I conducted with him for this book:

> Rio de Janeiro has always been questioned about its security ambience, as an inhibiting factor, for example, for tourist activities, and this is now the great opportunity to dispel this image. (Interview, 13 August 2014)

Rio's Security Secretary puts it in a similar way:

> A lot of people came here and thought that everything was fantastic. They left as ambassadors for Rio de Janeiro, which is priceless ... Even more so because Rio de Janeiro is known out there for having a very bad history. (Interview, 14 August 2014)

The mega-event security planning, as set out in this chapter and exemplified in these statements, can therefore be seen in the light of what a variety of authors have conceptualized in their thoughts about cities: on the one side conceptualized and imagined by its urban planners and architects, and on the other side as experienced by those who walk and breathe the city's streets. Michel de Certeau (1984) has theorized these contrasting visions of the city in a threefold process. The *concept city* is the one that urban planners imagine first, and it creates 'its own space' within which rational organization has to omit all the 'physical, mental and political pollutions that would compromise it' (de Certeau 1984, 94). Second, there is a mechanism of erasing all kinds of traditions that could jeopardize a totally 'plane projection' (de Certeau 1984, 94). And third, 'the creation of a universal and anonymous subject which is the city itself: it gradually becomes possible to attribute to it, as to its political model' (de Certeau 1984, 94). The idealization of mega-event security ties to this imagination of an ideal that had been dreamed of for many months in the preparations of the security scheme, as well as having been expressed in public declarations just before the World Cup and the Olympics. The words of the two secretaries build up the planner's view—their imagination. They create a dream of a city that overcomes its violent past through the mega-event security measures.

Another striking example stems from the press conference at the OMC in Rio de Janeiro a few days prior to the World Cup's start. Journalists insistently asked General De Nardi if Rio would be prepared to host the World Cup, which seemingly annoyed him:

> Rio de Janeiro has the right conditions because Rio de Janeiro's PM [Military Police] is *very good*. You can stay calm because they [the Military Police] are going to overcome any problem. Look at it carefully. I am saying it again: [the] armed forces, with their contingency troops ... with their infrastructure and strategies, are already acting. (Press conference, 10 June 2014)

Principally, the many press conferences and the continuous statements that Rio de Janeiro would be safe contributed to the totality of security ambitions and a discourse of total security. In his press conference statement, General De Nardi made it clear how *well prepared* he deemed Brazil's security strategy in a boastful and authoritarian tone of voice:

> Dear Sirs and Madams, good morning. It is a great pleasure to be here in a frank conversation with you to demonstrate how a globalized security is forming a trio: the public security institutions, the Ministry of Defence, and the Intelligence Agency, creating an ensemble called: Security of the World Cup ... Because Brazil is certain, dear Sirs, to be prepared in general terms to confront whatever problems may occur. (Press conference, 10 June 2014)

Here, the imaginary of a total security effort comes to light again. The General expresses a rational vision of Brazil's security efforts. They are prepared to *confront whatever problem*.

The General's statement works as a reminder of the construction of an official imaginary of the mega-event security. As James Donald (1992, 459) expresses it: 'The city is an imagined environment. It is an environment shaped by the interaction of practices, events and relationships so complex that they cannot easily be visualized.' The General, however, tries to construct an imaginary of security that is one of the planners; a vision of a static and perfect reality. To declare publicly, in front of the international audience, that Rio's military police is *very good* is a reduction and distortion of reality. During the 2013 Confederations Cup, as well as in numerous other incidents, Rio's military police had shown themselves to be the exact opposite of a police force *prepared* to deal with complex circumstances at street level. In other words, it indicates that there is another side to reality that differs strongly from the glossy paper brochures presented in Chapter 2 and by the statements of the General.

Jonathan Raban (1974, 21) demonstrates that city planners often imagine how the citizens should ideally live, and thereby underestimate the energy, complexity, and 'magic' that urban life brings with it. There is not only the side of the planners and their beautiful concepts. The idealizers of cities often share a common mistake of understanding those who live in the city as static and rational individuals. Reality, however, seems to be riddled with natural efforts at interpretation of everyday codes *on the ground* that cannot be grasped by a rational, rigid, inflexible, and fixed imaginary of what the city is (Raban 1974, 154). As Donald puts it:

> the *fact* of any city is always more diverse, more messy and more active than reformers find comfortable or comprehensible. The *concept* of the city can never get its full measure: an accurate representation would require something more like the experiential. (1992, 435; original emphasis)

It is here where I return to my earlier assertion that the security planners of Brazil's mega-event cycle have constructed a rational vision of *how* the mega-event security unfolds, and with *what* kind of measures the street level could be controlled. The vignette at the start of this chapter featured a scene about how I was removed from the core of the security operations in Rio. However, it opened up new opportunities to dive into the immediacy of the mega-event security at street level. It is to these spheres the book turns now and investigates how the total security vision was realized in the streets. In order to be able to experience the *real* city, one must come down from the elevated position and walk the streets, as de Certeau (1984, 93) asserts: 'The ordinary practitioners of the city live "down below," below the thresholds at which visibility begins.'

There is nothing to add for the moment, apart from to say: let the sport mega-events begin.

4

The Permeable Fortress

It is four in the morning. We step outside onto the street and I wonder where the police car was parked, the one Cléber mentioned on the phone. After walking for a little bit, we arrive at a black Ford Fiesta, one of the newer versions.

> This is a police car as well—you can just not see it from the outside.

The moment Cléber puts his stuff in the back, he asks me about my PhD programme and in which area I am doing my project. Cléber seems to know something about criminology and mentions Foucault and other thinkers. He wears a dark-green T-shirt and grey shorts. The apartment complex is clearly one of the better ones in that region of the city. He persists with Foucault and we enter the car. Once I am at his side in the vehicle, he pulls a huge black semi-automatic gun out of his trousers and checks, with a routine movement and a 'click', whether there is still a bullet in the gun's barrel and positions it upside down between his legs. We start driving while he, as if nothing strange had happened, continues talking about Foucault and the complexities of Rio de Janeiro's security. I notice that his right hand stays on his right leg very close to the gun almost the whole trip.

When we come closer to Police City (one of two civil police headquarters), we drive through the favela complex Maré. Cléber points to a black homeless woman using crack on the sidewalk.

> Oh lá, *crackudas*.[1]

Just a few seconds later we pass a police station. In front of it we see Brazilian army trucks and soldiers standing guard as the Maré is occupied

[1] *Crackudas* is a term Cléber attributes to women or men (*crackudos*) who use crack; more specifically, to people who already show the long-term, physically debilitating effect of crack use. The term is used in a very derogatory way. The appropriate translation would be 'crackhead'.

Policing Sport Mega-Events. Dennis Pauschinger, Oxford University Press. © Dennis Pauschinger 2024.
DOI: 10.1093/oso/9780192848055.003.0005

by the Brazilian armed forces. We turn into another street and see another *crackuda*. Approaching Police City, we hear funk music blasting loudly from the favela right next to the civil police complex. Cléber parks the car. He changes his clothes and positions the gun on top of the car's roof. He says, 'tá tudo errado, tá tudo errado' ('everything is wrong, everything is wrong'), blaming the corrupt politicians for all these situations. The funk music from the favela Jacarezinho, which surrounds Police City, is very loud.

> This is what the people want. They want parties, drugs, drinks. These parties are circuses of horror. Not only because of its music, but for what you would find there. Youth prostitution, alcohol, drugs. If you go and invade there now, you would find all of this.

While we are preparing to go to the evacuation exercise at the Maracanã, some Special Forces officers return from an assignment. They carry their heavy weapons, machine guns, and precision rifles; they look like they are from another planet: all dressed in black, tall, strong, and with determined looks. Cléber explains to me that we will need to be escorted by them. He takes me to the Special Forces office. They work in shifts and are often on missions at night. When we are on our way out, three of the Special Forces officers who just returned from a mission are going home after their 24-hour shift. One tall guy with a hoodie has two huge, silver, shimmering guns in his hands, and puts one in the front and the other in the back of his trousers. The three of them walk out with us.

Days later, on an official game day, another Special Forces team follows the gigantic black-and-white bus on which huge letters say 'Civil Police' in the very early morning hours. The mobile police station has everything you would find in a normal station: the crime registration desks, a little cell, and a separate room for the police delegates with a coffee machine, a small fridge, and a fresh drinking water dispenser. I sit in the front with Cléber who drives the bus at breathtaking velocity through Rio. We pass the Jacarezinho again, where Unidade de Polícia Pacificadora (UPP) military police, soldiers, and the armed forces patrol. We rush in the direction of the Maracanã and when we approach the area close to the stadium, Cléber sounds his horn and swears at the municipal guards who are not quick enough to open blocked roads, asking him for his permit to pass, although the blue lights and siren are unmistakable.

The bus passes several checkpoints and arrives at its destination, not far from where spectators come down the ramp from the stadium metro station. The mobile police station is positioned just beside the mobile command-and-control centre, which is meant to be the on-the-ground operation central for the integrated command-and-control centre a few kilometres away and the military police mission control base. Arriving very early in the morning, I can observe how step by step the stadium's surroundings are transformed into an isolated territory, a fortress. Car traffic has been banned, a multitude of different security forces—private and public—patrol and control the area, and helicopter air patrols and surveillance equipment installed around the stadium transmit images to the fusion centres from the military, the public security forces, and the private sports government organizations.

During these early morning trips through these different regions in Rio, it became clear to me how security was differently applied, distributed, and perceived. The words of Cléber, talking about Foucault during our first encounter, reminded me of the many writings I had read about the organization of sport mega-event security. In these writings, the interplay of Foucauldian security and disciplinary governance is mainly put forth to make analytical sense of the complexities, inner tensions, and different modes of mega-event security. My glances out of the window of the mobile police station during these early morning journeys made me think that in Rio there is something else that merits equal analytical attention: the military occupation of the Maré community and the efforts of gargantuan proportions to secure the Maracanã's surroundings forcefully makes me think of sovereign power as spectacle.

In this chapter, I start to develop empirically and analytically what I name the triangle of security governance. Foucault (2007, 107–8) said in the *Security, Territory, Population* lectures that, 'In fact, we have a triangle: sovereignty, discipline, and governmental management, which has population as its main target and apparatuses of security as its essential mechanisms.' I will do so by critically assessing the security plans presented in Chapter 3. In the first section, I will show how the imagination of the planners, of Rio as a controlled, militarized, and totally secure event city—as a spectacular fortress—materialized.[2] Going down to street level, I illustrate how this fortress was built up and how it was put into practice during the mega-events in Rio.

[2] To name the sport mega-event security architecture a 'fortress' is an idea also used by Minas Samatas in several of his writings (e.g. Samatas 2011a, 3352).

In the second section of the chapter, I will continue the view from below by drawing upon my interviews and my ethnography during both the World Cup and the Olympics, within and outside of the security perimeters. I demonstrate how the dream of the spectacular fortress as designed by the security planners has been porous and permeable, despite the 'total security' spectacle in Rio.

From Glossy Paper to the Real World

> Fortress: A military stronghold, fortified place; in mod. use chiefly one capable of receiving a large force; often applied to a strongly fortified town regarded from a military point of view.
>
> (*Oxford English Dictionary* online)[3]

Mario Andrada, spokesman for the Olympic organizing committee Rio 2016, said at a press conference prior to the Games that 'Rio will be the safest city in the world during the Olympics' (Arthur 2016, n.p.). The statement captures the topics addressed in this section. First, the quote is one of an imaginary that only can derive from a planner's view, not from someone who lives in the immediacy of a city. Second, it transmits how that imaginary of security was delineated: Rio de Janeiro was clearly pictured as a spectacular fortress. The following subsections, therefore, look at these imaginaries and illustrate how the fortress was put into practice.

Considerable literature exists on the ways in which cities have been transformed into ever more lockdown-like fortress cities in connection with fears of crime (Davis 1990; Low 1997), 'splintering spheres of security' (Klauser 2010), consumer culture and crime (Hayward 2004), or counterterrorism measures (Coaffee 2003, 2004). However, Brazilian cities have long been marked by fortified private homes and gated communities (Caldeira 2000b) and have been pictured as militarized battle spaces (Wacquant 2008). The metaphor of a *fortress city* is long known from Mike Davis' (1990) *City of Quartz*. However, a variety of authors have rightly asserted that to analyse how security unfolds in urban

[3] See www.oed.com/view/Entry/73732?rskey=iYIa9Z&result=1&isAdvanced=false#eid (accessed 7 June 2016).

space and how, more specifically, *governing through space* takes place (Hentschel 2015, 2), the *fortress* is not always helpful as an analytical tool. To grasp the complex intersections of security measures and how they refer to enclosure, isolation, and fortified enclaves, as well as to understand their 'psycho-immunological sphere' (Klauser 2010, 327), other metaphors may be more useful, such as 'atmospheres' (Klauser 2010) or 'bubbles' (Hentschel 2015). Klauser (2010) draws upon the work of Peter Sloterdijk (2001, 2003, 2004) and principally his contemplations ranging around the metaphor of a *foam city*. Klauser (2010, 331) develops this idea further and states powerfully that: 'Securitisation strategies not only separate, differentiate, and articulate distinct physical spaces; they also create and maintain carefully defended atmospheric differences.' For Klauser (2010, 331), Sloterdijk 'provides a suggestive account of how modern society architecturally supports both the isolation of individuals in built microcells (e.g. in the apartment) and the concentration of isolated entities into collective ensembles of cooperation and contemplation such as stadiums.' Hentschel (2015) embarks on a similar approach and states that security governance could best be understood as if it were happening in bubbles because this enables us to better grasp the complexities in urban space. Hentschel (2015, 47–8) argues that bubbles of governance are useful tools because they can compose an understanding that space does not exist without time. Therefore, spaces when understood as bubbles may resist decades of insecurity around them, and others may already have burst after a short time. Bubbles also seem to enable us to understand how certain places become a target because they are considered dangerous or as spaces that hold prestige. Bubbles are also able to grasp the differences and, more importantly, the common features of different places such as gated communities or favela huts; and bubbles concretely create the possibility of overcoming prior judgements about different modes of governance or 'formal and informal actors and private or public space' (Hentschel 2015, 47–8).

Although there are other notions of more flexible and less static metaphors, I here strive to use the metaphor of the 'fortress' for the mega-event city Rio as it connects with the security planning that was discussed in Chapter 3. Therefore, the notion of a fortress that is total in its security ambitions and imagined as *secure*, *safe*, and *static* corresponds to what the authorities have projected Rio de Janeiro to be during the mega-events.

Occupying Rio: The Fortress within a Fortress

The fortress was built up not only around the stadium and within the security perimeters; Rio de Janeiro's strategically important hubs were also marked by the strong and persistent presence of different police forces and the military. As observed in Chapter 2 on Rio, the UPP programme was conceptualized as a new form of urban militarism (Graham 2010). Police Special Forces operations within distinct territories have long been described as a sort of warfare for the participants, the police, and the drug dealers. Rio has been subject to interventions by federal troops several times (Viana 2021). One of the intrinsic features within the new military urbanism is the normalization of war and its perpetuation within cities (Graham 2010, 60). This has long been a persistent scenario in Rio and sheds light on the permanence of the fortress. Rio is a city that can be named a 'militarized fortress' independently of the mega-events. Nevertheless, what happened during the World Cup and the Olympics took on the new dimensions of a 'city under siege' (Graham 2010, 60). The besieged Rio experienced different strategies to secure, maintain, and amplify the fortress.

During both the World Cup and the Olympics, Rio lived up to very distinct and selective—as I call them—occupying policing efforts. Most emblematic perhaps was the Copacabana neighbourhood, where the beach sidewalks were patrolled by the Brazilian army in groups of three or more soldiers. In addition, a myriad of public and private policing institutions were present in Copacabana. Major attention was directed towards the Beach Volleyball arena on the division between the neighbourhoods Copacabana and Leme. The arena was completely fenced, and military police and soldiers patrolled its front streets and sidewalks. Between the fences, and at the entrance metal detectors, national force officers kept watch. Even war-ready Brazilian navy ships patrolled the Copacabana coast and helicopters flew over the region constantly. These kind of occupying policing efforts also played out in the surroundings of the Maracanã stadium, at the Olympic stadium in Rio's North Zone, and in the military zone in Deodoro, the fourth Olympic zone.

Copacabana was also an example of these strategies during the World Cup. For the FIFA Fan Fest in the Copacabana neighbourhood, a similar security scheme applied. Located directly on the beach, the Fan Fest provided visitors with a theme park that featured the whole range of the FIFA marketing partners. A cableway enabled fans to fly over the crowd and specialized lounges and a lively cultural programme helped to elevate the ambience. As the Fan Zones are now an integral part of World Cups, they are especially protected (Klauser 2011b). High metal fences surrounded the area; access controls at the entrance and technological camera surveillance devices made the Fan Fest one of the spaces that served to enclose certain populations and to control their access to the area. The very same mechanisms of fencing, camera surveillance, and access controls were applied during the Olympics at the volleyball arena. The spectacular mega-event security has also most obviously been visible within the military region at the Deodoro Olympic site in Rio's North Zone, where the armed forces positioned armoured vehicles in front of the entrances to the pedestrian path that led to the sport venues. This region and the military operation speak volumes about the militarization that had been put in place during the Rio 2016 Olympics.

The implementation of security perimeters—or security cordons—is a common strategy to secure mega-event venues and has been applied at a variety of World Cups and Olympics. These strategies have been widely observed and researched at different football tournaments in the past, such as EURO 2008 in Switzerland and Austria (Klauser 2013). In the London 2012 Olympics, for instance, these strategies derived from the 'rings of steel' that were set up in the London inner-city landscape after the 9/11 terrorist attacks in New York (Coaffee 2004), which were widely adapted for the London 2012 Olympics within 'Olympic spaces of exception' (Fussey and Coaffee 2011). In Rio security cordons were applied to build up a fortress within a fortress.

The security perimeters during the World Cup in Rio were a FIFA requirement to secure the stadium to the maximum. The Maracanã security perimeters were divided between private and public security forces: public security forces operated outside of and private security within the stadium. I named the area between the metro station and the ramp that led the public to the stadium main entrance the 'policing triangle', with the mobile command-and-control centre, a mobile civil police station, and the elevated observation platforms of the military police. Traffic on the main street was prohibited hours prior to kick-off on match days, and access was tightly controlled.

As much as certain neighbourhoods of Rio became a fortress, the Maracanã borough near the stadium was transformed into a fortress within a fortress. As a standard for mega-event security, the stadiums, or any other sport venues, were disconnected from their urban surroundings and transformed into so-called 'islands of security' (Fussey and Coaffee 2011; Klauser 2011a). The already-mentioned security perimeters around the Maracanã were furnished with multiple access controls. When I visited a game as a spectator, I counted six ways in which I was controlled by multiple and different forces. Approaching the stadium, I had to pass through the following control mechanisms: a national force barrier; two military police checkpoints; a metal detector control station run by private security; a ticket scanner with turning metal bars; and a final check by private security stewards before going to my seat. Finally, at the entrance to the seating area, my ticket was checked again. Another time, arriving via the metro station Maracanã, my tickets were already checked at the metro exit. To go to the stadium area, I needed to pass another cordon of military police officials on top of the narrow bridge that leads to the stadium's main entrance. I record from a day in the field on 15 June 2014 what global security requirements mean for a local host: five helicopters above the stadium (some of them from TV stations); thousands of patrolling military police with different heavily armed units and municipal guards equipped with long truncheons; mobile military police and the Centro Integrado de Comando e Controle (CICC) observer units; army divisions escorting the player delegations with motorized federal police officers; private security inside and close to the stadium doors; and multiple security checkpoints in an isolated area. The intensive controls, checkpoints, aerial policing, and isolation of the area invoke what Fussey et al. (2011, 140) have described as 'the spatial imprints of the "total security" model'.

During the Olympics, the security perimeter was principally applied around the Maracanã stadium on the days of the inauguration and closing ceremony. Here, the access roads to the stadium were totally closed down, even more than during the World Cup. Moreover, the main streets leading to the stadium were closed by the armed forces and afforded the scenery the air of a war zone or state of emergency as the Maracanã borough was occupied.

Yet, these fortress security measures were distributed selectively. Whereas the stadium area, for example, during the World Cup and the Olympics had been highly militarized and marked by lockdown strategies, other parts of the city that were also important for the safe and secure staging of events had a clear lack of protection. One of the major differences between the World Cup and the Olympics was the participation of the armed forces in policing Rio's streets. This happened for three major reasons: the first is related to an increased risk evaluation of possible terrorist attacks during the

Olympics. As shown in Chapter 3, terrorism was not a number one topic for the Rio 2016 organizers, but it is a major drive for mega-event securitization (see Fussey et al. 2011; Giulianotti and Klauser 2012). After the terrorist attacks in Europe in 2015, these preoccupations had come back onto the major risk list for the security organizers and international attention on Brazil increased. Second, the internal public security situation in Rio had worsened since the FIFA tournament and threatened the peaceful delivery of the event. Third, the financial crisis of Rio de Janeiro State contributed to the risk scenario and induced the participation of the national force and armed forces. These developments led to visible policing efforts and the attempt to fortify the fortress Rio.

Principally, the Olympics, where terrorism had become a late but immanent preoccupation for the security forces, exhibited such spatially selective security approaches. As outlined earlier in the chapter, neighbourhoods such as Copacabana and the Maracanã vicinity even saw the armed forces with war-ready ships patrolling the beaches. The security measures unfolded in some spots of the city with vigour, while other Olympic spaces were not secured at all. Counterterrorism measures, for instance those on the Bus Rapid Transit System lines, offer an example of such selective security deployment. Starting from the newly inaugurated metro station Jardim Oceânico to the Olympic Park in the Barra da Tijuca neighbourhood, the bus line did not see many police forces, let alone armed forces. The buses, however, were fully packed with Olympic spectators. There were even event days when I hardly saw any police patrolling at the stations or the metro entrances—only metro employees and metro security officers making their routine rounds. Furthermore, while the volleyball arena was totally fenced, one could easily walk around the arena and access the fences. Literally, one could stand between the arena, the beach, and the warship that was cruising the coast. In other words, if anyone had wanted to bring something into the arena or to explode a bomb, it would have been easy to do so in that area.

Henceforth, we may have to understand the deployment of considerable numbers of soldiers and CCTV in some areas, and the absence of those in other areas, for exactly what they are: selective notions of a spectacular security. As Boyle and Haggerty have noted:

> Security practices are increasingly fashioned for public consumption through mass media templates. Specified personnel serve as media

> security liaisons for mega-events, and the coverage of preparations for the Olympics, G8 meetings, or the World Cup are all now replete with details about the amount of money being spent on security, the number of officers involved, and the radius of restricted airspace around the event. Added to this mix are increasingly familiar images of police snipers, CCTV cameras at strategic locations and officers removing mailboxes and welding shut manhole covers. (2009, 264)

Their analysis is spot-on in relation to my observations in Rio. Nonetheless, I disagree with Boyle and Haggerty (2009, 264) about their notion that 'The spectacle of security must strike a fine balance so that it is not *too* spectacular' (original emphasis). In contrast, in Rio this was exactly what happened: the mega-event security turned into a spectacle *on its own* (also McMichael 2013, 115).[4] Another important point is that these total security efforts fulfil a specific function at such events, which convey notions of spectacle as the form that conditions everyday life in a mediated society (Debord 1992), attracts the audience to the dramatic, and legitimizes common materializations of 'political and economic power' (Larkins 2015, 13). The transformation of Rio into a fortress, marked by a spectacular security performance, is as much a consumption of security as it is, in Foucauldian terms, spectacle as sovereign power that here serves as a means to manifest state dominance. The scenes described above are here reminiscent of military parades where all the available arsenal of military power is shown to impress and transmit strength—both in materialistic terms and discursively by the many statements of military personnel as presented in Chapter 3.

This section of the chapter has demonstrated how far and concretely the planners' imagination went to build up a fortress in the World Cup and Olympic city. The planners' hard city had concrete and experienced effects within the soft city that materialized within these militarized spectacles. The following section demonstrates how the security fortress was permeable and porous.

[4] In contrast to my Foucauldian understanding of spectacle, Boyle and Haggerty (2009, 259) strongly draw upon Guy Debord's (1992) *Society of the Spectacle*. Debord (1992) has conceptualized a society of the spectacle within which it is inevitable to consume the images of capitalist production, conditions that lead the people into modes of consumption. For Debord, spectacle is the form that conditions everyday life in a mediated society.

Flawed Total Security: The Porosity of the Fortress

The ethnographic view from below, already illustrated in the first section of the chapter, continues within this second section. On the one hand, permeability is here understood in its sense of being able to disrupt a given stronghold or wall. The permeability of the mega-event security architecture is tellingly compared to Franz Kafka's (1926) novel *Das Schloss* (*The Castle*) when Pete Fussey writes:

> where despite an imposing appearance and seeming omniscience, it is unreachable and, on closer inspection, tenuously held together with elements flaking away—edifices of Olympic security do not always live up to their appearances of scale, cohesion and capacity. (2015, 219)

Despite the harshly reverberating policing schemes within the Copacabana and Maracanã neighbourhoods, the fortress-like security cordons displayed twofold serious deficits. The first reflects what was reported and researched at the 2012 London Olympics: security efforts create new risks (Fussey et al. 2011). The second dynamic within the fortress was that the fortress literally did not keep its promises: it had holes in its thick walls.

On the other hand, porosity is here comprehended in the sense of Carvalho's (2013) notion that although certain urban spaces may be forbidden for specific racial and social classes, there is a certain porosity in which these categories overlap. In these two steps, I analyse how permeability and porosity played out in Rio.

Scrutinizing Total Security

As I illustrated earlier, multiple security checks paved a spectator's way from public transport to the entrance of the stadium and to the seats during the World Cup. Besides frisk and search procedures and simple ticket controls, metal detectors were key to the security spectacle around the Maracanã. From my position at the mobile civil police station, I could perfectly observe the bridge that led to the main Maracanã entrance. Depending on the match day, the military police lined up on the bridge. They manned multiple checkpoints. The first one was right at the exit of the metro station; additional blocks were at the middle and end of the bridge and further controls were on the other bridge exits that led to the nearby public university. The closer the game approached, the more people naturally gathered on the bridge. The military police units asked the spectators to present their tickets before they let them through the first checkpoints. This provoked vast human congestion at the top of the ramp. Masses of spectators were trapped on the bridge, unsecured. Stated differently, the efforts to secure the isolated and highly monitored space created new security risks.

After the attacks on 11 November 2015 in Paris and on 22 March 2016 in Brussels, the same scenarios were repeated at national football games in France and many other European countries, as I witnessed at a Hamburg game in late January 2016. More severe entry controls provoked human congestions in front of the stadium, which transformed a measure designed to promote security and safety into an insecure, dangerous, and futile undertaking. These rather visible security measures in this particular moment created both security and insecurity at the same time, as is often the case with security practices (Jusionyte and Goldstein 2016, 9). Another example follows to support these inferences.

The above-mentioned military police checkpoints, and the fact that spectators were asked to present their tickets, created such additional and new security risks. One of the consequences included the following scene I observed on 15 June 2014 within the Maracanã security perimeter:

> Two hours before the game started, international and national fans came to the mobile police station to report that their tickets had been stolen while they made their way through the many checkpoints. One hour left until the game and the mobile police station was drowned in chaos: crying fans, screaming families, overwhelmed police officers. Many of those who had high expectations of seeing the game were now standing in front of us without their tickets to hand. The civil police officers did not know what to do. Some were brought to the FIFA ticket box office and were handed new tickets; others had to realize that there was no way to get into the stadium. In the background, Argentinean fans hoisted their national flag from the bridge, while one of their comrades, with a blue-and-white painted face and a blue-and-white flag around his neck, collapsed, crying desperately and screaming that he had saved money for months to see his team.

Notwithstanding the many security forces within the highly secured territory and the closed-circuit controls by the military police and other institutions, these measures had not prevented the ticket robberies. Perhaps this is even a rather normal scenario during mega-events that attract thieves who profit from overcrowded places. However, what happened here is that it was a requirement of the military police for spectators to present their tickets several times openly. This in itself provided the opportunity for ticket thieves to exploit the fans' excitement and their festive state of mind.

Moreover, the scene gives insight into the heart of the complex policing infrastructure around the stadium. The multiple policing forces performed their own roles but influenced the work of the others constantly. What we see here is a twofold problematic. First, it reminds us of the complexity of the security sector in Brazil which fights with these kinds of multiple policing institutions and their conflicting relationships. As I pointed out in Chapter 3, it was part of the Brazilian mega-event security vision that these conflicts could be bridged by the integration concept. This example, therefore, already anticipates what I will explore later in the book, where I investigate if this cooperation between the different institutions had worked as imagined and planned.

Second, this dynamic also refers to a common problem in the accountability of plural policing (Loader 2000; Jones and Newburn 2006). It is difficult to say who was responsible for what in which situation where 'new forms of institutional complexity ... erode democratic accountability by obscuring who is responsible for what and answerable to whom' (Loader 2000, 333). Here, there was an obvious absence of someone who could be made responsible for the problems narrated above. Chaos and improvisation, as well as conflicting actions, made up the policing efforts and were a steady companion at Rio's mega-events which made the fortress look rather fragile and brittle, as I will elaborate with further evidence in the next subsection.

Invasions from Below and Above

On 18 June 2014, the day of the group match when Spain played against Chile, 85 Chilean fans broke through all the security checks, ticket controls, and highly secured FIFA security perimeters and invaded the stadium. The fans reached as far as the FIFA pressroom within the Maracanã, where most of them were detained. After the incident it was widely discussed who was responsible for the failure and how such a lapse could happen. Although the integration concept between all security forces was a major project for and among the security officials, it seems that cooperation between state and private security was a problematic issue.

As stated already, around the Maracanã stadium there were at least three different security perimeters: an internal area within the stadium, an outer perimeter that restricted access to ticket-holders, and an external security area close to the stadium that extended way beyond the stadium limits. Private security was responsible for the inner and outer circle, while the public security forces were present within the outer and external security perimeter. Yet the invasion took place. A Local Organizing Committee (LOC) security officer recounts that everyone failed in that particular situation. The military police did not control the tickets correctly and check if the tickets were for the right game. The private security responsible for the inner security circle and for the gate where the Chile fans invaded left the door open and could not prevent the incident (interview, LOC security officer, 14 August 2014).

The protagonists on the stage of the press conference in the CICC on 20 June after the invasion incident seemed nervous and irritated, and were not as clear as the security officer. The multiple representatives from the involved state security institutions and the LOC, however, declared that the security measures would be augmented for the upcoming games. This decision reflects a common reaction after major security incidents, which is to augment the controls and lockdown strategies (Coaffee 2004). Still, the protagonists' arguments proved contradictory in practice. On the one side, they clearly stated that no one may enter the territory near the stadium without a valid ticket for the day of the match. On the other side, they openly declared that tourists who wanted to visit the stadium surroundings would not be banned from doing so (press conference, CICC, 20.06.2014).

Drawing on my own observations within the external and outer security perimeter, however, the declarations made by the public security officials were—neither before nor after the incident—completely realized. Before the incident there were, at some spots around the stadium, very strict controls by the military police, and whoever did not have a ticket could not access the area at these specific points. At the same time, watching from the position of the mobile civil police station near to the Maracanã metro entrance, I saw several pedestrians, cyclists, and street-food sellers walking around the stadium without being stopped. After the incident, in a similar way, I experienced both severe and rather flawed checkpoints and ticket controls.

The above elaborations are something that also happened during the London 2012 Olympics, where Olympic security operations were shaped by inherent tensions among heterogeneous organizations: 'Olympic security varyingly operates at multiple scales, across different temporalities, myriad spaces and for diverse purposes' (Fussey 2015, 213). These inherent tensions came to the fore in Rio during the World Cup in multiple situations, as shown above in the case of the Chilean fan invasion. Specifically, in Rio these tensions were also marked by pre-existing institutional conflicts among the police forces. In addition, there were also marked tensions between the discourse of the Olympic security officials and the severity of the ground policing operation, as will become more obvious with the next example.

Each of the Olympic venues during the 2016 Games was a fortress within a fortress. After arriving in the fortress with normal tickets, I was astonished that I could access areas that should never be possible for a civilian like me. At the same time as the Rio Olympics were announced as the safest and best secured ever, I could walk around behind the scenes of the Olympic Park arenas and was not checked once for any special credentials. This sheds light on how these events, even if secured to the maximum, were poorly safeguarded. On that day, I was able to bring things through the metal detector system and smuggle—on purpose—my water bottle through the national force checkpoints. The Olympic Park, fully controlled by CCTV, was not able to detect me wandering around in areas I was not allowed into. I even accessed areas where basketball players who had just played a game—among them several NBA stars—were waiting for the shuttle to their team hotel. The fortress within a fortress was a hollow security spectacle that would not have resisted any well-planned attack.

Tensions of such scale also found their way into more technological spheres. A drone pilot I interviewed during the Olympics, demonstrated how the inherent tensions among manifold institutions that policed the Olympics led to a tremendous permeability of the fortress. The drone pilot had flown over the volleyball arena in Copacabana with his DJI Phantom 3 to film the stadium for his customer, the Fédération International de Volleyball (FIVB). The national force, responsible for policing the area, demanded the drone be taken down as overflying these areas was not allowed. As the FIVB did not have permission from the International Olympic Committee at hand, they were brought to a civil police station. At first glance, this incident simply showcases the multiplicity of actors involved in the control of the Olympic spaces and how the different approaches conflicted.

Another example arose from the interview that illustrates the porosity of the fortress in Rio. The drone pilot showed me pictures where another drone was not even able to get close to the Olympic areas due to software updates that included GPS restrictions for the Olympic boroughs. Any drone equipped with the software update was prevented from flying ahead and forced to land safely. Yet every drone *without* the software update could easily transport objects into the Olympic areas, even in autopilot mode (interview, commercial drone pilot, 9 August 2016). This essentially challenges the total security claims and the imaginary of a security fortress for the Olympics. Moreover, interesting discussions could arise regarding whether the aerial space is *public* and how power relations are rearranged within these still rather new possibilities and visibilities of the aerial gaze (see Klauser and Pedrozo 2015; Pauschinger and Klauser 2020).

Although Rio was transformed into a militarized fortress, these incidents are further evidence that it was a rather *permeable fortress* within which security organization was, in fact, marked by chaos and improvisation. The highly secured fortress Rio de Janeiro proved to have various insecurities and leaks. The final subsection of this chapter provides a closer analysis of how we may understand security at sport mega-events within these highly secured spaces.

'Fuck It, It's Just Peanuts': Guarantee the Flow to Control the Space

A theme that accompanied the fieldwork in Rio de Janeiro was the more or less severe control mechanisms at the Maracanã security perimeter access points. During the World Cup I had no official police badge or FIFA working permission. Nevertheless, I was able to access the area with the help of a civil police officer. At other opportunities, I managed to enter the perimeter with a ticket from a different game day, and again on other days military police officers stopped me. During the Olympics the highly militarized and policed space around the stadium on the day of the inauguration ceremony was also porous. Military police officers prevented me from even getting close to or accessing the stadium front areas near the Maracanã metro station. The very same day and just a few minutes later, I could access the same area from the other side, taking a different exit at the other metro station, São Cristovão. The difference was that at the first metro station the military police controlled access to the restricted area and asked for tickets or working permissions. The armed forces only stood guard. On the other side, armed forces were in charge of controlling the area. They did not prevent my access and even informed me in which direction I should walk with friendly good humour. At the end of my walk, I took the exit where I was banned earlier that day.

The different approaches of sometimes more, and at certain times less, severe ticket and access controls have been a continuous problematic at mega-events. My experiences from the field are important to highlight as they lead towards my conceptual analysis of the Foucauldian triangle of security governance. To pursue this task, it is worth looking at the discussion set out by Klauser (2013) and Fussey (2015). Both use a Foucauldian understanding of security that matches with mega-event security. Both draw upon Foucault's (2007) lecture series, *Security, Territory, Population*. As a reminder, for Foucault (2007, 65), security relies on a constant movement of the objects and people that circulate within pre-existing territories, 'but in such a way that the inherent dangers of this circulation are cancelled out'.

In addition, it is essential to outline the particularities in Rio in contrast to the findings of Klauser (2013) and Fussey (2015). In Rio, surveillance and security measures similar to those at previous events like EURO 2008 and the London Olympics were applied, and the space at Rio's mega-events was equally *monitored*, *controlled*, and *assessed*.

Klauser (2013) writes in his paper on spatialities of security and surveillance, within which he depicts the mechanisms of security and surveillance at EURO 2008:

> More specifically, the key argument I am seeking to advance here is that surveillance (in its spatialities) has to be studied simultaneously with regard to fluidity and fixity, flows and presences, circulations and enclosures, external separation and internal organisation, because it is the articulation and reconciliation of precisely these contrapuntal pairs of logics that condition the functioning and implications of urban surveillance today. (2013, 291)

This quote is helpful in shedding light on the ground-level dynamics I observed in Rio: there was not, as already outlined above, just surveillance and control measures that pointed in only one direction or focused only on one particular object. On the contrary, surveillance and security measures were both fixed and mobile, focused on external separation and internal organization, and concentrated on enclosures and circulation—all simultaneously.

For EURO 2008, Klauser (2013, 292–6) explored and demarcated three main goals of the variety of surveillance and security measures. Swiss state authorities and private entities applied their catalogue of measures to ensure enclosure and access controls, to manage circulation, and to regulate the internal organization of the monitored zones. As Klauser analyses:

> Fan zones, stadium security rings, enclosed team hotels, training grounds and other secluded places stand for a particular spatial logic of surveillance. The aim is to guarantee the good functioning of selected, enclosed and hierarchically organised portions of space by controlling and filtering the flows of people and objects crossing their borderlines at specific access and control points. (2013, 292)

The 'dilemma' that Klauser (2013, 292) derives from his fieldwork in Switzerland is how to do both: on the one hand, *control* space, while on the other hand *allowing* the flow of people. Security authorities in Rio tried to control and guarantee access at the same time. These kinds of strategies not only applied around the sport venues but also came to the fore sporadically in different neighbourhoods. Take just the example of the border region between the neighbourhoods of Botafogo and Copacabana, separated by a mountain with the infamous Tabajara favela on top. As I often went to Copacabana by public transport, I mainly used the tunnel Alaor Prata. At the exit of the tunnel, the military police constantly controlled access to the neighbourhood, checking whomsoever they identified as suspicious. Obviously, those stopped, frisked, and searched were representative of what was understood as suspicious, criminal, and the common other in Rio: young black men on motorcycles or small, old cars with black drivers.

These dynamics shed light on the ways in which security is being sorted within and around these highly secured spaces, as well as within Rio during the Olympics, and perhaps even beyond. It reverberates with Foucault's (2007, 65) thoughts about a security apparatus that no longer envisions purely disciplinary spaces, which without doubt still continues to exist, but creates the possibility of filtering and monitoring who can actually access the controlled spaces and who should not. It is, therefore, a security apparatus that highlights a constant flux of people and prioritizes mobility. Graham's (2010, 145) 'passage point urbanism' is defined by Klauser (2013, 294–5) as an essential part of the event context and attributes three main characteristics to it: it must be flexible and adaptable; enable surveillance assemblages of people, objects, and different institutions; and ensure a relationship between circulation and separation which is complementary, while at the same time being contradictory and the root cause of conflict. In many ways these observations have materialized in Rio, as I will show in the following paragraphs.

One major aspect Fussey (2015, 219) found that differed from Klauser's (2013b) analysis was that access and control mechanisms varied in different urban environments like the Fan Zones and the stadium areas at EURO 2008. At the London 2012 Olympics, however, these access controls varied 'within the same setting. Here good flows were permitted and assisted in their traversal of borders and boundaries' (Fussey 2015, 219). Hence, at London 2012, protestors and all those that did not fit into the Olympic spirit and marketing strategy were not immediately—and sometimes not at all—banned and/or excluded from the venues. However, all the flows and categories of good and bad visitors were constantly watched, monitored, and placed under surveillance.

Within the World Cup security scheme around the Maracanã stadium, these complexities also came to the fore. Exploring the mechanisms that were deployed around the stadium, I observed how the surveillance and control dynamics served different actors in the field such as the LOC, FIFA, and the many state security entities, while being applied and used in completely different ways. On some game days, the bad were filtered and just monitored, whereas on other days, restrictive policies for all those who did not fit into the monitored and highly secured urban environment around the stadium applied. Nonetheless, as Fussey (2015) has argued for London 2012, access controls in Rio were different *within the same setting*. Moreover, the specificity in Rio was that these differences depended strongly on variables such as time and space within the same setting, *which actors* were responsible for certain areas, *and at what stage* in the tournament. In other words, it depended strongly on the temporality and which organization was responsible within these settings. Another example can offer further insight into this dynamic.

On many game days, I observed the movements at the mobile civil police station. The position was a very good observation spot from which not only to witness the many different dynamics in and around the security perimeter but also to keep an eye on the different approaches by the many security forces with their diverse working philosophies. The civil police station was responsible for registering any sorts of crimes happening in front of the stadium. During the seven World Cup games in Rio, many different crimes occurred within the security cordon, despite the official promise to maintain the imagined security fortress. The ways in which these were approached varied greatly throughout the tournament. As reported in the section on access controls, this changed after the invasion incident. The aspect of the temporal factor within the tournament is therefore crucial, as the ways in which crimes were approached were different before and after the invasion incident. Moreover, the severity of the access controls varied not only over the different time frames during the whole tournament but also during a game day. Whereas before the games the controls were overly severe, after the games had ended, the checkpoints started to relax, even though the teams and spectators were still in the area.

It is noteworthy, therefore, that the different institutions handled the control mechanisms in totally different ways. Some of the municipal guards, who often seemed highly motivated, brought illegal ticket retailers and street kids to the civil police mobile police station. Here, two things happened above all. First, the municipal guards applied Brazilian legislation that prohibits illegal ticket sales. Second, they applied an informal principle that poor, black, and homeless street kids would not fit into the area of the festive and globalized FIFA marketing machinery. Thus, those who were not wanted within the festive spaces were arrested, or at least banned from the area.

Within this very same setting, the civil police would act somewhat differently. One situation from the field exemplifies that difference. After a World Cup game and a long day of work, many officers of the different police institutions would hang around on the green space in front of the mobile police station. Shortly after the matches, illegal and non-FIFA-licensed street sellers walked around the stadium with a mobile charcoal grill. I was standing around with civil police officers when one of them approached the group. To my surprise, the policemen bought some peanuts from the informal seller. When one of the group said to a high-ranked civil police officer, 'Oh, the chief is buying illegal stuff', he answered in a laughing tone: 'Fuck it, it's just peanuts'. This example shows how differently distinct policing institutions had handled the same order, which was to keep the security perimeter free from those who did not fit there (from a security and FIFA marketing perspective). The complexity of the governed and monitored spaces at mega-events seems to make it impossible to maintain the totality of security and the prohibition mantra. In Foucauldian terms, the good and the bad were filtered. In the case of the World Cup 2014, it depended strongly on *who was in charge*, for *which institution*, who had to consider *who was good* or *who was bad* for the environment, and at *what exact point in time and space*. In other words, the temporality of the access controls was as important as which policing institution was responsible for them.

What can here be observed is this porosity of class and race relations in Rio. As Carvalho (2013) has pointed out, the back-and-forth between segregated urban space is always possible and happens still today daily. Think only of the numerous house servants, security guards, and chauffeurs that by matter of obligation transit between the favela and peripheries and the high-class apartments of economically prosperous Brazilian households. Throughout the many years I have been in Brazil, these possibilities of transiting through and across segregated spaces on micro and macro scales were for me always a matter of choice, but for the working poor were often permitted only in specific conditions of labour.

During the mega-events, this was stunningly visible in the sport venues, where the general cheering public in the stands was mostly white, while those selling merchandise and serving food were people racialized as non-white. Rio's security forces saw boys from favelas as falling into the common suspicious categories and barred them from entry at the mega-event security perimeters. In contrast, I could walk more or less freely around as someone corresponding with the stereotype of a legitimate and white spectator of a World Cup game. The peanuts scene is a reminder of these relationships in which the security perimeter around the stadium was highly secured before the game but became accessible and porous once the game was over, and the police decided to 'let in' those who served their needs.

A similar approach, related to my own positionality in my research, came to mind when I realized how I was able to permeate many of the secured spaces. During the Olympics, the highly militarized and policed space around the stadium on the day of the inauguration ceremony was normally not accessible. However, I was able to navigate easily around the Maracanã together with a civil police officer, who helped me infiltrate the security perimeters. Armed forces close to checkpoints on the Olympic inauguration day did not prevent my access, and even informed me in which direction I should walk in a friendly tone. At the same time, I could walk around behind the scenes of the Olympic Park arenas and was not checked once for any special credentials. As previously noted, I even accessed areas where basketball players who had just played a game were waiting for the shuttle to their team hotel.

Beside the security flaws, I also attribute this free navigation of mine to my status as a white foreigner, who is not targeted as the culturally and racially constructed other in Brazilian society (Misse 2006; Vargas 2016; Alves 2018). The project of whitening Brazil and erasing black Brazilian heritage by a politics of cultural and spatial exclusion and killing (Nascimento 1989; Vargas 2012), however, continued throughout the mega-events. Data produced by Terre des Hommes (2016, 10) shows that the city government actively 'cleared' Rio's wealthier neighbourhoods in the South Zone of street children or tried to prevent youth from the peripheries from coming into these areas. The report highlights that police killings increased before the tournaments and continued during the events: 92 shootouts were reported during the Olympics alone (19).

This chapter has highlighted that the imaginary of a total security dream was that of the planners, and stands in strong contrast to the lived experience of the soft city that happens at ground level. All these examples reiterate the need to move forward and to continue at street level. On the day of the World Cup final, which has been praised as an overall success by the security authorities, the military police brutally beat up Canadian journalist Jason O'Hara who was covering an emerging protest at the Saens Peaña metro station (Corbeil 2014). At the same time, hundreds of journalists worked freely within the security perimeter and in the stadium to cover how Philipp Lahm would raise FIFA's most valued marketing brand into Rio's dark sky: the golden World Cup trophy. The Cup's shiny appearance tries to blind the audience to what continues in its shadow. The book now turns to the everyday policing activities in some of my fieldwork locations and sheds light on the complexities, spheres, and localities that were not shown and protected by Rio's mega-event spectacle.

5
Working at the Edge in the Police City

> You know what happens? A lot of people say that something must be done. But very few really have the courage to come here and do it. If you really count the people—even among police officers—who go into favelas to confront an enemy when they fire rifle shots at you, these are very few ... Because everyone has a certain fear of dying. Some have it a lot less. I can say that here in the CORE, in the sector I work in, this fear is very low. But no one wants to die.

These words of the 33-year-old police officer I interviewed in 2014 roar loudly from my earphones and pound in my head that morning at the end of 2016. I had just discovered that he had been shot while he was off duty. He was on his way home from a dinner with his girlfriend and five armed assailants approached his car in a dark and narrow street. A refuse collection car had blocked the road and the robbers took advantage of that moment. As he always carried his firearm, he knew that if they discovered he was a police officer, he would certainly die. So, he made the first move and started shooting immediately. He killed one of the attackers, but had no chance of surviving the many bullets that perforated his body. One of the guys shot him in the face when he was already down. His girlfriend survived uninjured—physically.

When I read the news that morning and saw the headlines of a Rio newspaper that a civil police officer from the Special Forces had died in an armed assault, I searched for the victim in my recordings as the name didn't sound strange to me. I realized that I had engaged in a longer conversation with him that Olympic summer in Rio. I wrote to another of my participants from the police who was assigned to his group in the Special Forces. He

Policing Sport Mega-Events. Dennis Pauschinger, Oxford University Press. © Dennis Pauschinger 2024.
DOI: 10.1093/oso/9780192848055.003.0006

didn't answer. Another one answered and said, 'you know he is up the hills, they are looking for the guys with blood in their eyes, it's a war, it-is-a-war'. The next day I saw in the papers how his unit colleagues carried his coffin in their full equipment to pay him his last respects.

The police officer who had been killed was trained in the civil police Special Forces. Their headquarters is in the Cidade da Polícia, a complex run by the civil police between the favelas of Jacarezinho and Manguinhos in the North Zone of Rio de Janeiro which agglomerates many of the specialized police departments. It also houses the police's main administration, a theatre hall for festive events, and several training grounds for the Special Forces. Among these, there is an artificial favela that has been constructed to practise missions under the most realistic conditions possible.

Years later in May 2021, I had a similar situation again, in which I looked at Rio de Janeiro headlines and read the name of a police officer whom I had known from my fieldwork who had now been shot—this time in the favela Jacarezinho, in which the civil police and their Special Forces entered to arrest drug traffickers. The police officer was shot in the head the moment he stepped out of the armoured vehicle. What unfolded moments later was the most lethal police operation in the history of Rio de Janeiro and cost 27 lives. Outlets all over the world covered the story, showing the bloodshed in terrible photographs (e.g. Franzen 2021; Phillips 2021). The suffering and trauma of those who witnessed the scenes, among them children, of how police officers raid houses and kill are endless. The scenes of yet another funeral, accompanied by many in uniform and the police officer's 11-year-old son who cries on his father's coffin, are images from a senseless conflict.

These collateral incidents happened at the beginning of October 2016 and in May 2021, just a few weeks and years respectively after the last curtain of the mega-event spectacles had fallen. Many others happened in between and since these. The Olympics, the International Olympic Committee (IOC) president said at the closing ceremony, 'are leaving a unique legacy for generations to come. History will talk about a Rio de Janeiro before and a much better Rio de Janeiro after the Olympic Games'. In light of the narrated incident, the flagrancy of his words speaks volumes, and again evokes the question: *for whom?* A city within which such violent acts happen sheds light on the long-lasting patterns of violence that continuously shake Rio, despite the mega-event security plans; despite command-and-control centres full of surveillance technologies; despite the new weapons; despite the new armoured vehicles. Despite . . .

This chapter looks behind the scenes of Rio's security apparatus and projects a spotlight onto the spaces that have been hidden by the shadows of the spectacle provided by FIFA, the IOC, and the Brazilian government. Rio de Janeiro's police officers are working at *the edge*. Defined as the outer limit of something, as the moment just before something meaningful happens, or as a tense feeling (*Oxford Dictionaries* 2019), for Rio's police officers *the edge* constitutes both an emotional state of being and a spatial order. In this chapter, I explore police officers as 'edgeworkers' and how their emotional and spatial edging contributes crucially to the production of 'police territoriality', the attempt to establish urban order, and the making of everyday tensions in Rio de Janeiro. I do so by highlighting my observations and interviews with the police officers I accompanied for this work and down below onto street level. In the first section of the chapter, I specifically look at how certain defining dynamics of Rio's urban conflict continued completely unchanged by the mega-event security scheme. I then shed light upon how the police, and especially the civil police Special Forces, contribute essentially in producing the city as a space of war, which, equally, was not addressed by any of the mega-event security provisions, and which was intended to be hidden by the security spectacle.

Rio de Janeiro's Public Security Unchanged: Welcome to an Old World

The IOC marketing claim that paved Rio de Janeiro during the Olympics read 'A New World'. The narrative behind the marketing tools is suggesting, just as was the IOC president in his closing speech, that Rio de Janeiro would be a better place after the mega-events, including the city's security conditions. In contrast, this section of the chapter uses the tagline 'Welcome to an Old World'. The following subsections aim, therefore, to illustrate how these narratives contrast with the street-level observations from my fieldwork that plunge into the immediacy of the civil police, and which are a determining factor within Rio's public security. Looking behind the scenes of the civil police's work lays bare that it is an old and ugly world that continues in the shadows of the mega-event security spectacle, but washed to the surface in different moments during the events and years after.

Setting the Scene

It was one of those evenings during the World Cup in the police station. At the same time as I was helping a police officer to register a crime suffered by two German tourists, two military police brought in three black kids, not older than ten years. One of them the military police treated more harshly, pinning his arm behind to his back. I followed them to see what was going on in the back of the station, where the people that get caught committing a crime are processed. When I came around the corner, one of the military policemen, who were fully equipped with bulletproof vests, said to one of the kids in an aggressive tone of voice, 'cala sua boca, cala a sua boca porra' ('shut up, shut the fuck up'). He put his finger in the boy's face. The civil policeman told the boys in a rude manner to only speak when they were asked a question. The officer took the names of the boys who were only wearing T-shirts and were barefoot. The officer opened one of the cells and sent the prisoner in there into the other cell, so he could lock the kids up in one of the cells together.

In the front, total chaos had erupted. The waiting room was fully packed with a lot of people. Military policemen were securing guys who had done something. There was a lot going on at the same time. It was loud. People were yelling. Constantly, police officers were running back and forth in the station. Some were registering crimes. Others were occupied in coping with the number of handcuffed people in the back.

These recollections bring to the fore a routine dynamic of a civil police station during the World Cup. It was a constant change of scenes, from the public sector in the front to the hidden sector in the back. These dynamics stand in strong contrast to days where no exceptional events were on. Often, and especially during late-night hours, the scene would be filled with boredom and the police officers in the registration area would pass their time watching television or playing on their cell phones.[1] Others, responsible for the paperwork investigations, would continue their routine. The scenes from the record above also provide a first look at the circumstances that unfold in the spaces that were hidden for the majority of the mega-event spectators. The scene points towards long traditions within Rio de Janeiro's police work that throw doubt on the many claims of a changed public security landscape through the tournaments.

[1] Boredom is a core element of police work and is reported by many police scholars (Fassin 2013, 78).

A civil police station (Delegacia Policial—DP) is normally structured into different sections. In 2014, the year of the scene above, the civil police DPs had had 15 years of experience since the state of Rio de Janeiro reformed most stations as part of the so-called Delegacia Legal (Legal Station) programme, which was proposed by the social scientist Luiz Eduardo Soares who worked in the Ministry of Public Security of the state of Rio de Janeiro in 1999. According to Soares (2000, 85), the project mainly aimed to technologically modernize the DPs to reduce the possibility of police corruption. Soares wanted to digitalize the crime data collection and speed up the investigation process, which should restore moral confidence in police work. Following an extensive study by Vívian Ferreira Paes (2006, 151), this reform was intended to change the ways in which the police exercised the registration of crimes, to be able to cope with police activity and to try to govern police conduct. The reform may have digitalized the ways in which crimes are registered, but the police have found other ways to continue to base their work on the inquisitorial system, on secrecy, and on punitive control (Paes 2006, 151).

A Delegacia Legal consists of different sectors, some of which are worth describing here to better understand the dynamics in the next sections. The police officers of the GI (Grupo de Investigação) (Investigation Group) are responsible for the crime registration and work in 24-hour shifts, followed by 72 hours off duty. Each of these shifts has an officer who works in the SIP (Setor de Inteligência Policial) (Police Intelligence Sector) where fingerprints and photographs are taken. Other officers within the GI group work during commercial hours to pursue police investigations. An important section within the civil police station is composed by the GIC (Grupo de Investigação Complementar) (Additional Investigation Group) who work directly for the police station chief (Delegado de Polícia),[2] and are the so-called confidence group of the DP police chief. They normally work on cases that seem to have the possibility of being solved quickly, and they often go on small missions outside of the DP (see also Misse et al. 2010, 29–34). The hierarchies in a DP are relatively fixed. In each of the 24-hour

[2] The civil police has several hierarchical levels. The institution is divided between police officers and police station chiefs/delegates. The latter are the ones that hold administrative and decision responsibility. To become a chief, you must have studied law and passed a public tender. To become a normal police officer with the civil police, a university degree and a public tender is required. Within the station, there are many distinct positions that are not important to name here. See also Misse et al. (2010), Albrecht and Husain (2011), and Denyer Willis (2014).

GI shifts, there is one shift-station chief who is the person who actually decides about the immediate cases that appear at the station. In addition, the DP has one main chief who is responsible for the whole station and who reports to the directors of the civil police institution, and receives support from an assistant station chief.

In essence, the civil police has a diversity of different positions within its organization. Simplifying, I classified three main groups. The first are the *bureaucrats*. They are the ones who do the paperwork, the deskwork investigations, and the registrations of crimes during the 24-hour shifts. The second group are the *street investigators*, namely the small GIC group that works directly for the main police delegate who sends them on small missions that have the possibility of an immediate or at least a short-term success. Homicide detectives and other members of specialized police departments are also part of this category. Finally, the third group are the *combatants*. These are the civil police officers from the Special Forces.

Militarism and Hypermasculinity

As outlined in Chapter 2, An Olympic City at War, about Rio de Janeiro's public security circumstances, the civil police are one of two main forces within the Brazilian state and the backbone of the country's public security system (alongside the federal police that operates across state boundaries). Whereas the military police patrol the streets, civil police officers investigate crimes, interrogate suspects, and file cases with the judiciary, and can be seen as an agency of surveillance and an auxiliary branch of the juridical system (Kant de Lima 1995, 85). Although the civil police as an organization has a clear civilian character, it is anchored in Brazil's militaristic past (Zaverucha 2000, 9). This past still resonates today in its hierarchical, military, and hypermasculine everyday working environments.

In Rio's civil police Special Forces Coordenadoria de Recursos Especiais (CORE) (Coordination of Special Assets), this is especially obvious. As one of its members says:

> Here in Rio de Janeiro we use rifles, war equipment like helmets, bulletproof vests against rifles . . . This is military equipment, which for us has become a routine. The CORE is exactly this: within the civil police, we are a paramilitary force.

Although included in a civilian organization, the CORE unit uses AR 10 and M4 battle rifles and their uniforms and cars are all black. The CORE is the militarized special resources department and consists among other sectors of a bomb detection unit, a section with dogs, and a helicopter service team. One of the most important sector in the CORE is a relatively small group of approximately 40 men that work in 24-hour shifts (called Serviço de Operações e Táticas Especiais (SOTE) (Special Operations and Tactics Service)). Their main task is to support the specialized or normal district police stations in dangerous circumstances or in territories dominated by armed drug traffickers. All members are specially trained civil police officers who are selected by physical and psychological assessment, and often internalize a hypermasculine and militaristic way of perceiving police work.

Through my observations of the officers that work in many distinct positions within the civil police, I perceived how a fascination with militarism and hypermasculine attitudes are deeply embedded within the civil police. Masculinities are understood in the sense of Raewyn Connell (2005, 71) as 'simultaneously a place in gender relations', as well as 'practices' and the 'effects of these practices in bodily experience, personality and culture'. Connell's (2005, 77) concept of 'hegemonic masculinity' helps us to understand masculinity as a means of justifying men's superiority to women, principally when there 'is some correspondence between cultural ideal and institutional power, collective if not individual'. Hypermasculinity refers then to excessively masculine actions in a cultural criminological sense: in highly insecure and uncertain late modern environments, groups may exaggerate their own identity as ways of overcoming feelings of 'worthlessness', in order to establish their own 'superiority' (Ferrell et al. 2008, 60).

The characteristics of militarism and hypermasculinity have been above all visible among the members of the civil police Special Forces, as they are a unit trained like a military force and equipped just like the military police Special Forces Batalhão de Operações Policiais Especiais (BOPE). The CORE officers are all specially trained civil police officers who are selected by assessment in one of the most difficult police Special Forces courses in the world. Over several months, the police officers must bear physical and psychological pressure and prove their toughness through a series of inhuman exercises. This training is embedded within militarism and fosters forceful hypermasculine identities—which are based on muscle training and a fascination for weapons and battle—as is common in military training (Barrett 1996; Hinojosa 2010). At the end of the course, they are kept in custody for several days without any contact with the outside world until they are named members of the CORE. When I had the chance to witness one of the formation ceremonies, it was stunning how the congratulation speeches were furnished with a vocabulary of war, hypermasculinity, warriors, and heroism.

As one of the Special Forces officers said in a conversation about the protests by teachers prior to the World Cup:

> We, we need to know to divide . . . in a society, the bad and the good, the wrong and the right . . . For me, a vagabond is a vagabond, a good person is a good person . . . I go with full force against vagabonds, but against a teacher? What am I going to do? I will go there to shoot the teacher? (Interview, 13 June 2014)

The statement of the CORE officer gives us an idea about how the conflict in Rio de Janeiro is one that is framed by a military vocabulary and categories such as *enemy* and *friends*, the *good* and the *bad*—much as in the opening quote of the murdered Special Forces member. Thus, when you perceive your police work within a militarized framework, this consequently leads to forms of violence and to the right to kill—a right that is given to you by society as such, but that you justify for yourself within this stereotypical thinking.

These statements point to what scholars and human rights associations have long debated and criticized; that many police in Rio de Janeiro are trained with and have internalized a culture of militarism and war (see Muñoz Acebes 2016), which contributes to the violence in the city. As Kraska wrote:

> The interwoven scripts of militarism and masculinity provide the cultural foundation for organized forms of violence by militaries and police to further state power, and these scripts furnish a more diffuse but still pervasive social network of threatened and real violence among individual men. (1998, 103)

These notions of militarism and hypermasculinity play a key role when it comes to explaining the levels of police lethality and violence in Rio de Janeiro. The CORE Facebook profile photo at the time of this research speaks volumes about how the members comprehend their unit within a highly militarized framework. The photo shows the unit in action, with a background that transmits their activity as taking place in unusual and dangerous spaces, as if they were on a battlefield where explosions and fire mark their routines.

Masculinity and militarism go hand in hand and take place within the police station, and extend far beyond the militarized Special Forces unit. I recorded that one day, at five o'clock in the morning, the immediate investigation group got ready for a small mission near the police station. The institution of the civil police merely provides weapons and a bulletproof vest to protect the officers. However, some of the GIC members had brought their own supplementary equipment and looked like a military unit that would start an ambush in a matter of moments.

The fascination with military combat, weapons, and Special Forces has been a constant companion for this investigation unit's members. In other words, what we see in Rio is a civil police force that has no military hierarchy, yet has internalized a certain militarism that seems to be on the rise. Nonetheless, it is also important to note that the hypermasculine identities presented here are just one aspect of what I have laid out. I am aware that militarism is not a solely masculine activity. During the fieldwork experience I have seen women referring to the war allegories and the militarism framework in the same way as men, and they have also engaged in high-risk operations which are not exclusively dominated by men (see also Naegler and Salman 2016, 359–61). Women played an important role within the police station, as the station chiefs that overlooked and directed the police officers within the police station were almost exclusively women. However, women did not participate in the SOTE unit. With these backgrounds of unchanged public security dynamics in Rio, the chapter continues to look behind the scenes of the mega-events.

The Drying Ice Dilemma

In Rio de Janeiro, police officers continuously use a metaphor to describe their police work, referring to the act of *enxugando gelo*—to dry ice from a melting but ever-growing ice block. As one of the CORE officers told me in an interview:

> Well, we have a civil and a military police [institution], and two different budgets to do the same things ... In reality, they don't get there, they don't do anything. It's not that you don't want to do anything, it's that

> you can't. It's an expression which is often used today, *enxugar gelo* [to dry ice]. Every day you rub the ice and it's put back into the *cumbuca*, into the fridge, again and again, and each time with a little bit more water. And then again, the ice block returns and nothing that you have done pays off.

To dry ice is an impossible endeavour. The pointless attempt to dry the water from a melting ice block metaphorically exemplifies the everyday struggle of coping with daily insecurities in the city, while the ice block returns to the freezer after every shift and all the work starts over again the following day. *Enxugando gelo* expresses then the desperate attempt to change the public security landscape without the possibility of ever actually achieving this goal. As the officer expresses, 'nothing that you have done pays off', which verbalizes the feeling of powerlessness to change the wider picture, and principally it articulates the police officers' personal daily failure while they are trying to do their job.

The continuity and omnipresence of the drying ice metaphor were clear throughout my fieldwork. On several occasions, Special Forces members would tell me how they had to go to the same territories again and again, to do the same job, without actually seeing any change. The police officers find themselves in a dilemma. On one hand, they want to do their jobs, but feel desperately unable to do them. On the other, if they did not do them, the ice would grow even faster. Police officers are trapped in the drying ice dilemma, and are pushed to emotional edges, which has concrete spatial consequences.

This is a feeling of frustration significantly paired with the feeling that one's own work is not efficient at all. These frustrations dominated not only among the combatants or the investigators but also among the bureaucrats. When I once talked to some of the case investigators, the bureaucrats told me that each of them would have hundreds of cases to solve. This is an overwhelming task which cannot be fulfilled. Therefore, they are confronted with their daily and very personal failure. Drying ice stands for these unsolved cases that are piled up on top of cabinets in the police station, and reminds the officers of the work ahead. Most pressing, however, is that drying ice expresses the frustration that all my respondents felt when they carry out their police work. The expression of these feelings was commonly heard during my fieldwork with the police. With two examples from the field, I lay out what the drying ice dilemma entails for the police officers in their everyday working routines, and what it means for Rio's long-standing urban conflict.

Emotions and Violence at the Edge

One afternoon in October 2014 I witnessed a scene that involved a foreign couple. They had come to the station to report that someone had grabbed the lady's necklace on the beach sidewalk. The military police brought a possible perpetrator to the station, who was then identified under extremely murky circumstances as the police pushed the tourist to identify someone, although she was not sure if it was really him. For some officers, however, the same colour of skin and a similar baseball cap were sufficient to keep the suspect in prison. The suspected thief could not believe what had happened to him and started to yell and complain for hours in the cell. Thereafter the situation developed as I recorded in my fieldnotes:

> I sit with the officers in one of the station's rooms. We talk about all kinds of random things. The prisoner doesn't stop banging against the door. His yelling starts to become annoying. One of the officers loses his patience. 'Let's handcuff him, like this it doesn't work.' Three of them go into the cell and try to handcuff the prisoner to an iron pipe above the cement bench. He panics. He cries. He yells. He injures himself with the handcuffs as he pulls them too strongly away from him. Now he cries desperately, 'I didn't do anything.' One of the older policemen says that it is strange that he reacts like that. 'To recognize someone because of a similar cap is a fucked-up situation. He wouldn't yell like that if he had done the robbery.' Another responds: 'Man, they recognized him. It's the same cap and the same colour of skin.'
>
> Back in the room we hear the prisoner yelling. He doesn't stop. The officers start to imitate him. They imitate his desperate weeping and shout out things to him. 'Your mother is on her wayyy.' Accompanied by loud laughs. I catch myself from also yelling something. The situation continues for at least an hour and a half. We go out to have a coffee in the neighbourhood. Back in the station the prisoner continues to weep, yell, and bang the door. One of the younger officers can't stand it anymore. He takes a bottle of pepper spray and fills the cell with it. It doesn't help and makes the situation worse. Now it sounds as if someone is dying in there. 'Uaaaaaiiiiaaaaaaahhhh, heeeeellllppp, heeeeeeelp.' The spray scratches in my throat and eyes. I can only begin to imagine how it must be for the prisoner. He doesn't stop and gets even louder. The officers decide to go in, to transfer him to the other cell. It takes four police officers to bring him the two metres to the other side and into the other

cell. He struggles and they hit him. One of the officers turns to me and asks: 'man, what can we do?'

This scene gives an idea of how in the back of a civil police station, a house of legal authority and credibility (Kant de Lima 1995), violence is exercised in the weeks and months after the World Cup had unfolded only a few kilometres away from the station, and where the 2016 Olympics would take place just two years later. Furthermore, the situation can demonstrate how violence and fear play out in a way that offers insights into what actually happens in Rio de Janeiro's public security field. The above situation, however, illustrates a variety of dynamics (not least on my position within the research setting).

A first dynamic can be traced back the conditions that define the continuous lines of Rio's urban conflict that play out at large in this situation. Kant de Lima (1995, 134) demonstrated in his police ethnography the ways in which the police in Rio de Janeiro understand why they are committing acts of violence against the poor, and quotes one of his respondents who says: 'this is the only language these people understand'. This configuration of attitudes towards the poor reflects the idea of a 'criminal-person' (Grillo 2013) which emerges through the statements of the police officers and the English tourists in the above scene. They suspect the boy clearly because a random person in the street had pointed him out as someone with black skin who had been 'robbing the whole morning'. However, whether this is true or not cannot be verified in this situation. The young man who has several entries within the police database is judged by the police officer as the legitimate other who deserves to be arrested. He is treated as one of the *vagabundos* who are inscribed in the scripts of the racist stereotypical and historical patterns in Rio de Janeiro (Misse 2006, 77). Furthermore, the police officer seems to justify his actions by assessing his moral economy, something that also seems to stem from this myriad of structural reasons (Fassin 2013a).

These dynamics also point to another aspect that often happened in the police station and on several occasions during my fieldwork. One night I walked down the hallway into the back of the station to the SIC office where Gustavo, one of the older policemen, and another officer talked to a prisoner. I asked if I was disturbing them. 'No, no, not at all, we are trying to identify a *ganso*, a goose, here.' I asked them to clarify what they meant. They told me that a *ganso* is someone criminal, someone who looks around with a long neck to catch sight of something to steal or to commit another crime. The word *ganso* was consistently attributed to many of those who were brought into the station. In other words, the *ganso* is another description of a *vagabundo*.[3]

Stereotypical views about prisoners and people who were arrested have been paired with these narratives and are embedded within the dynamics that I have elaborated above. A common phrase was: 'we know these guys' or 'we can see whether they are perpetrators or not'. In addition, several of the younger and newer police officers, who had entered the civil police recently and came directly from the police academy, asked me more than once: 'Dennis, do you know this guy Lombroso? This man should become a saint.' Another common phrase was: 'Lombroso, this guy got it right, and we can see it in them just like him.' In an astonishing way the police officers seemingly believed that what early criminologist Cesare Lombroso had said about the physical appearance of convicted criminals was an approach worth following and taking for granted. Lombroso was convinced that there was a methodology that was based in a cultural practice of 'presenting and representing' that reveals the 'abnormal and the dangerous' in the physical appearance of people (Mossrion 2004, 68). However, rather than the police officers really relying on Lombrosian thinking, it is more that the concept of the *criminal person* paired with the societal racism is inscribed within Rio's urban conflict and runs through the veins of law enforcement.[4]

A second dynamic points essentially to the plethora of emotions that run through the everyday reality of police work in Rio. Several motives of the police officers played a role within this situation and clearly overlap. On the one hand, the yelling and constant complaints by the prisoner had a gruelling effect on the officers that I myself felt as the case unfolded. The situation demonstrates how the prisoner continued yelling for several hours and brought the officers to the edge of their endurance. After long hours in the station, the policemen could no longer bear how the inmate continuously cried and shouted for the police station chief.

[3] Contrary to this, Mingardi (1992, 35) in his police ethnography in São Paulo describes how the word *ganso* stems from police informants who look for any information that could help the police. Police officers also distinguish between a *trabalhador* (worker), a *cidadão do bem* (citizen on the good side), and a *vagabundo* (someone who earns money within the world of crime or someone who steals and does not work). See also Teixeira Pinheiro (2015, 82) and Denyer Willis (2015, 76).

[4] This view is not new within the civil police. Huggins et al. (2002, 113) report how a civil police officer at the beginning of the 1990s would make use of Lombrosian terms to describe a certain supposedly criminal individual. Kant de Lima (1995, 79) has also shown that Rio de Janeiro's police believe that they know by the appearance of a suspect if someone is a criminal or not.

The violence that unfolded afterwards was a reaction of the officers who were annoyed by the prisoner's 'show' and their irritation turned to rage. On the other hand, the drying ice dilemma played a vital role—when most strikingly one of the officers turned to me and asked me, justifying, 'What can we do?' He exempted himself and his colleagues from any responsibility for handling the case in a different way. It is exactly the question 'what can we do?' that evokes a direct reference to the frustration of *drying ice*. It seems to illustrate in a dramatic way that a structural approach is not enough to make sense of these reactions. What I witnessed and felt here are emotions that started with the humiliation of the prisoner and ended with his beating. Feelings such as rage and frustration are at the core of the unfolding dynamics. Furthermore, through such a situation, the officer may re-establish his feelings of a loss of police power when he tries (and fails) to change the wider picture of Rio's public security. Another emblematic scene from the field, below, illustrates this in an even more exacerbated way.

A year before the Olympics I went back to Rio de Janeiro for follow-up research. I tried to conduct more interviews, but also to spend time in the police station to investigate how things had developed since I had left. In the following recollection from June, I remember that:

> It was a calm night on an ordinary Monday in the police station where I conducted most of my participant observation. I met a police officer who had been on vacation and whom I hadn't seen at my previous visits to the department. When he saw me we hugged each other, and he was very delighted to see me again. We had spent the World Cup period in the station together and had done many shifts in the month after the tournament. We chatted for quite a while about all kinds of ordinary topics. He told me about his family life, vacations he and some friends had taken, and told me stories about girls. We also touched on the topic of the current political discussions in the Brazilian political landscape. Nothing too unusual for a calm Monday night shift.
>
> Around 10pm the military police brought four young boys into the police station. Two of them seemed to be brothers. They were all wearing almost the same clothes, dirty blue shorts. The older one wore a shirt with the letters *Real Gangsta*. These boys were accused of having committed a robbery. I went with the officer into the back of the station where we squeezed into the registration room, where the four boys needed to line up in front of the blue plastic measurement poster. All of them were black, poor, and between 11 and 14 years old. Only one was from a favela in the

region, famous for high homicide and violence rates. The registration process was very humiliating for the boys as the officer insulted them constantly and made it clear that if he caught them in the street, he would kill them. 'How can you be so stupid as to rob in your own area?'

One of the boys was fascinated by the fingerprint technology. He found it interesting how his fingerprints would appear on the computer screen after he had scanned them on the small fingerprint device. When it was his turn, he concentrated on doing it right. But he got distracted because he was looking at the screen and didn't manage to scan his fingers correctly, which made the officer even angrier. He shouted at the boy, asking him if he was too stupid to scan his finger. He took the boy's hand in a rough manner to scan the fingers. I could see the shame in the boy's face. The officer yelled at them, asking: 'Are you going to school?' They stammered that they didn't. 'And why is that?', the officer asked. One of them said, 'Because we don't have the school material.' The officer got even angrier. 'Fuck you boy, this is a lie, you don't go to school because you don't want to.'

At some point he turned around to me and asked, 'what should I do with them, Dennis, or actually, what can I do? What do you do with these sorts of boys? What is the solution? Hit them?' I wasn't sure what I should answer, unless he really intended to start a discussion on the Brazilian education system, racist social inequality, and a state that fails to provide security. Instead, I asked the boys why they were not going to school.

When the registration process was over, I relaxed because we all could escape from the tense situation. Suddenly, the officer made a step towards the boys and hit one with his flat hand in the face, punched another one twice with his fist on the head, and kicked the smaller boys violently. 'You are due a beating, you liars.' The boys started to whimper and scream, but the officer showed no mercy and continued, yelling at them that they deserved it and that this is the only way they would learn their lesson. After approximately 15 seconds he chased the two taller ones out of the room with ferocious kicks while the two younger ones embraced each other under the sink, trying to escape the violence. He waited at the door and ordered them to come out, yet his kicking caused them to weep more. Their eyes were filled with fear and horror. They hesitated to exit the room, accompanied by their helpless crying, knowing he would kick them again. Finally, they took all their courage and tried to pass through the door at the best moment possible so he wouldn't hurt them too much.

> When we returned to the front of the station the boys needed to sit in the waiting area, still shaking from both fear and rage. The officer, too, was still brimming with fury and looked at me, saying: 'What do they think? Tomorrow they are here again. That's the *only way to do at least something*!'[5]

This vignette exemplifies the emotional and spatial dynamics of the drying ice dilemma. The officer complained about the boys being out of custody quickly, and that he would need to do the same work with them again soon. These kinds of situations are not isolated phenomena but repeated everyday realities. I have observed multiple settings in which ordinary police officers deal with the same suspects several times: arrested, brought to prison or to children's homes, released, and back at the station a few days later for the exact same charges. At the same time, those officers that undertake the investigative desk work in the police department have to rummage through piles of case files that grow each day without really solving many of them.

The last statement by the police officer in the vignette, that beating would be the 'only way' of doing 'at least something', is as devastating as it is insightful. The officer expressed the essence of the drying ice dilemma with the fact that the boys would just be taken to a children's home and be released the next day. In his opinion, there was nothing he could do to prevent them stealing in the neighbourhood again. In other words, he was *enxugando gelo*. The drying ice dilemma pushes the police officer to his emotional edge and makes him an *edgeworker*.

As has been shown with the edgework concept (see the Introduction) when linked to criminal activity, humiliation is the direct emotional certainty that edgeworkers often encounter. The transgressive act can configure a compensation for this humiliation and channel it through another set of emotions grounded in rage and fury (Lyng 2005b, 29). Much as edgeworkers from economically privileged groups engage in dangerous motorcycling to escape the dullness of everyday life (Lyng 1998), the rage-driven activity creates a situation in which 'losing control of oneself, has the immediate consequence of imploding time and space distinctions' (Lyng 2005b, 29). Many criminal and violent acts in urban settings can be seen as

[5] The day of this incident, the same police officer treated another boy in a very friendly and different way. He said to me: 'you see, this one is a worker, and not a vagabond'. The boy carried the leftovers of a chewing gum package and came into the station saying he needed to go to a children's shelter as he could not get home at that hour. He also visibly had a handicap on his right foot and no criminal record.

an escape from a humiliation experienced in everyday life (Hayward 2004, 165). The humiliation is then channelled through rage or other emotional states, and can allow the edgeworker to overcome this emotional pandemonium (Katz 1988, 312).

The police officer tries to take control within a micro situation while he is unable to change the ontologically insecure and disordered world of the wider public security situation in Rio. While this does not justify his actions, it does make them palpable and understandable in the sense of a 'criminological verstehen' (Ferrell 1998). It is embedded in both the structural conditions of Rio's urban conflict, and the phenomenology of the police officer's emotional worlds marked by the drying ice dilemma. Using violence, he attempts to regain a bit of the control he has lost, or perhaps has never had, over the general public security dynamics.

This emotional reaction to the drying ice dilemma also has effects on the spatial components of police work. A police station is divided into a publicly accessible front part and a restricted area in the back for police officers. There is a territorial border that divides the station into an accessible public and inaccessible secret space. In other words, the police produce their territoriality in different ways in the front and in the back of the station (Goffman 1959). While police officers perform a publicly visible role in the front, the behaviour in the private backspace in police stations is expressed differently (Fyfe 1992, 477–9). In the example considered here, the relational and emotional component of producing territory comes to the fore (Raffestin 2012, 124). Driven by the emotions of the drying ice dilemma, police territoriality is here materialized in a *space of secrecy*. In this sense, the emotions provoked by the drying ice dilemma, the feeling of losing control, influence the production of police territory in a relational way where the emotions are as important as the structural components. The loss of control is, therefore, not only emotionally but also spatially felt, and it is expressed, shaped, and extended beyond the professional workplace of police officers, as we will see in the following section.

Vocation and Exposure: Rio's Police and Their Everyday Edges

The drying ice dilemma is paired with other narratives exposed in the opening vignette of this chapter, in which the CORE officer who died described his feelings, saying that 'everyone has a certain fear of dying. Some have it a lot less. I can say that here in the CORE, in the sector I work in, this fear is very low. But no one wants to die'.

This interview displays how police officers deal with being permanently exposed to the possibility of death. The officer shows us the intensive everyday reality, with both an exposure to dangerous and risky activities at work, and the routinely accompanying vulnerability. Another one of them said:

> We are ... in an urban war, but we don't have the legislation for a war. If we fail, we will be punished. If a shot aimed at a criminal ends up hitting an innocent, we will be punished for that ... we are in an urban war, but without the adequate weapons to fight criminality.

These passages pose a pressing question: why do police officers do what they do, although they experience their work as being permanently exposed to war-like scenarios, with worries about their own safety, and a subjective feeling of abandonment by the government that does not provide them with the material they 'need' to fulfil their duties? Stated differently, and this time in terms of the drying ice dilemma, why are these police officers still taking all these risks and doing their jobs, if they are just drying ice?

The following interview extract, where a CORE member explained to me how much they have to risk their lives in doing their work, may help to answer these questions. When I approached the issue of why he thinks he is doing his work—despite the fact that he had been close to getting fatally shot so many times—he started to search for words, his eyes filled with tears, and he started to cry, saying with a faltering voice: 'We say [pause] ... it's our vocation. It's because of that ... [pause] We like to do that.' The police officer's emotional breakdown makes us understand that he comprehends his police work, despite all the difficulties, as his duty and as an inner vocation that fills his work routine with sense—with meaning as 'an ongoing, everyday process of sense-making' (Ferrell 2013, 258).

The breakdown had filled the situation with emotions and laid bare the officer's pure human condition while he was deeply moved by the activities he carries out on an everyday basis. He moved from one emotional state (talking about his daily routines) to the other (breaking down), and uncovered his emotional metamorphosis (Katz 1999). The situation opens up a world of fragility and emotions that profoundly influences—beside the above-mentioned aspects of racial profiling, militarism, and hypermasculinity—the work of the civil police. More than that, the emotions attribute meaning to the police practices and enhance our awareness of how deeply involved the police officers are with their daily routines. The drying ice dilemma, however, damages this involvement and produces a humiliating factor that influences and questions the raison d'être of the CORE member in the interview. The police officer experiences the powerful force of drying ice on a bodily level, and the negotiation he must undertake to go out there, time and again, and dry ice.

The vocation of being a police officer, therefore, produces *spaces of exposure*. Police officers experience their daily routines in Rio de Janeiro as extremely dangerous. They feel unsafe when they are at work, go home, or commute around the city with their families. This makes them embody a 24-hour preparedness, as one of the CORE members once said: 'Even when I go to the toilet I take my gun with me. I am always armed.' These are not merely empty claims. I remember one morning when I arrived very early at the Police City in Rio's North Zone. That morning, a CORE officer prepared to go home after his 24-hour shift and, as I said in the first paragraphs of Chapter 4, this tall man with a hoodie had two huge, shimmering silver guns in his hands, and put one in the front and the other in the back of his trousers, to make his way home 'safely'. The possibility of death not only accompanies the officers during their working hours but is also present in their private lives as spaces of exposure. As an example, consider the death of the police officer from the opening scene, as much as other police officers from my fieldwork who died on duty while undertaking different missions.

The drying ice dilemma poses such emotional challenges to the police officers because they comprehend their job as a vocation that extends beyond their daily working routines. Furthermore, this turns them into even more vulnerable subjects in terms of their life outside of work. On one hand, the police produce territories of exposure through their work when they 'go into favelas to confront an enemy'. On the other hand, the city turns into a space of exposure for them outside of their daily working routines through the embodiment of their vocation. Territoriality as a system of relations between the physical and social environment (Raffestin 2012, 129) here appears in the ways in which the emotional states of police officers (the social) define their movements within the city's urban conflict (the physical). We here see how the activity of the police officers themselves, their acting as police in *and* outside of their working hours and—more importantly—in the spaces 'provided to them', produces territoriality (Raffestin 2012, 124).

This section has shown why the emotions invoked by the drying ice dilemma are so defining for police in Rio de Janeiro, as the officers understand their work as a vocation. In what follows, I explore how the work of the Special Forces is best understood with the edgework concept as a strategy to compensate for and escape from this dilemma.

'We Entertain Ourselves': Pleasure, Excitement, and War in Rio de Janeiro

A leaked video which was nationally broadcast by the Brazilian news show Fantástico in 2012 features scenes from a mission with a CORE helicopter. A police unit has spotted the drug dealer Matemático in a car in the North Zone of Rio. The helicopter roars above the highly populated area, following their target which rapidly moves through the narrow alleys of the city's outskirts. The police officers' voices are heard through their radios followed by automatic rifle fire. The images and dynamics from the video are reminiscent of war scenes, similar to those of the released WikiLeaks video showing the US military shooting at a van and killing Reuters photographer Namir Noor-Eldeen (McGreal 2010).[3]

Most pressing, however, are the ways in which—and more importantly in what kind and tone of voice—the officers communicate with each other. For a while their voices go on in a tranquil and controlled manner. But then, suddenly, they start to yell at each other with excited screams; with a high-pitched, almost hysterical sound they exhaustingly shriek 'shoot, shoot, shoot', only interrupted by the gunfire that kills the drug trafficker. In the following interview extract, a CORE officer narrates what it feels like to go on such a mission with his team:

> The people [his CORE colleagues] here are like me. They are here because they like it. What we earn here [pause] no, is not the reason, will not cover our risk. Will not cover what we do here . . . it is difficult to explain, it is the action, adrenaline, liking to do what is right . . . As I said, we are at home, if we hear anything, if we see there is a major operation within which there will be a lot of gunfire, we are leaving our home, we come here, put on our clothes and we go, because we like it. It is not that we like to get shot, no! . . . We like the confrontation, the togetherness of our team, arriving in the community [favela], *dominating* that community, arresting people and fighting. We like that . . . This is it, perfect. You know. In reality, first comes the conviction that we do the right thing . . . and the majority here likes the *adrenaline*, with *pleasure*, we even, I will even risk to say this in an abusive way: *we entertain ourselves*.

Here, the sense of vocation mixes with aspects of edgework, as the CORE members discern their work routine as central to their identity, as delivering by experiencing that adrenaline rush. In the helicopter operation video, the excited and frantic voices reflect how rage and frustration translate into an adrenaline blast during the battle. Often in edgework, the acts of risk taking are associated with the attempt to counteract a lack of identity in late modern and highly insecure worlds (Ferrell et al. 2015, 74). In this case, however, the highly risky activity is connected to the insecurity felt through the drying ice dilemma as the phenomenon where the police officers lose control within their everyday world.

It is clearly noticeable how the officer talks about the ways in which they enter a 'community'. The officer clearly asserts that they are doing what they 'like' to do. They also do something they *know how* to do. Something they are *trained* and *skilled* to do. Said differently, it attributes to them a notion of control over very specific circumstances: the 'domination' of a community in a situation that contains danger, insecurity, and uncertainty, namely the wider picture of the urban conflict, which they are unable to change. In this particular case, the Special Forces officers are looking for the adrenaline rush and their highly skilled job to regain a bit of the control they lose when they are trying so desperately to dry the ice. In other words, their agency is an act of consciously and controlled loss of control in order to experience a rush of adrenaline and 'to take control' (Ferrell et al. 2015, 74).

Per contra, the most striking part in the interview is how the police officer emphasizes the feelings of pleasure and excitement as essential aspects of what members of the Special Forces do. They are 'entertaining' themselves while they are performing their daily routines. These reflections point towards behaviours that seem to stem from an existential need to survive, a crucial element in the edgework approach as 'the participants in edgework perceive that there is a direct link between survival capacities and the survival outcome' (Lyng 1990, 873). This, in turn, gives meaning to police work within the Brazilian public security context, and allows us to understand their activity as acts of survival and an escape from the drying ice dilemma.

To fathom how the CORE officers as edgeworkers have direct implications for the production of territoriality, there is another significant emotional element at work. Special Forces' narratives about the classification of their activities have, in the end, crucial spatial dimensions and produce some parts of the city as *spaces of war*. One of the CORE members said about their team:

> In the SOTE we are only 37 in total. And really, we are functioning like brothers. Sure, there are some conflicts, disputes, discussions ... but we are one family. Everyone protects everyone; everyone helps each other ... everyone looks after the life of the other ... because we only have us, right? If we can't count on each other, we can't count on anyone.

Together with the other quotes in this section, this passage makes reference to what has been written about the experience of soldiers in battle. The exciting activity, the 'pleasure', the 'entertainment', and the connectivity between the members of the CORE team are all aspects that we find in accounts of paramilitary units (e.g. Kraska 1998) and soldiers in war zones. The book *War*, written by Sebastian Junger (2011), a journalist who spent over a year with a US platoon in Afghanistan, is interesting as it discusses how joy is among the most important aspects of what motivates and moves soldiers in combat. Three types of joy in Junger's book are of interest for this discussion as they resonate with the narratives of the CORE members: adrenaline rush in battle, comradeship among the members of the platoon, and the meaning and purpose the combatants take from being in the unit and in battle (Cottee 2011, 448).

Although war is clearly something horrific, many soldiers, once they have come home from the battlefields, miss spending time in war zones (Junger 2011, 233). Soldiers involved in war have shown in accounts how even the cruellest scenes hold very specific attractions and can even be 'captivating, especially for those whose lives are experienced as dull, unexciting, unfulfilling, meaningless and solitary' (Cottee 2011, 456). Fighting can become something that gives meaning and purpose, although it is highly destructive and may, in many ways, be 'fighting for its own sake' (Gray 1998, 52–3). For those involved in it, war can provide many things simultaneously. It makes the daily trivia visible and helps to overcome it; it provides purpose, and a reason to live; and it works as an 'exciting elixir' (Hedges 2002, 3).

In the case of the CORE officers, these elements are present, as the Special Forces experience their work as necessary and find pleasure and excitement within their daily battles, and in the performance of combat. They 'entertain' themselves by doing what they like to do. In addition, 'the delight of comradeship' (Gray 1998, 28–9), so important for soldiers in battle, comes to the fore in the narratives of the CORE officers who consider themselves as 'one family'. The CORE officers perceive themselves in a similar way to the platoon in Afghanistan: united, trusting only themselves as a group, and feeling an almost desperate fulfilment in battle, as the life outside can exhibit despair arising from the daily attempt to dry the ice. As the CORE officer in the interview says: 'We like the confrontation, the togetherness of our team ... and fighting.' The war-like activity, the Special Forces' routines, turn into an experience at the edge and serve as an effective leverage to make the drying ice dilemma less humiliating, less painful, and more bearable.

These war narratives expose how the CORE members regard their police work emotionally and in practice as war. Consequently, the officers also identify and produce certain neighbourhoods in the city as spaces of war. The ways in which the CORE officer in the interview above narrates how his team enters favelas, and likes to 'dominate' and to fight in them, are the very means through which police territoriality is produced by waging war. Urban order-making in these communities is here produced through the appropriation of territories, through the territorial marking and reclaiming of space by the police activity within it (Raffestin 2012, 124). The spatial edges of Rio, in this case the many favelas and peripheral neighbourhoods, are in this sense territorialized spaces of war by the emotional edges of the Special Forces. This comes at the cost of producing Rio de Janeiro as a city with such a violent urban conflict, and therefore as a 'bordered space' (Christensen and Albrecht 2020, 387).

In essence, what this chapter has shown is that the Foucauldian triangle's element of sovereign power as spectacle (Foucault 2007) is indeed in motion in Rio de Janeiro. It has become apparent how much sovereign power as an activity of killing, as an activity of an internalized logic of war is happening before, during, and after the mega-events. As said in the Introduction to this book, sovereign power through spectacle is very much at the centre of both Brazil's routine public security strategies and the Olympic security schemes.

What does this mean for the wider understanding of mega-event security and beyond? As was shown in the previous chapters, the mega-event security fortress was porous and permeable, despite the immense efforts to provide and deploy as much security as possible. This chapter focused on the hidden conditions during the mega-events. Chapter 6 will look at how other hidden dynamics unfolded during and after the mega-events, which stand in strong contrast to the official legacy discourse of the organizers.

PART III
CAMOUFLAGE

6
Security of Camouflage

The civil police headquarters in Rio de Janeiro's centre is an old and tall building near the famous Lapa arches. It is August 2016, and the Olympic Games are running at full speed now. My last visit dates back a year. During the World Cup I was here for the first time. Now, the last thing that remains of the tournament is a huge piece of graffiti that shows an excavator destroying houses to prepare the city for the mega-events. My talk with the civil police officers goes smoothly, and we chat about the civil police's participation in the Olympics security operation. Suddenly, one of them looks seriously at us, taking his eyes off his cell phone. 'It came in via WhatsApp just now. One national force officer has been shot in the Maré.' The ambience in the room changes from tranquil to tense. Now we hear a voice message that the other wounded officer had launched into a general WhatsApp group, which had quickly made the rounds among the police officers. His voice is hysterical and he gives an account of how they had accidently entered the wrong road and were welcomed with gun shots.

The next morning, the TV stations broadcast a live police operation in the favela complex Maré, the one near to the main airport road which had been occupied by federal troops. The police operation was directed from within the regional Integrated Command and Control Centre (Centro Integrado de Comando e Controle, CICC) and the special operations room for the Olympics. The incursion of the favela Vila do João in the Maré complex results in dead and arrested. Meanwhile, heavy daily shootouts in the favela complex Alemão and others occur, and a photo showing a creek of blood running down a favela alley goes viral. The Olympics, however, continue. The Olympic peace that is always declared prior to the Games is just a Twitter feed that glorifies the marketing machine of the International Olympic Committee (IOC). Rio de Janeiro, for instance, continues to be a city rattled by an urban conflict with too many victims in too many vicinities.

Policing Sport Mega-Events. Dennis Pauschinger, Oxford University Press. © Dennis Pauschinger 2024.
DOI: 10.1093/oso/9780192848055.003.0007

This field vignette puts on display how the traditional production of spectacular police operations in Rio continued during the Games. However, it also trains attention on how the spectacle in Rio de Janeiro acts on different audiences with differing intentions and purposes. Rio's mega-event security was not only infused with failures but also distributed selectively along lines of racial and social inequality. The security measures unfolded in some spots of the city—important as tourist zones like Copacabana—with vigour, while other spatialities (e.g. the outskirts and favelas) were not 'secured' at all, but instead experienced state power through militaristic police invasions. In Chapter 5 we saw how such selective distribution of mega-event security provisions has spared the hidden spaces and emotional worlds of police officers, who themselves contribute to the long-standing urban conflict in the city.

In this chapter, I continue to show how, for an integral analysis of both mundane urban security governance and sport mega-event security measures in Rio, it is best to mobilize the Foucauldian triangle of security governance in its entirety (Foucault 2007). I have argued that what happened in Rio during the mega-events can only be grasped in full if we consider spectacle as a form of sovereign power that continues to be exercised in Rio as an integral part of security politics. In this part of the book, then, I will highlight the purposes of such spectacular security strategies that lead towards what I have called the *security of camouflage.*

Spectacular Politics of Visibility

Rio de Janeiro's State Secretary of Public Security affirmed in an interview for this book that a secure event was the key to changing the city's image, and that it would be 'priceless' if the tourists could take home the feeling of a safe Rio (interview, 14 October 2014). Boyle and Haggerty (2012, 242) argue that mega-event planners calculate risks for the events under highly uncertain conditions, and therefore 'plan for the worst'. Within this mechanism, a security discourse unfolds to set out a series of reassuring imaginaries or 'cultural meanings' to convince the public that everything has been done to avoid risks (Boyle and Haggerty 2012, 255). The veritable security show at Rio's mega-events, then, served the purpose of producing images of total security and a government that is prepared for every eventuality, just as Rio's Public Security Secretary said. Clearly, there is also the political component of satisfying national and international expectations for a host within a Global South setting (Cornelissen 2011, 3227).

During mega-events and beyond, security has turned into such a spectacle that it seems to dominate all aspects of everyday life. As Campbell and Shapiro (2007, 133) outline, visual culture has become a powerful tool for the securitization of society and produces a double effect that first includes the visual and images in militarization processes to anchor them in society; second, these images help to contest these practices. Thus images, as well as making things visible, are a powerful tool to convey a certain message about security. In this sense, it is the performance and mediatization of security that plays out in these spheres and *makes* security. Stephanie Savell (2016, 61) helpfully refers to work by Jusionyte who states that:

> Security—both discourse and practice—is contested and negotiated between authors and participants in its processes, which are embedded in particular political and social, and institutional settings. (2015a, 7)

Savell (2016, 61) shows exactly this, namely how the military performs a mediated spectacle of security in the occupations of the favelas in Rio de Janeiro. While the military in this case wants to transmit a clear message of a 'humanitarian militarism', Larkins (2013, 565) affirms that 'highly visible performances of state power' constitute police work in Rio de Janeiro. I have observed these mechanisms during the mega-event cycle—principally during the World Cup and the Olympic Games—in the local police stations, as well as in the Special Forces operations of the CORE. It is, therefore, necessary to seek an understanding of why this occurred and what kind of motivation lies behind these mechanisms. A first step will be to look at the ways in which the mega-event security operations have played with this politics of visibility.

When I was observing what was going on within the CICC during the Olympics, I wondered why the public relations department was taking photographs of the flickering screens with surveillance camera images. When I saw the photos on the Secretary of Security's official Twitter feed, accompanied by explanations and descriptions of these images, I understood that their intention was to reproduce the security spectacle. A tweet before the start of the Olympics said the Olympic security was now all set up, with the hashtag #SecureGames, showing how military and police forces stood guard on an important highway. The production of visible security politics and the mega-event as a spectacle was accompanied not only by the many public statements of the security authorities but also by the work of the public relations department of Rio de Janeiro's Security Secretary.[1]

This politics of visibility provides an insight into the ways in which Rio's public security department relies on spreading images that render their security efforts more visible. Interestingly, the same dynamics have happened within the police station and the Special Forces units I have observed. Rio de Janeiro's Secretary of Public Security said in an interview, when I asked him about his policies:

> So what we need are visible, understandable, measurable and objective security policies so that the people see what is happening ... My preoccupation was and will always be with questions of urban criminality. With the people's sense of security. I think it's this that we need to pursue in public security, because you can have a lot of police officers in the streets and you feel unsafe, and you can have very few police in the streets and feel safe. (Interview, 14 October 2014)

These assertions point to the very fact that security politics under the Beltrame administration in Rio de Janeiro are driven by the belief in such measures as are typical for situational crime prevention policies, within which '[g]reat store is ... placed on increased physical security and, importantly, high-profile surveillance, both public and private' (Hayward 2007, 235). While the major mega-event security operations have turned into a mediated and visible spectacle, on a lower and smaller scale this is already common practice within Rio de Janeiro's police. As Lint et al. (2007, 1636) argue, the idea that 'control must be *seen* to be done is behind much police and security work'. The above statement refers to exactly this: that security *must be seen to be done.*

During my fieldwork I could observe how the civil police operated numerous times driven by a politics of visibility. Examples from the field can thus provide an underlying narrative of these politics of visibility that have played out on a much smaller scale, yet are an intrinsic part of Rio de Janeiro's police work (see also Kant de Lima 1995). On numerous occasions the police station served as a powerful example of how these politics of visibility are used within police work. The GIC (Grupo de Investigação Complementar)—the investigation team that responds directly to the

[1] The official spokesman, for example, tried several times to limit my and my colleague's access, and was furious when I was able to bypass his authority with my own contacts.

police station chief—is an emblematic case to demonstrate these assertions. During my stay in the station, I wondered several times what kind of work path they followed. The longer I stayed in the police station, the more I realized that the group's work was directed towards investigations that had a chance of bringing an immediate or short-term result. In a variety of conversations with other police officers, it came to the fore that the GIC group would 'only do what gives them visibility'. Larkins' (2013, 565) concept of police performance as an expression of state power can be found on a smaller scale here too. It is not only that Rio's State Secretary of Security has confirmed such an approach to their police work—performative and visible spectacles in the police station were also expressed in manifold forms. The politics of visibility serves two purposes, which are best described in terms of external and internal visibility of the spectacle.

The externally visible spectacular police performance addresses and acts upon the general public. How the police deal with the media serves as a vivid example. The police make their work visible by giving interviews and producing well-orchestrated media spectacles, wherein arrested people are presented to the press and the police delegate makes sure that the often black and poor individuals are presented to the press in a way that also reproduces the common stereotypes and the *pessoa-criminal* (Grillo 2013). Often the GIC group would set out confiscated money, credit cards, and other stolen goods in obsessive detail to present all this to the media.[2]

The second dynamic in the politics of visibility refers to internal visibility—the spectacle acting upon a different audience. There is internal competition among the different police stations, and principally competition among the police chiefs and their teams, to achieve the monthly target for crime reduction. In a situation in which foreigners had been arrested during the World Cup, one of the civil police officers came to me and said: 'You know, for me that's it already, I achieved what I wanted the most, to promote the police station. It's already in the WhatsApp group now.' Here the internal politics of visibility played an important role for the police officers, and thus for the public security system in Rio de Janeiro. The two processes comprising the politics of visibility suggest that the same mechanisms occur on a larger scale for the mega-events and on localized scales for Rio de Janeiro's public security. This said, I suggest that mega-event security

[2] See the Twitter feed by Christoph Harig on the ways in which Brazilian police forces visualize their apprehensions to the media: https://twitter.com/c_harig/status/1183750793062703105?s=21.

cannot be analysed by just considering it as something disconnected from local conditions. They are intertwined and follow similar paths in Rio.

The politics of visibility played a crucial role in the police station and the mega-event security efforts. However, *invisible* politics have been in the making in parallel to those that are visible, and complement the real legacy of the mega-event cycle. The concept of the *(in)visible-(in)security* provided by Jusionyte and Goldstein is helpful here when they write that

> everyday security arrangements provide security to some while creating insecurity and vulnerability for others. Security's logic is based on dichotomies, dividing 'us' from 'them'. Visibility and invisibility are key tools that security uses to enforce the separation between these empty categories. (2016, 9)

Security in their sense has the double function of representing *security* for some and *insecurity* for others, and they picture visibility and invisibility as crucial tools of analysis. Here, these tools are helpful for understanding the mega-event security in Rio. Take, for example, the CORE operations in the outskirts of Rio de Janeiro's North Zone. The CORE has a Facebook page and a Twitter account on which they produce visible images of their *successful* operations in these regions. Nonetheless, they only highlight the superficialities, the heroic images, and the production of action pictures featuring the combatants during operations that highlight their members and their work, as a way of containing the criminality problems that bring—in their view—*insecurity* to the region.

These missions, which are promoted by the proper institution as the necessary way to do police work in these areas, are applauded by an audience that shares this view, and that often thinks that the Special Forces are the last wall between them and evil. At the same time, these visible security missions obscure the consequences of such actions, which can routinely result in dead drug traffickers or civilians, and make life in the affected communities difficult.

Here, security certainly provokes consequences that are invisible for the wider audience, but very visible and insecure everyday dynamics for the affected populations. Reconnecting this to the Foucauldian triangle of security (Foucault 2007), the functioning of Rio's public security sector, spectacle as a mode of sovereign power has not receded at all and was extensively used in the preparation, staging, and aftermath of the Olympics. During the mega-events, this materiality of a spectacular security strategy was enacted by 'military parades', *eo ipso* the occupation of the city through the armed forces, the ostensive patrolling of the various policing institutions in strategically important neighbourhoods, the deployment of warships in front of Copacabana beach, and the many roaring military helicopters above the venues to serve the tourist and wider public audience. The police missions and the continuity of killings in other neighbourhoods dispelled spectacle as sovereign power (Foucault 1977) on the audiences in those affected communities.

The various ways of presenting images from surveillance cameras on the screens for Twitter followers, or deploying troops in Copacabana , are instances of such a demonstration of the spectacle, of sovereign power (Foucault 1977). However, at the very same time these measures are attempts to veil what happens within Rio's favelas, police stations, and suburbs. These kinds of measures are the ones that the mega-event officials, as well as those responsible for public security, do not want the wider public to see and want to render *invisible*.

Consider the following quote from one of my interviews with a civil police officer:

> I don't think that the state distributes the resources according to necessity. Unfortunately, here in Rio we see that the state's resources are distributed according to visibility . . . You can verify that there are areas in the interior of the capital or in the Baixada [Baixada Fluminense is a neighbour region of Rio de Janeiro city] and in the suburbs that present a higher criminal record, however have a reduced number of police patrols because these areas have less visibility . . . So, they try to transform the South Zone, which is a tourist zone, into a mirror . . . [and] this leads to a false sense of security. When a tourist comes to Rio, principally for this kind of event, he will not get to know reality. He will get to know a reality that was produced to preserve the image of the security of the state. (Interview, 24 October 2014)

Security here is clearly understood as something selective, and with a double purpose: to turn the security that is intended for the mega-event *visible* and to *hide* the consequences of the long-lasting urban conflict in Rio de Janeiro. This is the specificity of the mega-event editions in Rio de Janeiro, where this duality promotes forms of security that can no longer simply be called a spectacle or a politics of visibility. It must be named by its motivation, its intention, and its direction. Police operations are here recognized as a way of hiding away normalized dynamics of violence, while at the same time rendering the security that is intended for the mega-events *visible.* According to Savell, the spectacle, and thus the performance of security,

> demonstrates how visibility and invisibility are central to the production of security. A spectacle of military force occludes the suffering of citizens in its wake: behind the scenes of pacification, residents live through deaths, pillage, disrespectful treatment, and other abuses. A theatre of humanitarianism mutes discussions about social inequalities between favela residents and the rest of the city, effacing the structural roots of crime-related violence. (2016, 69)

The security spectacle is not only a way to demonstrate strength and an impression of security; it is at the same time an attempt to mask a conflict that has the potential to produce images that do not fit into the fantasy lands of the Olympics. In other words, what takes place in Rio de Janeiro is nothing other than a security that hides the roots of a long-lasting problematic within the security sector. As Goldstein asserts:

> And while spectacle is obviously an attempt to make certain things dramatically visible, it is also, by extension, an attempt to render other things invisible. The spectacle is as much about obscuring what performers wish to conceal as it is about putting on a display: controlling what is to be seen, when, and by whom. (2004, 16)

Mega-event security on the one side is a way of creating an image of a securitized city that *is* under control. However, it produces on the other side a shield that clouds the vision to the reality that pre-existed and will continue to exist after the mega-event caravan has left the city towards Tokyo 2020, Paris 2024, Los Angeles 2028, and so forth. How to understand these attempts at hiding and putting on display?

Spectacle as Camouflage

The politics of spectacular visibility in Rio de Janeiro's ordinary public security, and during the mega-events, is best appreciated with the act of camouflaging. Grounded in anthropologist Ieva Jusionyte's (2015b) concept of *States of Camouflage*, camouflage is an act that aims to distract from something else, or as Jusionyte (2015, 116) puts it, it 'implies the use of one symbolic and material order to protect another from being recognized by blurring the boundaries between the two'. In Jusionyte's (2015, 131) analysis, the state itself, as well as agents that use state identities, are involved in illicit activities and constantly use the camouflage techniques to actively disguise their own illegal actions.

For Rio de Janeiro, this is not new. As we have seen, state agents are involved in illegal and criminal patterns while they are on or off duty (see also Misse 2006; Cano et al. 2012; Grillo 2013; Larkins 2015). More than that, the camouflaging not only features state agents involved in criminal activities but is also produced to transmit an image and, principally, to omit what happens behind the curtains of the mega-events and the ordinary security spectacle. It is helpful to restate Jusionyte's notion of camouflage to understand such processes:

> Camouflage blurs the arbitrary yet consequential boundary between state and crime. More specifically, this notion enables us to examine how actors other than formal institutions participate in the performance of political authority by assuming its appearance: they deceive the state by indistinguishably blending with it. (2015b, 132)

This serves to describe camouflage as the ways in which state agents become involved in illegal activities but get away with it through the use of their uniforms and the performance to which the wider public is accustomed. In Rio de Janeiro this became apparent with the ways in which state agents are involved within criminal activities and transgress the borders of what they are allowed to do. As seen in the previous chapters, the illegal activities of police officers may be wrong before the law, but are not always so according to their own moral framework. From an analytical point of view, all these actions are techniques of a *security of camouflage*. This security of camouflage is a performance of political authority by blending with uniforms, while at the same time blurring the boundary with criminality (Jusionyte 2015, 131–2).

Such acts of camouflaging were present in Rio de Janeiro before the mega-events. However, they became intensified and professionalized during them. In other words, the obfuscations happening during the Olympics have existed before the Games, and will continue afterwards (see also Savell 2016). In what follows, I will make use of examples to fortify this argument and expose how the security legacy of the Games is one rooted in the fortification of a camouflage security, instead of actually improving any of the ground-level realities in Rio.

On the one side, I have shown how the police work towards an internal visibility. The external visible spectacle, however, is much more important here. Their way of presenting merely their results and the bright side of their work is an attempt to camouflage what happens within their police stations to safeguard their own image. These micro attempts at camouflage are certainly important. Nonetheless, it is crucial to look at the other side that also exemplifies the camouflage security, and which affects the police officers themselves. A few days before the World Cup started in 2014, the outside of the police station had been painted with fresh colour. This act of visibility symbolized the camouflage security that was at play. This attempt at camouflage could not paint over the many situations I witnessed during my fieldwork once I was in the station. Moreover, the station itself became a symbol for the fact that camouflaging is only a tool to hide from more pressing questions. While from the outside the station looked beautiful, its decline became apparent from the inside.

Already in 2014, the officers' sleeping conditions in the station were precarious, water dripped through the roof, and the printer was constantly broken. The conditions worsened when Rio's state government did not pay the salaries of the cleaning and maintenance personnel, so that by 2015 the station was in very bad shape. By 2016, there were huge holes in the ceiling through which the water had eaten its way, and the officers did not even have paper to print the crime registration documents. In another part of the station, the plywood panels on the floor buckled due to water infiltration from the broken air conditioning. All this damage symbolizes how camouflage security plays out. It hides, sometimes even successfully, the things that are not intended to appear for a wider public, yet under the surface of the polished security operations old traditions and deeply rooted problems continue to exist.

Hence camouflage security works within Rio de Janeiro's security sector, as well as within the mega-event security efforts. Relaying this back to the question of mega-event legacy, acts of camouflage are also revealing. As one of the CORE combatants said about the mega-event security in Rio de Janeiro, 'They armour the events. They armour the forces, they are armouring. What is not armoured continues bad and gets worse every day' (interview, CORE officer, 13 June 2014). In this framing, the use of camouflage is expressed very clearly. The sport venues are being secured with maximum force, while other parts of the city are exempted from any improvements. The security efforts have been highly selective. Moreover, it points to the notion of the invisible that has been overshadowed by the security spectacle. It forcefully demonstrates how the mega-event security spectacle was employed to secure certain event spaces, but at the same time served to occlude the violence in other territories. The armouring practice is a way of deciding what should be seen, when, and by whom (Goldstein 2004, 16).

A year after that statement, I received a WhatsApp voice message from one CORE officer who explained:

> Now that I am in the CORE ... the difference is that I see a completely distinct reality. It's as if I was in a daily war for real. When I worked in the police station, I already thought that some things were wrong, but I didn't see half of what I see now. You understand? It's like, you know, the reality we know from the South Zone it's a world totally apart, man. It's a world that I even like, but it's really not the reality of Rio de Janeiro. Here it's a hell. If you go to the North Zone, you see communities totally abandoned by the governors, things are infernal. (WhatsApp voice message, 15 September 2015)

Here, the notions of the visible and invisible are brought up again. According to Brighenti (2007, 327), the act of what we want to see and what should stay invisible is never just a 'technical matter', but is 'inherently practical and political'. The specificity in these interviews is not the mere decision of hiding or rendering something visible through spectacle; it is a mechanism that does both at the same time. The security of camouflage then is characterized by the power to actively decide that it *pretends* in spaces of whiteness to be a protective force, whereas it *hides* away at the same time the repression and violence in those spaces of non-whiteness and social disparity, while simultaneously staging spectacular violent actions to reaffirm its state power in both the favelas and the wealthy zones, acting on different audiences.

The newly appointed Special Forces officer on his side, however, now sees what he beforehand ignored or did not want to see. Moreover, the invisible that has always existed became visible for him. Yet, police officers of the Special Forces, who are essentially those that produce spectacle in the respective territories, who procure a way out of their everyday emotional dilemma of sensing their very police work as a vocation but expose themselves to deadly risks while carrying out their work, are thus both the products and producers of Rio's urban conflict (see Chapter 5; Pauschinger 2019).

As shown in the Introduction of this book, another example from the field is telling. The officer that was killed in the course of this work said the following during the Olympic summer, when I was back for a visit in the CORE unit:

> They besiege [the city] now so that the world doesn't see Rio de Janeiro's true reality. But after that, everything will turn back to normal: lots of shootouts, lots of dead, and lots of missions. You see these military forces at the Linha Vermelha [Red Line—route to the international airport]? They cannot move from there. They cannot do anything. They are here for those who come from outside to feel safe. But you know what, that is of no use. Near the military police base there, the drug trade controls it all. (Conversation with CORE officers, 19 August 2016)

The security plan for the Olympics in the quote of the CORE member here is pictured as a hiding away of what should not be seen by those who visit the city, yet it is also a camouflage of the factual security realities in Rio de Janeiro. As Jusionyte (2015b, 116) affirms, 'In hiding the predatory and brutal under the just and peaceful, camouflage could be viewed as the modus operandi of statecraft.' The CORE officer points to the fact that besides the military being just a figurative piece to confirm an appearance of security, the drug traffic still controls the area. After the Olympics and the Paralympics closing ceremony, the mega-event security camouflage falls away, whereas the camouflage politics continue trying to hide Rio's reality.

It seems that the mega-event security realities intended to hide what lies beneath the glossy paper surface of mega-event spectacles. Police officers from the police station said that 'After the World Cup the shielding ends and then it gets complicated again.' Whenever I started a conversation about the security legacy projects, the first answer was 'no, the World Cup didn't bring any change', or that maybe some material was finally bought, but this would only equip the police in a better way and not change any of the lived realities at street level within the city. Once some civil police officers joked when they showed me the new bulletproof vests they had gained before the World Cup and said, 'Here you see our legacy.' When I visited the police station in 2016, one of the shift police chiefs commented on the current political, financial, and social situation in Olympic Rio as follows: 'Our chaos became normality now.'

The world that the security of camouflage intended to hide appeared in another interview very clearly. The interviewee, who worked in a favela of Rio's North Zone in a public health post, told me that his institution had to be closed numerous times during the World Cup because of the police interventions: a stray bullet killed a sleeping child and the inhabitants of the neighbourhood were exposed to the steady urban conflict and kept in the crossfire of the police and the drug trade (interview, 2 September 2014). Thus, these politics of death were hidden—camouflaged—through the mega-event spectacle, but restricted to abandoned regions. However, with the Olympic closing ceremony, the spectacle as a form of camouflage fell off, and spectacular security politics returned with their normalized patterns of violence throughout the city—and not only in the abandoned spaces as described by the police officer. All too often, these missions are horrific incidents that would not have fitted into the 'New World', as the IOC advertised the Rio Games. In Chapter 7 we will look at the mega-event legacy discourses in Rio more closely.

7
Non/Material Legacies

> The money spent on the World Cup. It is not spent for the World Cup, it's for legacy.
>
> **(Press conference, South African FIFA Security Adviser André Pruis, 10 June 2014)**

> I think the only thing that justifies for a country to organize such an event of this nature, I am saying, a country with a development level like ours, is the legacy. It's the possibility of the legacy. It's you being able to achieve in five years what normally the history says would be done in 50.
>
> **(Interview, member of Rio mega-event planning staff, 27 August 2014)**

Rio's security governance strategies for the mega-events have focused, on the one hand, on both military occupation and community policing measures like the introduction of the well-studied pacifying police programme in peripheral and favela neighbourhoods (e.g. Richmond 2019). On the other hand, the introduction of digital security programmes such as camera surveillance schemes, command-and-control centres, predictive policing, and urban control systems has been prioritized, as these were also meant to integrate the widely dispersed and competing police forces (Cardoso 2013, 2019). Both strategies were intended to interrupt the vicious circle of violence to guarantee a peaceful staging of the mega-events, and to leave the city with what in the standardized Olympic jargon is called a long-lasting 'security legacy' (Armstrong et al. 2016; also Cornelissen 2011c).

Policing Sport Mega-Events. Dennis Pauschinger, Oxford University Press. © Dennis Pauschinger 2024.
DOI: 10.1093/oso/9780192848055.003.0008

This standard mega-event security legacy narrative was also repeated in Brazil. Rio's Extraordinary Sub-Secretary for Mega-Event Security, for example, depicts the mega-events as being a 'catalyst' and a 'window of opportunities' for long-planned security improvements that could be implemented more rapidly with the investments from the events (interview, 13 August 2014). Former Rio Public Security Secretary José Maríano Beltrame said, in an interview for this research, that 'Rio de Janeiro cannot afford the luxury of hosting these events and not keep a legacy from them' (4 October 2014). An official report into Olympic security at that time stated that the ambitious investments in digital security and urban management technologies should 'return to society as a legacy for the everyday life of public safety' (Brazilian Presidential Social Communication Secretariat 2016, 5).

In many of these kinds of statements from Brazilian mega-event security officials, the Olympic legacy was framed as twofold:

> I think the great legacy that remains is the material, the investments, the [security] equipment that I mentioned here, however [there is also] the non-material legacy [that] stays. Which is this junction of efforts of all the security forces. (Interview, Extraordinary Secretary for Mega-Event Security, 10 June 2014)

The two major frames of materiality and non-materiality have fundamentally marked Brazil's mega-event security strategy. The first referred to investments in visible *material* and concrete equipment and infrastructures, and the second has focused on less palpable and *non-material* efforts, such as integrating the work of the many different security institutions. Both are interrelated as the material was meant to technologically enable the non-material.

In the analysis of this chapter, I investigate how these *material* and *non-material* security strategy and legacy narratives played out in Rio de Janeiro during and after the mega-events. I will first do so by looking at the materiality of security, the command-and-control infrastructures, and the surveillance camera system; second, the chapter sheds light on the non-materiality of security, the integration strategy, and investigates how both aspects were nothing more than empty promises all too well known for mega-event organizers. In conceptual terms, this chapter equally sheds light on the fourth element that complements the Foucauldian triangle of governance with the 'government of things'.

Materiality of Security

The Brazilian government tried to overcome technologically and organizationally the long-lasting fight over competences of the many different police organizations by implementing the Integrated Command and Control System (SICC) that combines military command-and-control doctrines. These measures had already been introduced into Brazil's military planning in 2006 (Cardoso 2013, 131–3), but now were combined with a new managerial benchmarking philosophy based upon increasing efficiency by making use of statistical data (Cardoso 2019, 55). These kinds of systems are also a global standard in urban security advancements that are developed, tested, and further proliferated between Global North and South contexts, and an intrinsic part of mega-event security arrangements (Fussey and Coaffee 2012, 274).

The SICC system materialized in the Integrated Command and Control Centres (CICCs), infrastructures that were envisioned to regroup all the involved security agencies and to technologically enable the surveillance of both the mega-event security operations and the everyday urban security dynamics. Different national, regional, local, and mobile centres were connected over a network in the host cities and the venues during the World Cup and Olympics, and operated sophisticated surveillance camera systems. In Rio de Janeiro, the command-and-control centre was initially planned independently of the mega-events to centralize the state's emergency services and implement a surveillance camera scheme, but then advanced to be the most sophisticated centre due to the hosting of the Olympics and the federal investment in the facility (Cardoso 2019, 2014, 2013).

The military police colonel and general coordinator of the CICC in Rio de Janeiro described the planning of the centre as follows:

> You know, when we conceived of this centre—and I participated in the conceptualization of this centre—we first thought about the day-to-day life of the city . . . and within this work together with the Ministry of Justice I said the following: 'Look. We have one priority; [the] priority [is] the day-to-day life of the city. After that I will start working for the mega-events.' (Interview, 2 June 2014)

This statement showcases the official discourse of using the investments made in preparation for the mega-events for the everyday running of the city. Rio de Janeiro's Extraordinary Sub-Secretary for Mega-Events emphasized that the working and planning strategy can be summarized in two major principles: first, the mega-event must serve the city and not the other way around; and second, if the city is secure, the event is automatically secure as well. He observed: 'We worked with technologies and equipment that are useful for the day-to-day, however that also can be used during the World Cup' (interview, 13 August 2014). These statements echo the common strategies in mega-event planning: that the hosting of mega-events can bring both new developments in security measures and boost security projects long planned (Giulianotti and Klauser 2009), as well as fulfilling promises made to the country's population (Fussey and Klauser 2015).

Beside the building as such, the CICC features a series of technological artefacts that promise to remain in Rio de Janeiro and have direct consequences for the understanding of the everyday public security dynamics in the city. The technological matter that has been presented as one of *the* most important innovations in Rio de Janeiro's public security landscape was the surveillance camera system that has expanded its net around Rio de Janeiro. The CICC is therefore interesting as it is a space that has fixed boundaries, yet extends across these limits through the mobile and local CICCs, as well as through its surveillance practices.[1]

In the critical mega-event security literature, surveillance cameras have been indicated as one of the major legacies that remain in cities after hosting (Bennett and Haggerty 2011; Samatas 2011a). The camera surveillance scheme in Rio de Janeiro is not new, and can therefore not merely be attributed to the mega-event cycle, as it had already been planned and installed before the events became a reality in Rio. Undeniably, however, the mega-events have given these developments a major boost, and can be seen as an intrinsic element of the technological turn in Rio (Cardoso 2013, 123). During the events in Rio de Janeiro, different private and public institutions have used the camera surveillance systems. Among these different

[1] During a conversation with a former military police colonel, who was later responsible for the military police emergency call section within the CICC, he explained something interesting to me. The most important thing for the emergency call centre now is to reduce the time for a police car to arrive at an incident. Normally, there is nothing bad about that. Nonetheless, it shows that the official approach is now focused on using the technology to become more efficient and accountable. This can produce numbers and can be shown to the public. However, it does not at all change the police work once the patrol has arrived at an incident. For reasons of space limitations, it is not possible to elaborate upon this further. It is, however, a topic of future research that should investigate how technology seems to distract from important questions of the police officer's work with the public (see also Manning 2008).

institutions were FIFA, the International Olympic Committee (IOC), and the state security forces. Although surveillance camera strategies were a matter in Rio de Janeiro before the mega-events (Cardoso 2012), many of the cameras that deliver images to the CICCs today were installed very selectively during the seven years prior to the mega-event projects.

How then can we possibly understand the surveillance camera legacy in Rio? The camera surveillance mechanisms have taken some rather complex turns, as there were fixed as well as mobile cameras, operated by at least four different entities: federal, state, municipal, and private forces. I record the many hours I spent in the control centre during the Olympics, and how important the camera images were for the actors in the control rooms. The images from the cameras served as a way of making sure that the flow of the objects and of people was guaranteed. Consider only what the general CICC World Cup coordinator describes in the following quote about how camera surveillance has been an important working tool for the mega-event security:

> The whole work was based upon permanent monitoring, right? This is what we call 'situational awareness' . . . The more situational awareness, the more elements you have got to decide from . . . [and] you don't decide in the dark. (Interview, general coordinator CICC-R, 1 September 2014)

The coordinator states that ubiquitous camera surveillance can serve as a facilitator for decision-making and provides a better overview in complicated situations on the ground. It seems as if cameras, at least in this case, serve as a way of reducing complexities and sheds light on a situational crime prevention philosophy that is salient within many of my interviews. More to the point, the 'situational awareness' is the expression of a desire to have control over *everything* and it transcends the goal of total readiness that proliferated among the authorities (see also Krasmann and Hentschel 2019).

It is also interesting how the security solution company Avigilon, which provided many of the cameras in the centre, advertises on their website new surveillance camera solutions that would bring among other features 'situational awareness' to the surveillance camera operators. The coordinator's quote—as well as the fact that the CICC has been built upon the premise of camera surveillance and, in addition, has camera technology as its core element—sheds light on the ways in which technological camera surveillance is one of the predominant security measures for securing the mega-events in Rio de Janeiro. The coordinator's statement provides insight into a thinking that is induced by the belief that technology can and will actually enable those who operate the cameras to see everything and to monitor everybody. However, the quote above builds upon the view that camera surveillance is actually able to serve as the 'almighty eye' and provide, as the coordinator said, an overall ability to control.

As Bruno Cardoso (2013, 140) points out, the technological innovations, and principally the camera surveillance, in Rio have been imagined and planned as if the technology would bring improvements *on their own*, and the humans responsible for operating these systems are only a secondary component which results in an 'overvaluation of technology'. Practices rely on the human factor just as a facilitator and centralize the technology, whereas the humans are mediators within this process. However, it is highly questionable if the investments in these surveillance technologies actually fulfil the needs of public security in Rio. Nevertheless, high-ranking security authorities are convinced that the cameras could help to reduce criminality, prevent and solve crimes, and even help arrest someone *in flagrante* (interview, Sub-Secretary of Command and Control, 2 September 2014).

The views on the camera surveillance systems are, however, contested within the CICC. A federal road police officer expressed a different viewpoint in one of the interviews. He said that experience has shown that a handful of officers cannot pay attention to the '1,600 cameras in the state' all at once and observe everything to obtain 'situational awareness'. Besides acknowledging the limited use of these many cameras, the officer emphasized that the use of automated warning systems can make surveillance work (interview, federal road police officer, 13 October 2014). Although this statement reveals a consciousness about the limited capacity of police officers to look at screens for many hours, it also confirms a view that puts technology at the forefront of a solution for the complex public security conditions in Rio.

The Foucauldian security apparatus also helps us understand the camera surveillance distribution in the mega-event city and these kinds of statements in Rio. The camera surveillance scheme has been mainly distributed over very selective parts in the city. The majority of cameras are concentrated in the regions that have been important for the mega-events, such as the World Cup regions and thereafter the Olympic areas. These areas are the Copacabana neighbourhood and principally the beach regions; the Olympic Park in the West Zone in the neighbourhood Barra da Tijuca/Recreio dos Bandeirantes; the Maracanã borough; and the Deodoro military area where Olympic competitions also took place. Moreover, the city centre is sprinkled with cameras, as it is equally important with its Olympic Boulevard at the newly inaugurated Museum of Tomorrow in the Port area. However, the North Zone of the city and the Baixada Fluminense region do not have the same number of installed cameras and have not been such a priority, as was confirmed to me in many conversations within the CICC. The unequal distribution matches with the socio-economic divide of the city (Gaffney and Robertson 2016, 11).

Foucault (2007, 65) talks about the filtering mechanisms that security enhances and the corresponding efforts to separate out the bad from the good. Whereas digital technologies may be fundamentally new to the equation, the techniques as such are not. The mechanisms serve to leverage an exclusionary politics that has been commonplace in Rio de Janeiro since the beginning of its urbanization and long before democratization, and that has only proliferated since then (see, for example, Fischer 2008). The system filters those who are wanted from those people who are not wanted in the spaces where the cameras are installed. Stated differently, the camera surveillance scheme fortifies and follows old traditional patterns of Rio de Janeiro's exclusionary and death politics. Thus, the legacy of the camera surveillance system that has been built for the mega-events, and that remains in place afterwards, does not address the security conditions in Rio.

Interestingly, these insights into the ways in which the human and the non-human are applied here produce a direct link to the technopolitical turn in Rio de Janeiro and elsewhere (Barry 2001; Ceyhan 2002; Hecht 2011; Gaffney and Robertson 2016). In Foucauldian terms, what we have seen here is not only governance through and with different modes of power like discipline and techniques like security; what I observed in the CICC can also serve as an example of a *veritable* 'government of things' (Lemke 2015, 2021). Yet, it here also reiterates that technopolitical governance is about the governance of both humans and non-humans, or as Foucault (2007, 97) has said, 'That government is concerned with things understood in this way as the interaction of men and things … to govern means to govern things.' And this makes it so interesting at this point, as what we see is how the apparatus of security works here together with what Foucault has outlined with the government of things. Whereas it is true that the security apparatus, principally with its mechanism of filtering, is an analysis that works perfectly in Rio de Janeiro before, during, and after the Games, it is only by considering this fourth dimension that we can understand how the security apparatus works in the digital era.

It is worth recapturing what I outlined in the Introduction: that what we can actually take from this is that what Foucault means with the government of things is different to the ways in which he conceptualized sovereign power. In that sense, and thanks to Lemke's (2015, 2021) helpful writings, the government of things comes closer to what Foucault essentially laid out as how power in essence gets mobilized, that power is a mode of action that 'structure[s] the possible field of action of others' (Foucault 1982, 790). In other words, power in itself does not exist. It is, therefore, not just a substance or property of specific actors, as it 'exists only when it is put into action' (Foucault 1982, 788). For the French philosopher it then became a question of how—that is, through which mediating techniques—power is being exercised (Foucault 1982, 786).

If we do relate this back again to the apparatus of security, we can now understand that if the Foucauldian security is concerned with the filtering of the good and the bad, and with enabling circulation, it is the circulation by objects *and* subjects, and the filtering exercised by humans *and* non-humans as actions upon the actions of others, that is meant here. Thus, this invites us to contemplate the security apparatus not as different to the governance of things but as a complement towards an understanding of the ways in which the human and non-human, the material and non-material, are working together. Within the CICCs, or so it seems, the CCTV camera system is managed by and manages humans in both spaces of enclosure (discipline) and territorial control mechanisms of openness (security apparatus).

Non-Materiality of Security

Standing in the middle of the mega-event operation room in the CICC in Rio, I watch how helicopter images from Sepp Blatter's and Angela Merkel's escorted cars are transmitted onto the flatscreens on the video wall. A few hours after the World Cup final, the leaders of the different police institutions give speeches over a microphone to thank everyone present, to thunderous applause. The military police colonel said emotively: 'The major legacy of this World Cup is the *integration* of the public security forces.' One of the civil police delegates echoed his words, elaborating: '*Integration* came to stay and will never vanish.' These fieldwork vignettes serve as a reminder of how deeply enrooted the non-material security narrative was among Brazil's security authorities.

As laid out earlier in this book, to implement and continue this non-materiality of security, the Brazilian government founded the Extraordinary Secretary for Mega-Event Security (SESGE). As a sub-secretary of the federal Ministry of Justice, it had responsibilities 'to plan, define, coordinate, implement and evaluate the actions of the public security [sector] for the mega-events' (SESGE 2012, 7). This strategy was important, as the Brazilian public security sector suffers from a disintegration of the many police forces, and their well-defined but practically complicated division of responsibilities that have often resulted in mistrust, miscommunication, and fights over competences (e.g. Soares 2000). The event organizers knew that they had to better integrate the different police forces, mainly in cities like Rio.

Cardoso (2013, 132–3) elaborates that the command-and-control strategy is a military doctrine that has been established in the Ministry of Defence in an official document that derives from the internationally well-known Command, Control, Communication, Computer and Intelligence or simply C4I systems; these are well known from the Olympics security scandal around Athens 2004 (see Samatas 2014). In an interview for this book, the technician of the CICC confirmed that the command-and-control strategy has a military origin which is also used by NATO. Following the Department of Defence *Dictionary of Military and Associated Terms*, command and control means 'The exercise of authority and direction by a properly designated commander over assigned and attached forces in the accomplishment of the mission. Also called C2.'[2] This strategy is supported by technological devices, software, intelligence, and control centres alike. The command-and-control architecture has not only found its way into Rio de Janeiro to become a defining public security policy but has also expanded to all the state capitals in the Brazilian federation. In Graham's *New Military Urbanism* the author writes:

> A fourth new component of contemporary urbanism is that the everyday spaces and systems of urban life are colonized by militarized control technologies, and as notions of policing and war, domestic and foreign, peace and war become less distinct, there emerges a massive boom in a convergent industrial complex encompassing security, surveillance, military technology. (2010, 73)

[2] See https://irp.fas.org/doddir/dod/dictionary.pdf.

Although I would not share the view that all pieces of Graham's new military urbanism apply to Brazil's reality—as we have seen, militarism has played an important role for a long time in Rio and there is nothing new about it in Graham's sense—the above quote, however, stunningly explores what the CICC architectures mean for the future of Rio's public security sphere. Now equipped with new military software, a military command-and-control strategy, militarily framed command-and-control buildings, and truly powerful technological surveillance material, militarization on a more inconspicuous yet nonetheless visible path has taken over in Rio de Janeiro. Cardoso (2019) has equally shed light on these developments, which he analysed as the 'managerial-militarized logic', in which military doctrines are combined with neoliberal management strategies and security technologies that organize and structure Rio de Janeiro's public security sector in the preparations for, and in the aftermath of, the mega-events. The risks involved in such a system are, as Cardoso (2019, 69) depicts, that the military dominance can question the conditions of basic rights and democratic structures.

Integration in Practice

Having outlined how the authorities have presented the integration philosophy as an overall important tool during the mega-events in Rio, it is worth looking at the ways in which the much-praised integration has worked among the different ministries, and the private and public security forces. Mega-event security patterns are most often complicated and twisted, as many distinct institutions participate with their own traditions and working philosophies. The orthodox ways in which institutions execute security practices at mega-events can sometimes permeate the original security planning (Fussey 2015, 220). The tensions within and among the many security institutions in Brazil gave the complicated mega-event organization a special touch, and laid bare integration problems between ministries, private and public security forces, and state police forces.

While overall the orchestrated mega-event security operations worked out to the extent of a more or less secure staging of the Games, from the beginning the strategy was not as cooperative as intended. While the SESGE organized and oversaw the mega-event security scheme, the Ministry of Defence also had an important role. Within the host cities, the state and municipality administrations had to work together with the federal forces. More importantly, the three-dimensional Brazilian state structure led to a competition between the Ministry of Justice and the Ministry of Defence over funds designated for the mega-event security, and resulted in tensions in the planning process which produced many visible and un-integrated infrastructures. This was strikingly apparent when I was able to visit the military facilities in which the armed forces had set up their very own command-and-control centre similar to that of the CICC. As a result of these two parallel command-and-control structures, the government had to create a special commission that would establish communication canals on high-ranked command levels, because the armed forces would not accept a civil policeman commanding a military representative within the CICC in Rio. As the member of the planning staff from the mega-event security project in Rio de Janeiro emphasized, 'Here you still have the culture of who commands … It's not easy to plan mega-event security here in Brazil' (interview, 27 August 2014). At the same time, the integrative working philosophy also did not work out between the public security organs and the private organizations like FIFA and the IOC and their local organizing committees (LOCs). The problems with the implementation of the integrative working philosophy often entailed different imaginations about the presence of public security forces in the privatized urban spaces, such as security perimeters in and around stadiums.

These different imaginations gained a specific complexity because the private entities implemented new forms of stadium security that were not present in Brazil.[3] During interviews and conference presentations by state officials, it became clear that the LOC and FIFA did not participate in preparation meetings as much as state security officials had been promised (interview, civil police officer, 11 September 2014). Moreover, LOC members stated in interviews that they had problems working with the state officials (interviews, LOC security officers, 28 May and 14 August 2014).

During the Olympics, different tensions between the Rio 2016 LOC and state police forces over the installation of police departments within the Olympic spaces led to serious juridical tensions (informal conversation, civil police officer, August 2016). On 7 June 2014, an evacuation exercise gave insights into a relationship rattled by inherent tensions: LOC officials, nervously talking into their radios, gave rude commands as to where the mobile police station could be positioned, and there was more a

[3] FIFA established the steward security system in the World Cup stadiums, a system unknown in Brazil where, normally, the military police provide the safety and security provisions.

goading of each other than a good working relationship. Many of my interview respondents told me about the difficulties in working with the LOC during the planning of the World Cup. While, due to personal relationships,[4] some of the officials on both sides described their relationship as good, I could also observe substantial complaints from others. Principally at a pre-meeting for the stadium evacuation exercise on 6 June 2014, it became clear how much the state forces struggled with the private entity that, in many respects, had taken over the city. In other words, communication and cooperation, as well as professional relationships, have been marked by disappointments and mistrust from both sides; however, these incidents strengthen the view that FIFA and the IOC interrupt local security conditions and impose a preconfigured model that has to be adapted and accepted (Bennett and Haggerty 2011, 12).

Unsurprisingly, cooperation has also been highly contested within the state police forces. An incident on 18 June 2014 during the Spain and Chile game highlights this. I remember how I took a tour around the stadium within the security perimeter with a civil police agent. When we were almost finished with our walk around the stadium, during which we inspected and discussed the different spatial distributions of the security scheme, we were stopped by military police personnel who did not want to let us pass. The incident unfolded as follows:

> The security perimeter around the stadium, crowded with fans just an hour before, now contained only FIFA staff, security and safety agents, and some lost fans, late for the first half of the match. The flashing of red military police lights was the only thing disturbing the stillness, other than the sound of fans chanting: 'Chi, Chi, Chi, le, le, le, viva Chile!'
>
> Almost at the end of our tour of the perimeter, we ran into a military checkpoint. Around ten military policemen stared at us. In the moment we wanted to pass, one of them, seemingly the leader of the group, asked my companion what we were doing there. Felipe answered that he was from the civil police and showed him his police badge around his neck. 'And who is this guy?', pointing in my direction. My walking partner immediately said that I was with him. The military policeman wanted to see the civil

[4] The LOC security section was equipped with many military or federal police officers. The 2023 book *The Sensation of Security* by Erika Robb Larkins goes into detail about these intertwined private and public security relationships in Brazil.

policeman's working permission and his police ID. He refused and insisted that the police badge was his ID. The military police official explained that he had the direct order to not let anyone pass without working permission. Felipe repeated: 'I am a policeman and I am working over there', pointing to the mobile police station. But the military police refused to let us pass. Felipe said with a firm voice that he would now continue walking and indeed started on his path. I timidly followed him. The military policemen started to surround us and blocked the way. When Felipe realized he could not pass, he returned and called a colleague.

A civil police SUV with red flashlights came driving in our direction and stopped. The driver was one of the civil police officers. He was a rather tall guy and wore glasses, blue jeans, and a military camouflage T-shirt with big black letters: *POLICIA CIVIL*. As all others, he carried a gun. Felipe stepped into the car's front passenger seat and I sat in the back behind the driver. The military policemen gathered around the car and made no effort to hide the fact that they would not let us pass. Pedro opened the driver's side window. Before he started to talk to the military police, Felipe had explained the situation to him.

'How are you doing guys? I came here to pick up my colleague. We are working over there and a bus full of Chilean fans just arrived. What's happening here?'

'We have the order to not let pass anyone without working permission and your colleague did not want to identify himself as a policeman. It is a very uncomfortable situation. And you know [now talking to Felipe], I cannot and will not let you pass without seeing your identification, although you seem to be police as your colleague came to pick you up.'

From the back of the car, I could see how furious Felipe was getting. He said loudly before Pedro could finish his attempt to mediate the situation:

'Is this what you want? Are you certain this is what you want?'
'Yes, exactly this.'
'Okay, alright. Here you see my ID.' He showed his ID in his wallet.
'Alright. Now you may pass. But surely all this wasn't necessary.'
'Aren't you still a police trainee, a police academy student?'

'Yes.'
'Alright, then be my student now.'

Felipe stepped out of the car again and approached the military police official who indeed seemed to be a police trainee. For the World Cup security, many police aspirants were used. Otherwise, the state of Rio de Janeiro would not have been able to fulfil the security planning requirements. Felipe, who is a civil police academy lecturer, wanted to teach and disabuse the trainee. Quickly the other military policemen came over to support their comrade. In my head pounded Felipe's words he had told the aspirant when they first met 15 minutes ago: 'A civil policeman is always on duty.' Now I cannot follow their conversation as I had stayed in the car, cautious about what might happen. I just witnessed how the aspirant removed himself from Felipe because he didn't want to listen to him and made derogatory movements with his hands. His other colleagues held Felipe back.

Meanwhile, Pedro was desperate. He loudly talked about the many Chileans in that bus at the mobile station. Another military policeman came to his window and Pedro started a conversation:

'You know, we are all together in this here. All together. We are all working for the same mission. We just have different structures and orders. And you all know that the big company here [FIFA] complicates our lives a lot. She gives the orders but we need to stand together. A lot of orders and a lot of people in command.'

Felipe came back into the car and Pedro continued talking to the military policeman. Pedro managed, somehow, to end the discussion and off we drove. Pedro continuously repeated: '*Estamos juntos aqui*' ['We are all together here']. Passing the rest of the military policemen, he showed them the elevated thumb and repeated: '*Estamos juntos, estamos juntos*.' The drive only took a few seconds. My adrenaline went down slowly and my heart rate normalized. Both of the civil police officers discussed the situation. 'How dare they?' and 'too many people commanding here'. Afterwards, Felipe started working immediately. Regarding the chaos at the mobile station, Pedro turned to me and said, laughing: 'You've got a lot of things to write about in your report, did you see this man?'

This incident with the two policemen during the Chile–Spain game demonstrated how complex and, at the same time, intractable access and crowd-control mechanisms, as well as security and risk issues, can be. As Fussey (2015, 218) rightly depicts, a common problem in the planning of mega-event organization and ground operations since Munich 1972 has been the failure to 'overcome the fissures between the plates of different security organisations'. Moreover, as already expressed differently, the organization of Brazilian police forces complicates such an endeavour even more. Therefore, it is almost unsurprising that the policing institutions had hostile encounters, different convictions, and, sometimes, even hampered each other's work. This is clearly detrimental to the whole security operation and can lead to perilous situations, which was tangible on numerous occasions. The above episode reveals how the *integration* concept had not reached the ground levels of the institutions involved.

A sentiment expressed by one of the civil police officers in the scene presented above caught my attention: 'There are too many people commanding here.' This statement paves the way for understanding how the tensions are shaped among the variety of actors in the field. The various private and public partnerships in the security organization at the mega-events in Rio (e.g. FIFA/police) shed light on debates about the myriad actors involved in matters of security—private and public—and how the problems in their work relationship are not value-free, nor can these working relationships be understood as simple gatherings of different actors (Klauser 2015, 233). They are the very opposite: complex and tense. As Klauser challenges:

> Thus implementing specific security and surveillance measures is not so much a question of universal principles than of everyday negotiations and micro adjustments between different actors, interests and stipulations. (2015, 233)

This discussion can be extended to the integration policies that have been widely announced, not only to improve the work between the public security forces after the mega-events but also to bridge the lack of cooperation during the events in security and surveillance areas. Several other scenes from the field have indicated that the cooperation among the distinct security institutions did not work. The mobile civil police station's coordinator had to discuss every time of his arrival within the Maracanã borough with municipal guards so that he could position the station at his designated slot. The interrelations between the civil police, the military police, and the municipal guards were shaped by mistrust, disgust for one another, and miscommunication. To put it bluntly, the representatives of the different institutions did not know about each other's tasks within the field, as the above scene has illustrated. In other words, in the middle of one of the major security operations for the World Cup, ground forces would not cooperate with each other. A similar problem was observed at the London 2012 Olympics when different units of the British Transport Police and the London Metropolitan Police policed the same Olympic sites. The institutions had very distinct ideas and experiences of how to deal with counterterrorism missions, which led to different approaches, causing tensions and contradictions (Fussey 2015, 220). Nevertheless, the specificity of the Brazilian public security history and its organization renders the organization of such mega-events more difficult and a special integration policy had to be set up.

The mobile version of the command-and-control centre (CICC-M) is another example of how the imagined plans did not work within the lived experience of the mega-event security schemes. Following the general CICC coordinator in Rio, 'The CICC-M was conceived to be a meeting place for people of various institutions, but already on an operational level' (interview, 1 September 2014). Moreover, the mobile centre had been planned to serve as an emergency decision centre from which local troops could be coordinated. The statements by the key figures above set out the premise that the mobile centre would be working independently of the command-and-control facility in Rio, in terms of its decision-making power and crisis management. It is essential, therefore, to explore the following interview with a higher-ranked civil police officer:

CIVIL POLICE OFFICER: I was there every game. The functioning of the police station was important, I was observing way more than the work of the police station. I was observing the positioning of the military police, I was observing the type of registers within the station, to be able to communicate with the CICC-R [the Rio CICC], with my colleague[5] in there, so that he could communicate with the officials of the military police to redirect [the troops] I was observing, I was getting information from the South Zone in case I would need to communicate with the Police City[6] for bigger incidents like those during the Chile game ... So

[5] I have decided to use 'my colleague' instead of writing out the name he refers to.

[6] With 'Police City' he refers to the civil police's base in the North Zone.

I was just beside the CICC-M, this truck within which nothing was happening, just the images, I went in there sometimes to get information …

ME: Didn't it work?

CIVIL POLICE OFFICER: No. It worked, but no one there had decision-making power.

ME: Ah.

CIVIL POLICE OFFICER: That's what I am saying. What you had there were military police officials, a municipality guard official, a fire brigade official, and me going in there sometimes. None of them had decision-making power, the only person who had decision-making power there, who could actually talk in the name of the institution, was me … Each of them there would have had to call their commander in the military police or, at least, their sub-commander, to ask for authorization to do something. So I gave my colleague the exact picture of what was happening in the street, and at the same time, I was in a position, if there had been a crisis, an explosive artefact, something, a hostage, I was the only one who had decision-making power there. The other institutions would have needed to report to the centre, while I would turn off the centre and say: 'from now on, the person who decides is me'. (Interview, 12 August 2014)

The interview exposes how the integrated command-and-control structure was not working in the way it was planned on paper. While the mobile centre was planned and positioned as a mobile crisis-management tool, in reality it could not serve as such due to the ranks of the officials working at the ground level. This coincides with the situation narrated earlier: how the civil and military police officials collided during the Chile game while both were simply trying to fulfil their duty and do the right thing. However, the military police official just followed his orders, which discloses his inflexibility and his hierarchical and military education. As the police officer rightly asserts, 'a military police official may well realize that a positioning is wrong, but is hardly likely to tell his superior' (interview, 12 August 2014). In fact, what happened on the ground during the World Cup is that the tensions among the different security forces were far from being integrated. As we have seen in the situation from the Chile game, different commands had been distributed to a variety of police forces, each of them fulfilling their tasks without knowing those of the others. In emergency situations, as the civil police officer reports in the interview, the integration command-and-control philosophy would have failed or, at least, taken too long to effectively solve the problem in the field.

Therefore, the situation suggests that regardless of how well the integrated command-and-control structure may have been set up, it was operationally incapable of fulfilling its role. It shows how the different institutions worked, in many respects, with their own working philosophies, within their own traditional and culturally anchored values and mechanisms. The civil police, in this case, acted within the integrated system, but with their own independent strategy, while many other institutions maintained the strategy that was planned, whether or not this was the best option, at least from an operational perspective. Furthermore, one has to bear in mind what has been said before; the Brazilian military hierarchies, this culture of 'who commands' (interview, staff member SESGE, 27 August 2014), feeds into this part of the chapter as well. Even if there had been a crisis at ground level, the high-ranked civil police officer would not have been able to give orders to the military police on the ground because, although their institutions may have worked together for the World Cup security, there was no official way for him to command the military police troops.

Improvisation had to take over in moments of tension around the Maracanã stadium and communication was crucial to overcome institutional vanities and conflicts. While in many moments it worked, in others, as exposed with the scene between the military and civil police above, it did not and could have led to more serious incidents.

As we have seen, communication and data sharing between police forces have traditionally been very difficult in Brazil and elsewhere. Moreover, it is a typical example of how a practice is imagined on the planners' level but does not work in reality at ground level. The imaginary of the security dream continues here in the sense that the above situation of the police officers was full of lived experience or, as Raban (1974, 155) has put it, 'to live in a real city is to live in just as indomitable an environment as any valley full of rocks and stones and trees'. These stones and trees on our way cannot be calculated without encountering them, thus knowing about them, at street level. It seems that the glossy paper plans were detached from the reality of the streets.

It seems, furthermore, that the integrated command-and-control architecture has worked rather better at high-ranking management and coordination levels than on an overall institutional level, let alone at the street level, as seen in the scenes presented in the previous sections. The statements of key figures in the World Cup security planning have perpetually emphasized that the integrated system of command and control was unmistakably the most important basis for both a successful mega-event and for better public security in general. Despite the multiplicity of actors involved in the system, it is still very difficult to make it palpable, if at all. It is indeed something that only sometimes appears in its visible forms, and often stays hidden within personal interactions and micro situations that we need to observe and analyse. Whereas this section highlighted further evidence that the declared legacy of integration is a flawed model to address the current public security complexities in Rio de Janeiro, the next subsection investigates if it has any chance of becoming a long-lasting public security policy.

A Long-Lasting System?

From the scenes above follow the fundamental question of whether the so-called material and non-material legacy—the infrastructures and the integration strategy—would actually stay at all if it already presented such tremendous problems at the planning and operational levels. Three aspects stand out that raise some doubts. A first aspect to come closer to such an analysis is the very fact that the technologies implemented in the integrated command-and-control system need constant software updates, maintenance, and training for the officers that run them (Cardoso 2016, 12). It is more than questionable if the state of Rio de Janeiro can afford to continue on such a path.

The second aspect may be even more pressing. Undeniably, the integration policy has improved the interpersonal relationships among the different members of the manifold institutions within Rio de Janeiro's command-and-control centre. Nevertheless, the mega-events furthered *cooperation* between the different forces and did not, as frequently emphasized, create *integration*. Narrowed down, it was rather cooperation between many different security forces and institutions that worked towards the smooth staging of the tournament. As a federal road police officer clarified during the World Cup, the cooperation was excellent among individuals rather than between the institutions (interview, federal road police officer, 13 October 2014). Another federal police officer told me during the Olympics the experience of working with so many institutions had been wonderful; however, 'if tomorrow they change the teams, we start all over again'. According to this officer, who had a decisive role in Rio's command-and-control structure during the Olympics, the federal police had a key position within the integration efforts, but would not be present within the CICC that would continue to work on the everyday running of the city.

Other authorities clearly stated that the integration must be seen as a process that takes a long time to effectively materialize, and during the mega-events the forces had not yet reached this goal, although the policy-making level had announced its achievement.

The third and more pressing aspect casting doubt upon whether the integration concept will become a long-lasting public security policy lies within the Brazilian mega-event organization itself. The Extraordinary Secretary for Mega-Event Security, SESGE, had a decisive role in the integrated command-and-control system strategy (SICC). The many different CICCs during both the World Cup and the Olympics were coordinated by the SESGE. The SESGE team always emphasized in conversations that they worked as a facilitator or mediator. They saw their main task as gathering information from all the involved security forces and feeding this into shared data banks. In other words, the integration system worked through the mediation of the SESGE. In a Foucauldian sense, then, the SESGE was responsible for guaranteeing the flow and enabling the circulation of information, filtering the important (good) and unimportant (bad) objects (Foucault 2007, 65). The SESGE here has the position of letting things happen. As Foucault puts it:

> It seems to me that in the apparatus of security ... what is involved is precisely not taking either the point of what is prevented or the point of view of what is obligatory, but standing back sufficiently so that one can grasp the point at which things are taking place, whether or not they are desirable. This means grasping them at their level of nature ... grasping them at the level of their effective reality. The mechanism of security works on the basis of this reality, by trying to use it as a support and make it function, make its components function in relation to each other. (2007, 46–7)

Foucault (2007, 47) sees the mechanism of security as different from the law that 'prohibits' and the discipline that 'prescribes', though security makes use of both, the law and discipline, to cancel out the reality to which security responds; it 'nullifies it, or limits, checks, or regulates it'. This regulation mentioned by Foucault is organized and translated in my case study of Rio de Janeiro by the SESGE, an organization that acts as mediator in the CICC to ensure that the other institutions involved in the CICC relate to and communicate with each other. Much as Foucault says in the above quote, the SESGE 'grasped' the work of the involved institutions, took them at their very 'nature', to ensure that they produced 'security' together.

As the SESGE was an agency that was dissolved after the Olympics, the natural question is therefore what happens when the facilitating agency is not present to mediate anymore. The SESGE was mainly equipped with federal police officers who also played only a subordinated role within the daily running of the control centres and Rio's quotidian public security. Many of the involved officers I spoke to were worried about the legacy of integration when the SESGE stopped exercising its facilitating role. Another point that adds to this is that it seems that the command-and-control structure, which is based upon a flexible network structure, does not fit with the old-fashioned, hierarchical, bureaucratic, and vertical Brazilian public security system (Cardoso 2013, 141).

In an online event organized by the University of São Paulo in which I participated in 2021, the question was raised whether the planned systems for the mega-events in Brazil prevailed.[7] And indeed, what stayed are the buildings, the infrastructures, the cameras, and the philosophy of a military doctrine combined with managerial vocabularies of how to organize public security. The integration and real improvements seem to have vanished, or at least this was the dominant opinion among the participants. Bruno de Vasconcelos Cardoso said something enlightening at this event. He combined his studies about the technological advancements in the public security sector in Rio de Janeiro with his sharp analysis of the 'managerial-militarized logic' as something that prepared the ground in the preparation and realization of the mega-events for what was yet to come. Three years after the election of Jairo Bolsonaro, and many years after his ground-breaking studies, Cardoso seems to have foreseen the risks that such a system could be extended as an authoritarian state security politics, as the characteristics of the security politics of the Brazilian president are exactly these: militarism and extreme neoliberal economic politics combined. In the final part of this book, the Conclusions, I extend this analysis to what such security politics also mean: nothing other than the politics of insecurity and death.

[7] Public Security, Technology and the Legacy of the Sport Mega-Events, NEVUSP, 25 June 2021, www.youtube.com/watch?v=LKZXpTAXizc.

Conclusions

Insecurity and Digitalized Necropolitics

At daybreak on 20 August 2019, black Brazilian Willian Augusto da Silva boarded a bus heading towards the city of Rio de Janeiro. At 5.40am, when the vehicle was crossing the famous bridge that connects the cities of Rio and Niterói, 20-year-old Willian took the 39 bus passengers hostage, threatening them with a Molotov cocktail and a gun. Rapidly, the Special Forces and emergency services arrived at the crime scene, blocked the traffic-jammed bridge, positioned snipers on top of fire brigade cars, and started negotiations. Rio's smart city centre released messages to redirect the heavy traffic, and the police followed the scenes from within their command-and-control room filled with cutting-edge digital technology. The hostages communicated their hopes for rescue with their smartphones from inside the bus. Nearby, random spectators and myriad TV crews gathered to observe the scenes and to transmit the unfolding tragedy to millions of households watching the morning news.

Shortly after 9am, and the release of six hostages, Willian was hit by several deadly sniper shots while getting back on the bus after he had come out for an instant. Willian's death was broadcast live nationally, and it could be seen how the 'successful' sniper stood up, lifted his fist into the air, and celebrated from atop the fire brigade vehicle. Sounds of jeering from the people and reporters filled the air in response. Moments after that, Rio de Janeiro's far-right governor Wilson Witzel was filmed descending from a helicopter as it landed on the bridge, running towards the police officers, and cheering as if he had just scored the winning goal in a football game. His personal assistant was closely following him, recording the arrival with a smartphone for social networks (Betim 2019). The public and live broadcast of the celebration—by police officers, political figures, and the general public—of an act of killing perpetrated by government forces, and closely followed using digital technologies, is symptomatic of our current political moment, one in which state violence, far-right populism, and the digital connect in a new way.

Increasingly, Big Data, algorithms, and emergent technologies are integrated in everyday security governance. Contrary to expectations, however, police forces globally still rely on repressive and lethal forms of state violence that co-exist and intermingle with smart and predictive public security strategies. In the literature about contemporary security politics, the conceptions of the shift from spectacular punitive state power to more disciplinary forms of societal control are mostly taken for granted and are applied universally as an analysis of our contemporary reality. The targeted sniper shot on the Rio–Niterói bridge that killed 20-year-old Willian serves also as a reminder that the police are often the only legitimate force that have the right to kill within democracies, representing and defending the state's sovereignty. Nonetheless, interpretation of the legitimacy of police killings is the subject of controversial societal debates. Recent events across the globe, like the deadly 8:46 minutes the white officer kneeled on black American George Floyd's neck (Hill et al. 2020), have repeatedly shown that police killings can only be fully understood by considering the historical and contemporary aspects of race, gender, and class (Ystanes and Salem 2020). In Brazil alone, 6,357 people were killed by the police in 2019—79.1% of them were black (FBSP 2020, 12–13). In 2022, the number of people killed by the Brazilian police was even higher, climbing up to 6,429 (FBSP 2023, 14). Willian's death poses, therefore, fundamental questions about how we can understand police killings in a time in which racial and class polarization is heavily increasing, most pressingly in a country like Brazil, in which the colonial past of slavery still echoes, and which can serve as an example for the global analysis of the past, present, and future of state violence.

In this book I have argued that another way of approaching these issues is by assessing and joining conceptual debates that ask how we can possibly understand security governance in times in which digital technologies find ever more entry into the organization, management, and deployment of urban security tactics, both at sport mega-events and—more generally speaking—in cities of post-colonial settings, by considering forms of sovereign power as still in place and active in these spheres.

Looking at the security politics in Rio de Janeiro before, during, and after the mega-events, I have argued that security production in Rio follows specific socio-spatial patterns along lines of class and racial inequalities that are historically rooted in projects of policing and killing the poor. Security politics in Rio are routinely carried out by using different forms of spectacle as a reaffirmation of sovereign power by multiple actors in the field. Mega-event security has transformed the city into a fortress, however, putting on display a security spectacle that I have conceptualized as a security of camouflage that has hidden away the brutal, oppressive, war-like police missions in the favelas and outskirts. Despite the many forms of security mechanisms such as the total control, perimeters, camera surveillance, and use of militarized policing, the fortress was porous and permeable. The forms of spectacular security operations and the traditional routines of killings were still operating and important. Thus, the organizers produced a security of camouflage to render unseen and invisible the official security politics—their politics of death.

The incident on the bridge points equally towards a much-needed analysis of how technology and security politics intermingle. The digital has had an essential function in the enrolment of the event, as the security forces, the general public, and the political leaders used technology to secure, watch, and promote the tragedy. Rio de Janeiro has been the perfect place to study this technopolitical relationship between technology and security politics, as everyday life in the city is marked by a violent urban conflict in which daily shootouts between the police and drug-trafficking groups co-exist with ambitious investments in digital security and urban management technologies. The city's efforts to permanently render Rio 'smart' and 'resilient' by implementing cutting-edge security technologies such as camera surveillance, command-and-control centres, predictive policing, and urban control systems, as well as to shift violent forms of urban policing to improve the public security scenario in the wake of the Olympics, are unprecedented (e.g. Cardoso 2013; Pauschinger 2020).

I have therefore investigated how the official material and non-material security strategies and legacy claims by Brazil's mega-event organizers have been implemented in the context of Rio de Janeiro. Materiality has been present with the emphasis upon security technologies like surveillance camera schemes and the mobilization of military forces. The non-materiality was meant to be the integration strategy intended to better unite and coordinate the myriad public and private security organizations.

With the empirical details I have presented in this book, I invite the reiteration of two main theoretical points towards the Foucauldian framework. First, the analysis brings to the fore how contemporary security arrangements in highly violent places like Rio de Janeiro cannot be analysed from Foucauldian perspectives that set out from the assumption that discipline and the apparatuses of security have substituted or pushed into the background forms of sovereign power. Much to the contrary, it is a question of the hierarchical positioning of these different security governance techniques that are more or less strongly alive depending on the societal context. To repeat Foucault's (2007, 107) own words, 'In fact, we have a triangle.' I have conceptualized this as the *triangle of security governance* which is composed of sovereign power (best understood in the terms of Mbembe's necropolitics), discipline, and security apparatuses, which all operate together simultaneously.

Second, I argue that to properly appreciate the imbrication of the widespread deployment of digital security technologies and repressive and deadly state violence, the triangle is best understood in combination with the agency of materiality in what Foucault conceptualized as the 'government of things' (Lemke 2015). With the example of the material legacy of the camera surveillance system that was built for the mega-events, and that has remained in place since, I have shown how there is a continuation of necropolitical conceptions of security in technological terms. A Foucauldian government of things must therefore be thought together not only with how it technologically sophisticates disciplinary spaces and the functioning of security apparatuses but also with how it is intrinsically interwoven with how power is delegated to technology to continue longstanding exclusionary politics.

Security governance in Rio can therefore not just be considered as enabling circulation and controlling access to distinct territories by and with the help of human and non-human entities. It is meant to bring necropolitics to the next level. Consider only the military occupations and the technological control mechanisms set up in and around favela neighbourhoods before, during, and after the mega-events. Here, the filtering works upside down, as the access control is not meant to define who can enter the favela; rather, it is about who can exit it. More than that, military occupation in this sense is also about the control *within* these territories. And here, a different kind of filtering takes place, in which the non-material has material consequences. The killings by both Rio's police forces and the army in the favelas are not isolated incidents but are part of a long-lasting insecurity death politics that clearly filters out who is 'good' from who is 'bad', and thus who is disposable and who deserves to live, along lines of race and social inequality, with the help of security technologies.

Continuities of Camouflage, Permeability, and Violence

Despite its manifold attempts, however, the security of camouflage cannot always conceal the different layers of reality. It is, therefore, more a process and a strategy than an impenetrable shield. This study has shown how permeable this shield can be. Hence a key question that has haunted this work throughout is that of: *security for whom?* This book has, therefore, highlighted the ways in which the mega-event security has been carried out. It did provide security very selectively within distinct zones of the city, and produced insecurity for many others. There are two sides to this story.

On the one side, there are the many human rights violations that took place during the mega-event preparations in Rio de Janeiro. Following a report by the World Cup and Olympics Popular Committee of Rio de Janeiro (2015, 36), 22,059 families were removed from their homes. At least 4,120 of those families were evicted as a direct result of the mega-events, while the rest are linked to the wider mega-event projects. The most emblematic and well-known case was the small favela of Vila Autódromo, which is located just beside the Olympic Park. The reasons for the removal of the favela were purely economic, as the land on which the settlers built their houses has turned into highly valuable territory. Today, there is nothing left except the simple houses of 20 families that resisted (Boykoff and Zirin 2016).

Furthermore, numerous organizations have presented reports to document the human rights violations. Among these, the state commission to prevent torture in Rio de Janeiro (MEPCT/RJ: Mecanismo Estadual de Prevenção e Combate à Tortura Rio de Janeiro) issued an extended document that highlights how Rio's security forces repressed public protests with lethal and non-lethal weapons. The commission reports how the security forces arbitrarily imprisoned and beat activists; how Rio's prison population increased from 29,045 prisoners in 2012 to 38,568 prisoners in 2014 (MEPCT/RJ 2014, 44); and how through 'social cleaning' strategies state police forces (along with municipality guards) violently collected homeless street kids in tourist areas (MEPCT/RJ 2014, 86).

According to the Amnesty International (2016, 13) report 'A Legacy of Violence', the Olympics have not made the city safer for everybody; rather, the police killings and the violent repression of protests are the 'real' legacy of the Olympics. Although these dynamics have been a common companion of Rio's public policies, many of the abuses have had a direct link to the mega-events, as they had intensified prior to the Games' inauguration.

Furthermore, Terre des Hommes (2016, 10) also shows that the city government actively 'cleaned' Rio de Janeiro's wealthier neighbourhoods in the South Zone of black and poor street children, or tried to prevent young black youth from coming to these areas. The report highlights that police killings increased before the events and continued while the Games were running. During the Olympics alone, 92 shootouts were reported (Terre des Hommes 2016, 19). The security of camouflage has attempted to hide these insecurity legacies of the mega-event cycle in Rio de Janeiro from the very start.

These silencing strategies through killings are inscribed in Brazil's history as a continuum, from slavery to the well-known bloody massacres of organized police violence against prisoners (e.g. the Carandiru prison massacre), street kids (e.g. the Candelaria killings), and unarmed favela residents (e.g. the Vigário Geral shootings), to today's daily favela incursions in Rio de Janeiro. The 2018 assassination of black Brazilian city council member and human rights activist Marielle Franco, who was born and raised in the favela complex Maré, symbolizes the preliminary climax of such death politics. The persons who pulled the trigger were part of a militia, yet who ordered the killing is still unknown. And, not long ago in 2021, the police incursion of the favela Jacarezinho just beside Police City is another chapter of such death politics.

On the other side, it is therefore important to note that the security of camouflage not only aimed to hide away human rights violations but was also intended to divert one's gaze from the picture this book has painted of the inner world of Rio's public security spheres. The recent killing of George Floyd in the United States has revealed the necessity of a more global and public discussion about racist police brutality, and shone a light on the pervasiveness of racism in organizational structures of police forces. The highlighting of such institutional racism by civil society has raised calls for deeper public transparency within police structures. Such transparency would benefit police forces too, brokering relations to repair trust with communities and to protect their own officers.

The governor's cheering and the sniper's killing from the initial scene in this concluding chapter thus can only be grasped in the light of both global developments and the specific conditions in Rio de Janeiro. Governor Witzel joins a league of globally ascendant extreme right-wing populists in times that Enzo Traverso (2019) has recently named 'post-fascism', and in which far-right authoritarian populism is advancing across continents, questioning basic standards of human rights, the free press, and sciences, and openly promoting racism, homophobia, misogyny, and class discrimination. During previous fieldwork in 2014, one of the Special Forces officers told me, 'we are in an urban war, but we don't have the legislation for a war. If a shot aimed at a criminal ends up hitting an innocent, we will be punished for that'. At that time, the police officers in the Special Forces were already showing me videos from the then still relatively unknown Bolsonaro, saying he would be the only one giving them the moral authority to do their militarized police work. Years later, it seems as if Bolsonaro and Governor Witzel have 'finally' awarded the police officers the necessary support to police the city in the ways they have longed for. When Witzel took office in January 2019, he advocated the use of snipers for targeted killings of drug traffickers in Rio's favelas, and filmed himself flying over communities with Special Forces who fire rifle shots down into the alleys. In the first eight months of Witzel's government, the police killed 1,249 people, the highest number in more than two decades (Ruge 2019, 2020). This number climbed to 1,810 people killed by state forces that year—the highest number since the start of the measurement in 1998 (BBC 2020). Although state violence and police killings were an unwritten rule in Rio, we can now ask if targeted killings have become an official political agenda induced by far-right politics.

In non-material terms, conversely, the roots of this material order of death lay in the non-materiality of the necropolitical that is engrained in Rio's urban conflict. During my fieldwork, stereotypical views about prisoners and people who were arrested have been paired with narratives and common phrases like 'we know these guys' or 'we can see whether they are perpetrators or not'. Another officer once told me, 'I was in the Mangueira Samba School and I saw a guy with shorts, sandals, and a huge golden heart around his neck. That moment I knew, he is a *vagabundo*.' Once I was driving with three officers to verify an incident in a nearby apartment block. In the car, the oldest of them narrated the events of the previous Sunday. It was September 2014, and the beaches of Rio's South Zone had started to become crowded as the temperature rose. On weekends, it is common for the youth of the suburbs to come to the beaches. At the beginning of the summer, collective robberies would eventually happen when young men raided the beaches.[1] The officer continued his story. When a military police patrol wanted to stop a public bus with around 50 young men and women

[1] For more details on this, see Penglase (2007).

that were on their way home, the officer told the driver not to stop and to take them 'as far away from here as you can'. The older officer told the other younger police officers in the car how the bus was overcrowded, as one of them said in response: 'Yeah, they resemble cockroaches. It would be best to take a sword and go through the bus, like St George from his horse.'

These statements are a mirror of how Rio's society at large racially judges and dehumanizes these youth from the favelas and the suburbs. They demonstrate how the police are a mirror of a Brazilian society that lives with these embedded racist stereotypes, and which are difficult to overcome in a climate that is riddled by fear of violence. These fears are nourished by politicians and a media that use the topic of violence for their own populist purposes and to advocate a harsh policing strategy that 'privileges the right to kill over the right to life' (Denyer Willis 2015, 132). These circumstances play a vital role in Rio's urban conflict and have not been addressed by the mega-event security schemes. In a countless number of instances during my research, I came across scenes in which I heard state agents justifying war-like scenarios without the need for any legal accounting. Numerous times, I participated in conversations with police officers who cheered the death of suspects, or in which I have witnessed state violence unfold.

In this book, I have therefore argued that police officers' emotions contribute fundamentally to the ways in which urban order is produced in Rio de Janeiro. I have explored the police as edgeworkers and shown across three instances how the emotional has concrete spatial effects. The three elements must be understood as different, but interrelated, aspects of how the emotions of the police contribute to police territoriality and add necessary spatial components to the edgework concept. Considering the role of emotions in the production of police territoriality, and complementing edgework with a spatial component, leads to a better comprehension of the ways in which the police shape and are shaped by space.

First, I have shown how Rio de Janeiro's urban conflict creates an emotional world defined in the book as the drying ice dilemma that officers sense as a loss of control. On one hand, the dilemma undermines the possibilities for the police officers to do their jobs. On the other, the drying ice dilemma allows us to conceive how emotions have materialized effects on the practices of producing police territoriality in the city. On its micro scale within a police station, it produces the spaces of secrecy within which the police officers work outside the view and control of public accountability.

Second, and to get to the core of the extent to which the drying ice dilemma represents an issue for the police officers in their everyday routines, I explored how approaching their jobs as a vocation produces spaces of exposure. The vocation and the exposure are two sides of the same coin. The officers have to navigate these spaces of exposure by dealing with their conditions at work and the many dangers they encounter when both on and off duty.

Finally, I have shown how pleasure and excitement as components of edgework are strategies to find ways to re-take control, and to overcome the drying ice dilemma which produces emotional and spatial strategies of war. The Special Forces (CORE) officers' emotional universe is comparable with the narratives of soldiers in war zones. The war-like activities themselves reward them with meaning to compensate for the dilemma. It is noteworthy that this produces the territorialization of spaces of war in the many favelas and outskirts of Rio. Taken together, these three elements comprise an emotional approach to the understanding of the police and their contribution to the urban conflict in Rio and beyond. I have shown how the urban conflict in Rio and the inner emotional life of the police officers are mutually interrelated. Territory is then produced by the human activity within it; that is, in this case, the police officers as edgeworkers and their emotional edging and its consequential spatial expressions. Yet, these emotions are produced by the conditions that are immanent to Rio's public security complex. In other words, one does not exist without the other. Put differently, the urban conflict produces the drying ice dilemma, and the drying ice dilemma produces the urban conflict: it shapes the police as edgeworkers who find strategies to overcome the dilemma, and who by doing so produce the conditions of the urban conflict.

Coming back to the scene in which the police officer hits little children in the police station from Chapter 5, this can serve to demonstrate how the emotional and spatial edges of police officers produce a vicious circle of violence in Rio's urban conflict. By the use of violence, police officers try to re-establish a moral order that in their view has been lost (Fassin 2013a, 106). The specificity of this moral order in Rio comprises the police officers' daily struggles with the ice block and the attempt to dry the ice. It is flanked with the emotional component, and the ways in which they perceive their position in society as one that lacks respect, a decent salary, and safety. The drying ice experience is felt as humiliating, as the officer's vocation is seen in relation to a never-ending spiral of not being able to and still wanting 'to do at least something'.

This can lead to acts of violence within a civil police station, as officers can use violence to compensate frustration and anger (Garmany 2014, 1250). Here, the humiliation is channelled through the officers as edgeworkers, and their rage-filled beating of children serves as a means to compensate for the emotional edge of the drying ice dilemma. Similarly, the Special Forces escape from the dilemma as edgeworkers by performing war-like activities that pump adrenaline through their veins, produce pleasure and excitement, and create the possibility for them to do what they are highly skilled and trained to do. Taking these assertions seriously, and pairing them with the statements of the CORE officers, indicates that their war-like battle serves a very distinct purpose. It compensates for the daily failure of police officers and, most importantly, it gives meaning and grants control where control has been lost. In essence, the war-like activity itself offers the CORE members meaning and entangles them in a fatal vicious circle. This work at the edge, however, encompasses spatial dimensions by producing spaces of secrecy, spaces of exposure, and spaces of war. Dramatically, these emotional and spatial dimensions of police work and violence affect black populations more than any other group, and racism has both emotional and spatial effects in and for police work (Alves 2018).

It is noteworthy that the emotional worlds of the police officers within the police station and the Special Forces are also targets of camouflage politics. Their struggles, their difficult everyday routines, and their insecurities should be the subject of future research. Only by understanding *their* side can one come closer to improving Rio's security sector. The findings of this book are supported by a recent study that investigated the reasons for military police lethality in Rio de Janeiro. Two results stand out. First, the war doctrine that is so deeply embedded in Rio's police forces contributes significantly to the use of lethal force (Cano and Magaloni 2016, 89). Second, the use of lethal violence by police officers is highly correlated with their emotional universe and their frustrations with their daily working routines (Cano and Magaloni 2016, 113). This book has also found that the war logics correlate with the police officers' emotions. The battle furnishes them with meaning to compensate for their frustrations. A key policy priority should, therefore, be to address these worrying dynamics so as to interrupt the deadly round of urban conflict in Rio de Janeiro.

With the theoretical posture of a scalar approach (Glück and Low, 2017), combining socio-spatial thought and ethnographic methods, I have been able to start from the bodily experienced emotions of police officers to say something about how the city is produced as a 'bordered space' (Christensen and Albrecht 2020, 387). The insights gained from these considerations advocate for more research that looks behind the scenes and into the immanence not only of public security rationales but also, first and foremost, police officers themselves. The police are often rightly criticized and held responsible for the violence they commit and the ways in which borders are enacted, enforced, and configured within the urban. Very much in the sense of a public anthropology of the police (Fassin 2013c, 2015; Mutsaers et al. 2015), however, there is a need for engaged scholarship that goes beyond much-needed criticism and opens the lens for police officers' emotional entanglements, their bodily experiences, and their intrinsic motivations, fears, passions, and sufferings. We can only come towards a better understanding of how police shape space and vice versa if we dive more into the immediacy of what moves police officers themselves. This is even more pressing in Rio de Janeiro where far-right populists, currently in power, promote more police lethality as the way forward to tackle criminality. Yet, this strategy will push the police and the city even further towards emotional and spatial edges.

Between Past, Present, and Future

There is no pause in Rio. While this book was in the making amid the Covid-19 pandemic, Brazil had emerged as the world's new epicentre, and Rio de Janeiro's government was obscuring the number of deaths (Lima 2020). Accompanying the pandemic concerns is a marked increase in favela operations of 27.9% by police in April 2020, compared to the same month in the previous year, with a parallel increase of 57.9% in the number of people killed in the course of these missions. One of the latest victims was again a 14-year-old black boy from the Salgueiro Complex in São Gonçalo, a city of greater Rio. João Pedro Matos Pinto was shot when Special Forces stormed the favela; his body was taken away by a police helicopter. It was only the following day that his parents found his body in the morgue (Ruge 2020). As said, police work in Rio de Janeiro has long been embedded in 'highly visible performances of state power' (Larkins 2013, 565), targeting populations racialized as black, to whom the state demonstrates through deliberate, almost public killings in a process that Mbembe (2003, 39–40) has conceptualized as necropower, within which entire populations in certain territories are deemed to live in 'death worlds' where sovereignty is exercised by deliberately deciding who deserves to die, and who to live. These killings are organized as a form of 'police terror' that 'becomes a tool for the spatial arrangement of racial difference' (Alves 2018, 61) in Brazilian cities such as Rio de Janeiro. Within the triangle of security governance in which I have argued that Foucauldian sovereign power must be understood as equally important to discipline and the security apparatus, the element of sovereign power is best understood as necropower that exercises control through killings (Medeiros, 2019, 86).

And state violence continued in intensified forms after the Olympics and also raises fundamental questions about the exercise of such state violence in our current political climate. The example put forth at the beginning of this chapter is telling: how Rio de Janeiro's far-right governor Wilson Witzel was filmed, three years after the Olympics, descending from a helicopter on the Rio–Niterói Bridge, running towards the sniper who had killed a hijacker, cheering. The composition of the materiality—the spectacular performance—and the non-materiality—the discursive encouragement of killing, authorizing death, and deciding who deserves to die and who does not—best illustrates how it is indeed the Foucauldian triangle that is at work in Rio de Janeiro. Here, sovereign power, discipline, and the security apparatus are working hand in hand. In contemporary Rio, however, sovereign power is exercised as necropolitics, in which killing becomes a form of security governance.

The technopolitical turn in Rio de Janeiro and the induction of a techno-fixated belief in technology can be perfectly combined with the triangle of security governance by considering the government of things. If we comprehend the Foucauldian government of things as the governance of both the human and non-human, and if we want to take seriously my proposition about the need to consider the three elements of the triangle as essential to the understanding of contemporary security governance in places like Rio de Janeiro, then the triangle and the government of things must be understood together. The camera surveillance system and the command-and-control centres are an example of how new technologies now work hand in hand with already-established ways of producing security. Viewed as the 'essential mechanism' (Foucault 2007, 108) of a government of things, the camera system allows circulations while 'controlling them, sifting the good and the bad' (Foucault 2007, 65) within and around both artificially created spaces of control and in already-given territories. Here, the government of things then means nothing else than the filtering of and by humans *and* machines.

The insights gained from this book will hopefully spark more scholarly investigations into the camouflage mechanisms of both contemporary security politics and at sport mega-events at large. Both too often work with the shimmering and shiny, while they hide the brutal under the supposedly just and peaceful. Camouflage, so I have argued, plays an important role within these mechanisms as the modus operandi of ordinary and sport mega-event security politics in Rio de Janeiro and beyond.

In sum, the book's findings have significant implications for our understandings of mega-event security in a Global South and post-colonial setting. The research shows what happens when the standardized mega-event security models are dropped into high-crime societies with such pre-conditions as in Brazil's public security sector. The book therefore provides evidence that the global security models associated with mega-event security had locally adapted to the Brazilian security conditions. These models have only *intensified* the previously existing security conditions in Rio de Janeiro, thereby increasing insecurity and doing little to improve overall security. Boykoff and Fussey (2014, 261) conclude in their study about the London 2012 'shadow legacies' that 'a repression-ready security state' is one of the Olympic legacies for the metropolis. In Rio that repressive state was already in place long before the Games were awarded to the city. However, the mega-events *improved* it with the manifold investments in new materials, new technologies, and new buildings for its security forces.[2]

Nonetheless, the generalizability of these results is subject to certain limitations as the special pre-conditions of Brazil's and Rio de Janeiro's public security spheres are unique in scale and intensity. However, mega-event security can only be analysed in full if the phenomenology of local security players is interwoven with the historical and structural pre-conditions in host cities. Moreover, it is only then that we may learn what it means for *global security to go local*. Most often, when sport mega-event security operators talk about visible *security spectacles*, what we should read in their words is that they refer to a mostly invisible and hidden world of *insecurity*. This world co-exists at the same time and setting as the visible spectacle of a *security of camouflage*.

The research was also not able to evaluate in depth the pacifying police programme (UPP) in relation to the Brazilian mega-events. Even though policy-makers have said that the UPPs would have been implemented independently of the World Cup and the Olympics, there are serious doubts about these claims. Further and future research might explore the

[2] The Brazilian government passed important legal amendments for the sport mega-events that have further criminalized the right to protest, and which can even classify protestors as terrorists. These amendments remain a covert legacy after the Games—see World Cup and Olympics Popular Committee of Rio de Janeiro (2015, 107).

intersections between the mega-event cycle and the UPP programme in more detail. This is certainly also valid for other research areas that could have been investigated more thoroughly throughout this research. The effectiveness and the long-term effects of the camera surveillance system and the integration concept are certainly worthy of future academic inquiry. The research material from the ethnography within the police station could provide the basis for a totally different future research project on the detailed dynamics within a civil police station in Rio de Janeiro.

An additional factor that was only addressed at the margins of this study is the private security sector. Two aspects would provoke challenging research projects in the future. First, one could investigate the private security departments of the local organizing committees of FIFA and the International Olympic Committee (IOC). As many of the security officers were former Brazilian policemen, this raises interesting questions about the overlapping of private–public security practices in mega-event security. Erika Robb Larkins' 2023 book, *The Sensation of Security: Private Guards and the Social Order in Brazil*, sheds important light on these dynamics. A second research project could investigate the private security corporations that provide the technologies used at mega-events. In Brazil these were mainly national corporations. What is the nature of these private security corporations' connections to a globalized security market? What is their future influence within the Brazilian public security sector? As Cardoso (2016, 12) has already indicated, these companies have long-term maintenance, training, and software update contracts.

The sport mega-event circus travelled to its next hosts, and Brazil has long passed out of the global political sports spotlight. However, the sport mega-events' consequences for the people of Rio remain. The real mega-event *legacy of insecurity* may only be fully understandable in a few years' time. It is, therefore, now even more pressing to conduct further research in Brazil and in Rio de Janeiro to fully grasp the long-term effects of the World Cup and the Olympics, as the people who suffered from the Games deserve this. The IOC president and Rio's mayor Eduardo Paes have repeatedly declared that Rio would be a better city after the Olympics. Clearly, more work is needed to demonstrate that this has not been the case. Hopefully, this book has contributed to this endeavour at least a little.

In 2023 a different Brazil seems to rise. President Lula and his third term spark hopes for a different and better Brazil. Yet, Bolsonaro's movement—the Bolsonarismo—will certainly remain (Franzen, 2022). Despite the hopes in new governments in Brazil and elsewhere, close attention should be paid to how, from the killing of George Floyd in Trumpist America to the deadly attack on Marielle Franco in a Brazil deeply marked by Bolsonarismo, the implementation of digital security technologies, the use of state violence, and the rise of far-right populism merge in worrying ways. While these developments have traditionally been studied separately, much more attention should be paid to how these phenomena coalesce, influence each other, and are essentially lived, negotiated, and contested. There is an urgent need to better explore how material and non-material forms of the technopolitical intermingle with necropower, and how power is ever more delegated to digital technologies. In the end, the same question remains in all these developments: *security for whom?*

Appendix: A Methodological Note

During the research for this book, I went through a series of very challenging situations that brought me to the edge of my capacity as a researcher. This methodological note aims to bring some of these challenges to the table, as I think doing so can help to better understand the ways in which the data of this book has been gathered and what it entails to do research in Brazil, in a city like Rio, with its police forces. I will therefore bring forth the questions of ethnographic bias, the moral ambiguities of doing research with the police, how I gained access, and how I dealt with questions of complicity and betrayal.

Ethnographic Bias

The trust and confidence I earned during my stays in the police stations and other fieldwork localities raise a number of serious issues about objectivity and my position within the field. Cultural criminology's ethnographic sensibility requires that the researcher cross boundaries that other disciplines would consider as 'no-go areas' of scientific objectivity. The *criminological verstehen* explained in the Introduction is an attempt to rupture such borders as an effort to immerse oneself within the culture under study. Yet, much criticism is directed towards ethnographic accounts as being simple descriptions and uncritical adaptations of what the researcher has experienced within the field.

Mitchell Duneier (2001) reminds us of the 'ethnographic fallacy' put forth by Stephen Steinberg in a conference paper about Gans' *Urban Villagers*. Duneier (2001, 343–4) writes that Steinberg alerts us that ethnography sometimes tends to take reality with all its details for granted, without making the effort to interpret and situate findings within wider structures that are hidden in the backgrounds of that which is observed. There is no easy way to escape this problematic: it requires both some confidence from the reader towards the ethnographic writer and the ethnographer's effort to situate the observed phenomena in their wider political and social-economic backgrounds (Duneier 2001, 343–4).

Jock Young (2011, 133–4) approaches this problematic in a similar way: 'We have to be constantly aware, then, of the underlying narrative about the subjects which the ethnographer is communicating to the outside world.' He suggests adopting an 'ethnographic lens' that is marked by a twofold layer of narratives. A first narrative is the ethnographic text or the 'subjects' story'. A second one is a 'meta-narrative' that is shaped and influenced by the personal history of the ethnographer where she or he provides the 'interpretative structure, the discourse within which the narrator interprets the story'. Such a process can lead to a problematic 'ethnographic othering' within which the ethnographer tends to depict the studied group and culture through her or his own lens, and may not do justice to those portrayed (Young 2011, 133–4).

Thus, ethnography requires reflexivity about the researcher's position within the field. It is important to know the ethnographer's social position and political stance, and *how* the researcher relates to the field. Moreover, this means adopting the principle that while ethnographic methods move beyond the normal boundaries of scientific objectivity, they do so in a conscious way: the research performance as such is a deeply political activity. Put differently, there is no such thing as a classical scientific objectivity that many positivistic researchers claim for themselves.

At a conference in Hamburg 2015, a famous Olympic economist told me that 'we as scientists should have a neutral distance to the events and simply evaluate the facts'. The conference took place in a climate when almost the entire interdisciplinary German sports science embraced the city of Hamburg's bidding ambitions to host the 2024 Olympic Games, regardless of all the related social and economic risks. In the moment the economist told me about his 'scientific neutrality', he probably had forgotten how immersed he already was in the political world of sports, as he had not found it strange that his suit was adorned with a 'Hamburg 2024' bid supporter's pin. As stated above, there is a need to be open about our own biases.

The present research is truly influenced by my aversion to the ways in which sport mega-events, and especially the FIFA World Cup and the Olympics, are organized. I engaged in the Hamburg 'NOlympia' campaign and released with a group of colleagues a position paper that asked for a more holistic approach within the bidding process that assesses openly and honestly the risks and dangers for a city that hosts the Olympics.[1] Yet, this does not free me from a thorough analysis of my fieldwork findings—including when they do not converge with my own political opinions. Therefore, what Ferrell (1998, 25) argues holds some truth for my own position, and for this present work: 'These perspectives further emphasize that methodologies inevitably intertwine with theoretical stances, political choices, and the social situations in which they are practiced.' Furthermore, the striving for total objectivity and research without bias is not possible. As Howard S. Becker (1966, 247) famously put it, we 'can never have a "balanced picture" until we have studied all of society simultaneously'.

Reflexivity extends to the researcher's own social status. I am certain that my good access to the field had also to do with the fact of being a white, European male who holds a degree from a German university, and whose joint UK–German PhD research has been financed by the European Union. In other words, I am part of what one would probably call the European educational elite. At the same time, however, I might have had an advantage over someone who had never been in Brazil before. I worked and lived for three years in São Paulo in a social organization that develops social activities in three favelas. Through the marriage to my black Brazilian wife, who comes from that very place, (black) Brazilian culture and Brazilian Portuguese have been part of my everyday life for the last 20 years. This had a crucial influence on my position in the field. Often in Rio, I was referred to as a 'gringo', a term used in Rio to identify foreigners across the ranges of race and class (Moutinho 2006). Yet, there is no way of negating that being identified as a foreign, white, and hetero man

[1] See www.olympiakritik-aus-der-wissenschaft.de.

came with tremendous advantages of access, treatment, and recognition. This, of course, always has an influence on my own reflections, judgements, and decisions in my research, as it also influences how others judge me, as Flavia Medeiros (2018) has shown in her work as a black woman from Rio de Janeiro doing fieldwork with police officers.

On the one side, it helped me to *get in* at ease, in the sense that I was able to participate in conversations, narrate jokes, and laugh at the right time. It even got to the point that some of the police officers thought that I was a Brazilian from the South.[2] As the civil police mostly work in plain clothes, I was confused for a police officer in numerous situations. These personal conditions enabled me to witness situations that I otherwise would not have been able to access. It was also of advantage to be *visibly* alien to the societal conflicts in Rio de Janeiro. Many respondents were eager to explain circumstances they would have hardly done if I had been a Brazilian.

On the other side, the advantage I had in terms of language and basic understanding of Brazilian culture did not free me from learning the language, codes, and practices of the field (Van Maanen 2011, 13).[3] My non-governmental organization (NGO) work in a favela had marked me profoundly. The topic of violence, criminal networks, and the police started to interest me when I witnessed the attacks of the criminal network PCC[4] in São Paulo. The *crime talk* in São Paulo's periphery, and my own experience of police violence, marked me tremendously and let me adopt a certain view and a certain cultural and linguistic vocabulary alien to the world of police (Caldeira 2000). When I initiated the research, I first decided to *choose the side* of the urban poor, as I was totally immersed in the fight against the 'poverty of rights' (Fischer 2008). In other words, I had to learn the language and codes that predominated among the people in my field: the Brazilian public security agents.[5] However, this experience challenged my pre-existing opinions about Brazilian police officers, as it showed me that there are no winners on either side.

Ethnography with the Police and Its Moral Ambiguities

Choosing Sides

Rio de Janeiro's police fundamentally shapes and is shaped by the ongoing experiences of insecurity at the city's manifold edges. Much has been written on the responsibility of the police for these processes within the favelas of Rio de Janeiro from the perspectives of the drug traffickers and the community's residents.[6] However,

[2] In the south of Brazil there live many German descendants that speak Brazilian Portuguese with a slightly different accent.

[3] Language was a major issue for this work. As a native-speaking German, writing in English with data in Brazilian Portuguese was challenging. See also Maclean (2007) and Caldeira (2000).

[4] Primeiro Comando da Capital (First Command of the Capital).

[5] See also Goffman (2014, 230).

[6] For example, the classic writings by Zaluar (2004) or new publications by Arias and Barnes (2017), Larkins (2015), Lessing (2017), and Savell (2016).

very little is known about how the police officers themselves live with and engage in the urban conflict, and how they deal with being at the epicentre of these everyday urban uncertainties. In this book, I argue that the conditions of Rio's urban conflict, in which police officers try to establish urban order, produce emotional states that actively generate experiences of insecurity in the city. More than that, I argue that we have to take the perspective of those who were at the forefront of the mega-event security imaginaries and realities in order to understand how, for whom, and with what consequences security was organized.

The decision to develop an ethnography with the police, however, was not what I planned in the beginning. Initiating the fieldwork in Rio de Janeiro, I still held the belief that I could cover the police and the side of favela residents. Rapidly, I realized that this was too dangerous and complicated. How could I do research while being on both sides at the same time? Becker (1966, 239) famously reminds us that it is impossible to stay neutral: 'the question is not whether we should take sides, since we inevitably will, but rather whose side are we on'. So, I chose to be on the side of the state security forces. However, just because I was on their side does not imply that I was blind to the other side.

Becker (1966, 242) takes a clear stance towards the political project of research in the social sciences when he suggests that the researcher should be on the side of the powerless in order to swing the power balance towards the weaker. Instead, I tried to approach it like Didier Fassin (2013), who tried not to choose *any* side when he did and wrote his ethnography on police work and the youth of the Parisian periphery. Instead, he aimed 'to combine interactionist and structuralist approaches' by first exposing the ways in which the police treat the youth; second, relating that to more 'sociological characteristics' of those who carry out these actions; and third, placing these situations in the wider picture of public security policies directed to the *banlieus* (Fassin 2013, 641). Bearing in mind this approach, I tried to deal with ethically complicated situations during the research and writing process. A recent and important paper by Jaime Amparo Alves (2021), however, rightly questions such an approach in times of increased racist police brutality and asks the question whether we can still withhold the position I just justified. It is truly important to have this discussion. In the moment, I have not yet answered this question for me entirely, but what I write here reflects my reasoning when I did my research and analysis of my material.

Getting In

Getting in is not so much a matter of obtaining formal authority (if this is at all possible/necessary) to access a given research field; it is more a matter of earning the trust of those we want to study (Duneier 2001, 336). To get into the field is therefore not a reference to just the locality or a territory but rather about how we can possibly get close enough to those under investigation in order to participate in their activity. Through conversations with research colleagues, I rapidly realized that my access to my field of study was extraordinarily good and provided me with a way into normally rather restricted areas. Thus, it is worth shedding light on how this access was guaranteed, and how I was able to open so many important doors.

To put it bluntly, my initial contact with the civil police was a coincidence. When I was on a family visit in São Paulo 2013 before the PhD started, I was already on the hunt for possible subjects and research sites. I visited several NGOs in São Paulo and participated in meetings of the committee that was founded to oppose the ways in which the World Cup and the Olympics were organized in Brazil. At that time, I was not yet sure which city—São Paulo or Rio de Janeiro—would be better suited to carry out my research plans. My inclination was towards São Paulo, as I knew the city from the years I lived there, and as all eyes would be on Rio for the mega-events, I thought it would be more interesting to write about São Paulo. However, I also knew that Rio de Janeiro would be more compelling due to its specific security conditions, and because not only would important World Cup games take place there but also the Olympics.

A retired friend of mine in Rio de Janeiro worked for many years at a Brazilian bank, and one of her clients was the civil police chief in Rio in 2013 when I initiated this research project. My friend suggested that she could arrange a meeting for me with the police chief. First, I was not very enthusiastic because I knew that the civil police would only have a minor role in the World Cup security. Nonetheless, I knew that this could be a good contact for coming closer to Brazil's security authorities, so I decided to go for a three-day trip to Rio. The meeting with the civil police chief at that time was pretty short. She asked me straightforwardly, 'what can we do for you?'. After I had briefly explained the purpose of my research, she brought me to the office of the civil police operational sub-chief. He was the one who oversaw the whole World Cup security strategy for the civil police. After I waited for a while in his office, he came in and greeted me. I presented my project and he told me that I could have access to whatever I wanted. The short Rio trip had been worth it.

I went back to Europe to start the PhD programme in September 2013. Since the visit in Rio, I had hoped to accompany the sub-chief in his work directly during his daily activities. Some weeks before I would return to Rio to initiate my fieldwork in April 2014, I wrote to the operational sub-chief to announce my impending arrival. To my shock, he told me that the police chief had left her position to run for the state parliament elections, and that he now had to wait for whoever would be announced as the new chief of the civil police. I already saw my whole plan collapsing like a house of cards. The only thing I could do in that situation was to wait. Then I learned that he himself was appointed as the new civil police chief and I thought it could probably not get better than that, and that I had a lot of luck.

After some weeks of painful waiting, the police chief fulfilled his promises and delegated someone else to take care of me. Luckily, this person brought me into contact with a policeman who was responsible for the civil police in the Integrated Command and Control Centre, the heart of the World Cup security operation. I met him the very same day, and was able to record an interview with him. He directed me to the Special Forces and the police station where I would later spend many day and night shifts. He wrote a recommendation letter with which he authorized from the highest police levels that I could do research, but explained: 'It is totally up to them if they want you to be around or not. We have this policy that we authorize you, but they decide if it is alright for them.' The letter worked at the Special Forces headquarters and they allowed me to come and go whenever I wanted. The same happened with the police station. The station chief granted me access to the station and suddenly I was in. Nonetheless, it was one thing to have the official authorization of the station chief and another to be accepted by the many police officers that worked there. This was maybe the hardest part.

In the beginning it was very difficult to relieve the suspicion about me. The World Cup was a crucial trust-building dynamic when chaos and confusion erupted and I started to help the police as a translator. These circumstances brought me closer to the police officers. Trust grew substantially due to my regular visits and late-night research shifts. I started to go for dinners with small groups of police officers, ride in their police cars, and develop friendly relationships with some of them. When I arrived at the station, some would say things like, 'come on in, you are already one of us here'. However, this was not the case with all of the police officers, as some had serious reservations towards me. My presence at *their* workplace seemed to bother them and restricted my access within certain situations.

Throughout my time with the police, I recognized how they liked that someone was interested in their work and their side of the story. They suffer a lot from the ways in which they are portrayed in the media, and feel a lack of respect towards themselves and their work from the people in general. There is no need to reiterate that this has to do with the long list and history of human rights violations and abuses of power by the police; still, my insistence in staying with them at the station and showing real interest gave me the possibility of access too.

Between Betrayal and Complicity

One given day I went to the registration room within the back of the police station with one of the police officers who had to take the fingerprints of four black boys. After the humiliating registration procedure, the police officer suddenly hit the boys violently in the face and kicked their legs brutally. The boys wept and cried.[7] My first thoughts when I witnessed the incident were blinded by rage. *This is all senseless.* However, after I came home very late that night, I started to process the experience, reflecting on writing about the ethical questions related to doing ethnographic research.

Ned Polsky's (1967) notion of 'guilty knowledge' helps to assess some of the questions. If we study criminal behaviour, we have to be morally prepared to witness, accept, and sometimes even to participate within criminal activity. Polsky (1967, 140) asserts that we 'will not be enabled to discern some vital aspects of criminal lifestyles and subcultures unless he [the researcher] (1) makes such a moral decision, (2) makes the criminals believe him, and (3) convinces them of his ability to act in accord with his decision'. This notion of *guilty knowledge* is related to what was laid out earlier in terms of the *criminological verstehen* put forward by Ferrell (1998) and cultural criminological research methods that pledge for a direct involvement within the immediacy of the research field (Lyng 1998).

[7] For a detailed description of the situation, see Chapter 5.

Doing ethnography implies being aware of ethically challenging and sometimes antagonistic questions that will arise during the research. Several ethical issues have marked me during the research which refer to what Clive Norris (1993, 123) mentions as 'the dilemmas posed when the researcher is faced with direct evidence of misconduct by those he or she is researching'. Beyond that, what happens when the researcher himself or herself participates in situations that are ethically and morally questionable? This can be narrowed down to issues of *reaction*, *intervention*, *complicity*, and *betrayal*.

Reaction. Did I react in the right way? Is there any correct way to react? Basically, I watched the incident without a lot of reaction at all. It happened quickly and did not last more than 15 to 25 seconds. If, and I am sure about this, the officer had continued the beating, I would have said something to stop him. The incident provoked me to think: until when do we need to remain in our *neutral* observer position? Is this at all possible? When do we need to step up? Is there any need to do so? To what extent are we crossing a moral line when we let things happen, and who is it that sets this line? All these questions can be narrowed down to our own moral standards that may vary from those who read the ethnography and can expose the work to heavy criticism. The following and second issue may provide some answers.

Intervention. The question of intervening involves a series of issues. Once the situation was over, I asked myself several times: what's next? Should I go to his superior to report what he had done in order that he cannot do it again? But what about the trust I gained from the officer? Can I violate it? To whom do I owe loyalty in this case, the boys or the officer? On the one hand, we have to be aware of the cultural differences and values that exist towards the treatment of children in different cultural contexts.[8] On the other, an intervention could have provoked a series of totally unknown and maybe dangerous consequences for the research process, the access, and myself. As an answer to some of the questions above, I decided not to intervene in the situation as I stood on the police officers' side—I was *with him* in that moment. I evaluated that my task was to make sense of the situation later within my writing.

Complicity. What responsibility did I have in the whole situation? Did he do it because I was there? Did he want to show off? Did he feel the necessity to demonstrate power? Alice Goffman refers to this kind of question in her own ethnography *On the Run*. She asks herself if she would augment the risk of her participants being stopped and frisked by the police because they walk around the neighbourhood with a white girl, as she had read in older policing literature. Through her own experience she realized that even without her, the police stopped her participants equally frequently: 'In order to understand whether one's words or actions are creating something strange and foreign, one must first learn what is normal' (Goffman 2014, 236). In this sense, it was paradoxically reassuring that I had witnessed the

[8] As a classic example see Scheper-Hughes' (1993) *Death without Weeping: The Violence of Everyday Life in Brazil.*

same officer beat another boy in a different situation where he was unaware of my presence.[9]

Betrayal. The ethical question of *betrayal* is directly connected to the question of trust and a current problem for ethnographic research within security forces. The issue accompanied me during the whole fieldwork period, as 'fieldwork can be a morally ambiguous enterprise' (Duneier 2001, 336). During the research in Rio I felt such a moral ambiguity that is directly connected to my own biography. As I had always been on the other side and not with police officers, I had continuously criticized the Brazilian police for their violent actions in favelas. During the fieldwork I learned that the police themselves are trapped in the complexities of the Brazilian public security system and are more the *powerless* than the powerful.[10] However, to earn the trust of the police, I needed to show clearly on whose side I stood. In order to do that, I was not forced to lie; nevertheless, I had been more discrete about some aspects of my personal background.

Yet, my fieldwork was accompanied by a constant preoccupation that some of my respondents would discover what I had said in newspaper articles and conference talks before my research: that the Brazilian police has a violence problem. I did not want to appear as one of those 'idiots from the human rights movement' the police officers talked about so often, as this could have closed my access. After a few months, however, I engaged in vivid discussions with some officers on such topics and defended my standpoints, as the intimacy was greater than the political differences. Furthermore, I experienced several situations where I engaged in more or less humiliating action towards suspects myself. I witnessed interrogations and sometimes asked the prisoners things that made the police officers laugh out loud and made me earn respect. Nonetheless, this made me realize how quickly one can be overwhelmed with and immersed in certain situations.

The question of *betrayal* and *trust* reappears again when it comes to writing up the research. It is then that we have to decide what details from the field observations can furnish the narrative of the ethnography without betraying the trust of the respondents (Fielding 2006, 287). After the scene from the field narrated above, the officer had said to me: 'Better you don't put this into your book.' However, the scene with the boys appeared to be crucial for the book as it touches on some of the most pressing research questions. I decided to use the scene within my work.

Still, there is something that bothers me profoundly with that decision. Again, it comes back to the question of trust and betrayal. During all of the fieldwork, on numerous occasions my respondents would make jokes and more or less serious comments about my motives, my status, and my research aims. They sometimes even joked that I was a *X-9*, a popular expression for a spy that would write a report criticizing their actions. I sensed two things. On the one side, I can imagine that my respondents would not like to see published some episodes I describe within the book.

[9] There can also arise a series of legal questions involving ethnography. Principally, Alice Goffman's (2014) book has been the subject of controversy. See Lubet (2015a, 2015b) and Lewis-Kraus (2016).

[10] Graham Denyer Willis (2015, 131) dedicates a whole chapter in his book *The Killing Consensus* to whether the police are the powerful.

On the other side, many of them were happy to know that someone would write about *their* positions and *their* working conditions.[11] Almost all of my respondents were committed to doing the right thing, and felt that it was impossible to always stick to the legal rules 'as this is the only way to do the job'. The police officer from the scene above gave me the reason why I should not describe the scene in my book: 'It could be bad for my superior.' The reason was not because he had felt uncomfortable with what he had just done, but that it would not be good for the police's reputation.

Two further reasons helped me to decide what to do. First, I do not reveal the time, place, or identity of anyone involved in illegal action. Second, I have never withheld from the participants that I would describe everything that I see. As stated above, I presented the scene not to blame or denigrate anyone. The scene serves purely to help understand the circumstances that lead to such incidents from the viewpoint of the police. For me it is important that what I report within this research is not meant to condemn or to accuse any of those I have studied. On the contrary, I am aware of the nuances and complexities of Rio's public security sector and its realities of violence within which the police officers and the high-ranked authorities have to constantly improvise how to act.

During my fieldwork, these realities of violence materialized as I have illustrated in this book. One of my respondents was killed in an armed assault, another one during service, and several others reported the psychological and physical scars they carry from being police officers exposed to highly dangerous situations. Not least because of these realties, it is an endeavour to do justice to the research subjects. Fassin (2013, 640) puts this fear of betraying one's own research subjects into context by saying: 'Carrying on an ethnography is cumulating debt.' Writing it is then a form of 'repaying' this debt. We therefore owe most to those we have worked with. However, for Fassin (2013, 640) there is a second dimension: we also owe to those 'primarily concerned by the issues on which we conduct research'. This relates back to what I have pointed out, namely that it is not only a matter of *choosing sides* but of putting what we observe into context, and trying to understand why things happen and why people act as they act.

In other words, I will and have to follow my conviction to portray the world I saw as the world I saw. This includes without doubt my *ethnographic lens*—my personal filter—of what I want to transmit within the chapters, which first and foremost serves to answer my research questions. As an endeavour, a cultural criminological sense of ethnography is presenting what stays hidden and is considered 'dangerous knowledge' (Young 2011, 174). At the core of this research lies a central question expressed by cultural criminologists:

> Cultural criminology's goal is to expose that presence [of structures of inequality and injustice in everyday life and crime] to those who might not see it, thereby helping ourselves and others to understand and confront the everyday reality of injustice ... And for cultural criminology that's just the question: How

[11] Denyer Willis (2015, 124–8) explains how he was positively surprised when he exposed the grievances about police work in São Paulo in an article for the *New York Times*. It was massively criticized by officials high up in the ministries and very much welcomed by the police officers he had worked with.

> best can we endanger existing arrangements of predatory crime, punitive criminal justice, and pervasive late modern exclusion? (Ferrell et al. 2008, 192)

The ways in which mega-events and contemporary urban security measures are organized these days produce a series of losers. The inequalities and injustices may not only be on the side of the urban poor or those deprived of civil rights; they may also be found on the sides of those acting within the Brazilian public security spheres. And everything can be brought down to the question of: *security for whom?*

References

Abrahamsen, R., and M.C. Williams. 2011. *Security beyond the State: Private Security in International Politics*. Cambridge: Cambridge University Press.

Adorno, S., and F. Salla. 2007. 'Organized Criminality in Prisons and the Attacks of the PCC', *Estudos Avançados* 21(61): 7–29.

Agamben, G. 2005. *State of Exception*. Chicago, IL: University of Chicago Press.

Albrecht, P. 2020. *Hybridization, Intervention and Authority: Security beyond Conflict in Sierra Leone*. London: Routledge.

Albrecht, J.F., and S. Husain. 2011. 'Severe Challenges Continue in Policing Brazil during the Twenty-First Century', in J.F. Albrecht and D.K. Das (eds), *Effective Crime Reduction Strategies: International Perspectives*. Boca Raton, FL: CRC Press, pp. 191–236.

Alegi, P. 2008. '"A Nation to Be Reckoned With": The Politics of World Cup Stadium Construction in Cape Town and Durban, South Africa', *African Studies* 67(3): 397–422.

Alegi, P., and C. Bolsmann (eds). 2012. *South Africa and the Global Game: Football, Apartheid and Beyond* (reprint edition). Abingdon: Routledge.

Alves, J.A. 2014. 'Neither Humans nor Rights: Some Notes on the Double Negation of Black Life in Brazil', *Journal of Black Studies* 45(2): 143–62.

Alves, J.A. 2016. '"Blood in Reasoning": State Violence, Contested Territories and Black Criminal Agency in Urban Brazil', *Journal of Latin American Studies* 48(1): 61–87.

Alves, J.A. 2018. *The Anti-Black City: Police Terror and Black Urban Life in Brazil*. Minneapolis, MN: University of Minnesota Press.

Alves, J.A. 2021. 'F*ck the Police! Antiblack Statecraft, the Myth of Cops' Fragility, and the Fierce Urgency of an Insurgent Anthropology of Policing', *Focaal* 2021(91): 100–14.

Alves, M.H.M., and P. Evanson. 2011. *Living in the Crossfire: Favela Residents, Drug Dealers, and Police Violence in Rio de Janeiro* (C. Pedroza de Faria and J.V. Palacios Vilches, eds), Voices of Latin American Life. Philadelphia, PA: Temple University Press.

Alves dos Santos Junior, O. 2015. 'Metropolizacao e Megaeventos: Proposicoes Gerais Em Torno Da Copa Do Mundo 2014 e Das Olimpíadas 2016 No Brasil', in O. Alves dos Santos Junior et al. (eds), *Brasil: Os Impactos da Copa do Mundo 2014 e das Olimpíadas 2016*. Rio de Janeiro: E-papers, pp. 21–40.

Alves dos Santos Junior, O. et al. (eds). 2015. *Brasil: Os Impactos da Copa do Mundo 2014 e das Olimpíadas 2016*. Rio de Janeiro: E-papers.

Amnesty International. 2016. *A Legacy of Violence: Killings by Police and Repression of Protest at the Rio 2016 Olympics*. London: Amnesty International.

Amorim, C. 2010. *CV-PCC: A Irmandade do Crime* (10th ed.). Rio de Janeiro: Editora Record.

Anderson, P. 2016, 21 April. 'Crisis in Brazil', *London Review of Books* 15–22.

Araujo Silva, M.C. de, and M.B. Carvalho. 2015. 'Circuitos Políticos em uma Favela Pacificada: Os Desafios da Mediação', *Dilemas: Revista de Estudos de Conflito e Controle Social* 8(1): 63–76.

Arias, E.D. 2006. *Drugs and Democracy in Rio de Janeiro: Trafficking, Social Networks, and Public Security*. Chapel Hill, NC: The University of North Carolina Press.

Arias, E.D. 2014. 'Violence, Citizenship, and Religion in a Rio de Janeiro Favela', *Latin American Research Review* 49(2014): 149–67.

Arias, E.D., and N. Barnes. 2017. 'Crime and Plural Orders in Rio de Janeiro, Brazil', *Current Sociology* 65(3): 448–65.

Armstrong, G. et al. 2016. *Policing the 2012 London Olympics: Legacy and Social Exclusion*. London: Routledge.

Arthur, B. 2016. 'These Rio Olympics Are Bending, Not Breaking: Arthur. Toronto Star', *thestar.com*. Retrieved 20 October 2016 from www.thestar.com/sports/olympics/2016/08/10/these-rio-olympics-are-bending-not-breaking-arthur.html.

Baasch, S. 2011. 'Event-Driven Security Policies and Spatial Control: The 2006 FIFA World Cup', in K.D. Haggerty and C.J. Bennett (eds), *Security Games: Surveillance and Control at Mega-Events*. New York: Routledge, pp. 103–19.

Balko, R. 2013. *Rise of the Warrior Cop the Militarization of America's Police Forces*. New York: PublicAffairs. URL (consulted November 2016): http://kentuk.eblib.com/patron/FullRecord.aspx?p=1113910.

Barad, K. 2007. *Meeting the Universe Halfway: Quantum Physics and the Entanglement of Matter and Meaning*. Durham, London: Duke University Press.

Barbosa, A.R. 2005. *Prender e dar Fuga: Biopolítica, Sistema Penitenciário e Tráfico de Drogas no Rio de Janeiro*. PhD Thesis. Rio de Janeiro, RJ: Universidade ederal do Rio de Janeiro. Retrieved 10 November 2023 from http://objdig.ufrj.br/72/teses/632556.pdf.

Barcellos, C. 2008. *Rota 66: A História da Policia que Mata* (9th ed.). Rio de Janeiro: Editora Record.

Barnes, N. 2017. 'Criminal Politics: An Integrated Approach to the Study of Organized Crime, Politics, and Violence', *Perspectives on Politics* 15(4): 967–87.

Barnes, N. 2021. 'The Logic of Criminal Territorial Control: Military Intervention in Rio de Janeiro', *Comparative Political Studies* 55(5): 789–831.

Barrett, F.J. 1996. 'The Organizational Construction of Hegemonic Masculinity: The Case of the US Navy', *Gender, Work & Organization* 3(3): 129–42.

Barry, A. 2001. *Political Machines: Governing a Technological Society*. London: Athlone Press.

Battibugli, T. 2009. 'A Difícil Adaptacão da Polícia Paulista ao Estado de Direito (Pós-1946 e Pós-1985)', *Dilemas: Revista de Estudos de Conflito e Controle Social* 2(3): 1946–64.

Becker, H.S. 1966. 'Whose Side Are We On', *Social Problems* 14(3): 239–47.

Beltrame, J.M. 2014. *Todo Dia é Segunda-Fiera*. Rio de Janeiro: GMT Editores Ltda.

Bennett, C.J., and K.D. Haggarty. 2011. 'Introduction: Security Games: Surveillance and Control at Mega Events', in C.J. Bennett and K.D. Haggarty (eds), *Security Games: Surveillance and Control at Mega-Events*. New York: Routledge, pp. 1–19.

Bernhard, D., and A.K. Martin. 2011. 'Rethinking Security at the Olympics', in C.J. Bennett and K.D. Haggarty (eds), *Security Games: Surveillance and Control at Mega-Events*. Abingdon: Routledge, pp. 20–35.

Betim, F. 2019. 'Witzel usa operação contra sequestrador para justificar ações indiscriminadas em favelas', *EL PAÍS*. Retrieved 7 October 2020 from https://brasil.elpais.com/brasil/2019/08/20/politica/1566323586_607069.html.

Bicudo, H.P. 1977. *Meu Depoimento sobre o Esquadrão da Morte* (5th ed.). São Paulo: Pontífica Comissão de Justica e Paz de São Paulo.

Bigo, D. 2006. 'Internal and External Aspects of Security', *European Security* 15(4): 385–404.

Bigo, D. 2008. 'Security: A Field Left Fallow', in M. Dillon and A.W. Neal (eds), *Foucault on Politics, Security and War*. Basingstoke: Palgrave Macmillan, pp. 93–114.

Biondi, K. 2010. *Juntos e Misturados: Uma Etnografia do PCC*. São Paulo: Editora Terceiro Nome.

Biondi, K. 2018. *Proibido Roubar na Quebrada: Território, Hierarquia e Lei no PCC*. São Paulo: Editora Gramma and Editora Terceiro Nome.

Boykoff, J. 2016. *Power Games: A Political History of the Olympics*. London: Verso.

Boykoff, J., and P. Fussey. 2014. 'London's Shadow Legacies: Security and Activism at the 2012 Olympics', *Contemporary Social Science* 9(2): 253–70.

Boykoff, J., and D. Zirin. 2016, 17 August. 'One Community's Resistance Will Be the Rio Olympics' Longest-Lasting Legacy. The Nation'. Retrieved 20 August 2016 from https://www.thenation.com/article/archive/one-communitys-resistance-will-be-the-rio-olympics-longest-lasting-legacy/.

Boyle, P. 2011. 'Knowledge Networks Mega-Events and Security Expertise', in K.D. Haggarty and C.J. Bennett (eds), *Security Games: Surveillance and Control at Mega-Events*. New York: Routledge, pp. 169–82.

Boyle, P., and K.D. Haggerty. 2009. 'Spectacular Security: Mega-Events and the Security Complex', *International Political Sociology* 3(3): 257–74.

Boyle, P., and K.D. Haggerty 2012. 'Planning for the Worst: Risk, Uncertainty and the Olympic Games', *The British Journal of Sociology* 63(2): 241–59.

Brighenti, A. 2007. 'Visibility: A Category for the Social Sciences', *Current Sociology* 55(3): 323–42.

Brogden, M., and C.D. Shearing. 1993. *Policing for a New South Africa*. London: Routledge.

Brownill, S. et al. 2013. 'Olympic Legacies and City Development Strategies in London and Rio; beyond the Carnival Mask?', *International Journal of Urban Sustainable Development* 5(2): 111–31.

Buzan, B. et al. 1998. *Security: A New Framework for Analysis*. Boulder, CO: Lynne Rienner Publishers.

Caldeira, T.P.R. 2000a. *Cidade de Muros: Crime, Segregação e Cidadania em São Paulo*. São Paulo: Edusp Editora 34.

Caldeira, T.P.R. 2000b. *City of Walls: Crime, Segregation, and Citizenship in São Paulo*. Berkeley, CA: University of California Press.

Caldeira, T.P.R. 2006. '"I Came to Sabotage Your Reasoning!": Violence and Resignifications of Justice in Brazil', in J. Comaroff and J.L. Comaroff (eds), *Law and Disorder in the Postcolony*. Chicago, IL: University of Chicago Press, pp. 102–49.

Caldeira, T.P.R., and J. Holston. 1998. 'Democracy, Law, and Violence: Disjunctions of Brazilian Citizenship', in F. Agüero and J. Stark (eds), *Fault Lines of Democracy in Post-Transition Latin America*. Miami, FL: North-South Center Press, University of Miami, pp. 263–96.

Calvo-González, E., and R. Ventura Santos. 2018. 'Problematizing Miscegenation: The Fact/Fiction of Race in Contemporary Brazil', *Journal of Anthropological Sciences = Rivista Di Antropologia: JASS* 96: 247–54.

Campbell, D., and M.J. Shapiro. 2007. 'Guest Editors' Introduction', *Security Dialogue* 38(2): 131–7.

Cano, I., and T. Duarte. 2012. *No Sapatinho: A Evolução das Milícias no Rio de Janeiro (2008–2011)*. Rio de Janeiro: Fundacao Heinrich Böll. URL (consulted January 2014): http://biblioteca.univap.br/dados/000002/0000024D.pdf.

Cano, I., and B. Magaloni. 2016. *Determinantes do Uso da Força Policial no Rio de Janeiro*. Rio de Janeiro: Editora UFRJ.

Cano, I. et al. (eds). 2012. *Os Donos do Morro: Uma Avaliação do Impacto das Unidades de Polícia Pacificadora (UPPs) no Rio de Janeiro*. Rio de Janeiro: LAV/UERJ.

Cardia, N. 2000. 'Urban Violence in São Paulo', *Comparative Urban Studies Occasional Papers Series* 33: 1–32.

Cardoso, B. de V. 2012. 'The Paradox of Caught-in-the-Act Surveillance Scenes: Dilemmas of Police Video Surveillance in Rio de Janeiro', *Surveillance & Society* 10(1): 51–64.

Cardoso, B. de V. 2013a. 'Megaeventos Esportivos e Modernização Tecnológica: Planos e Discursos Sobre o Legado em Segurança Pública', *Horizontes Antropológicos* 19(40): 119–48.

Cardoso, B. de V. 2013b. 'Câmeras LegisLativas: VideovigiLânCia e Leis no Rio de Janeiro', *Revista Brasileira de Ciências Sociais* 28(81): 49–62.

Cardoso, B. de V. 2014. *Todoso Os Olhos: Viedovigilâncias, Voyeurismos e (Re) Producao Imagética*. Rio de Janeiro: Editora UFRJ e FAPERJ.

Cardoso, B. de V. 2016. *Security as a Commodity: Mega Events and Public Security in Brazil* (e-Paper). Berlin: Heinrich Böll Foundation.

Cardoso, B. de V. 2019. 'A lógica gerencial-militarizada e a segurança pública no Rio de Janeiro: O CICC-RJ e as tecnologias de (re)construção do Estado', *Dilemas: Revista de Estudos de Conflito e Controle Social* Edição Especial Nr. 3/2019: 53–74.

Carvalho, B. 2013. *Porous City: A Cultural History of Rio de Janeiro*. Liverpool: Liverpool University Press.

Cavalcanti, R.P. 2020. *A Southern Criminology of Violence, Youth and Policing: Governing Insecurity in Urban Brazil*. Abingdon: Routledge.

Cavelty, M.D. et al. 2015. 'Resilience and (in)Security: Practices, Subjects, Temporalities', *Security Dialogue* 46(1): 3–14.

de Certeau, M. 1984. *The Practice of Everyday Life*. Berkeley, CA: University of California Press.

Ceyhan, A. 2002. 'Technologization of Security: Management of Uncertainty and Risk in the Age of Biometrics', *Surveillance & Society* 5(2): 102–23.

Chandler, D. 2014. *Resilience: The Governance of Complexity*. London: Routledge.

Christensen, M.M., and P. Albrecht. 2020. 'Urban Borderwork: Ethnographies of Policing', *Environment and Planning D: Society and Space* 38(3): 385–98.

Clavel, A. 2013. 'Armed Forces and Sports Mega Events: An Accepted Involvement in a Globalized World', *Sport in Society* 16(2): 205–22.

Coaffee, J. 2003. *Terrorism, Risk and the City: The Making of a Contemporary Urban Landscape*. Burlington, VT: Ashgate.

Coaffee, J. 2004. 'Rings of Steel, Rings of Concrete and Rings of Confidence: Designing out Terrorism in Central London Pre and Post September 11th', *International Journal of Urban and Regional Research* 28(1): 201–11.

Coaffee, J. 2012. 'Resilience through Lockdown: Reflections on "Total Security" Preparations for London 2012', *British Society of Criminology Newsletter* 70(Summer): 7–10.

Coaffee, J. 2013. 'Towards Next-Generation Urban Resilience in Planning Practice: From Securitization to Integrated Place Making', *Planning Practice and Research* 28(3): 323–39.

Coaffee, J. 2015. 'The Uneven Geographies of the Olympic Carceral: From Exceptionalism to Normalisation', *The Geographical Journal* 181(3): 199–211.

Coaffee, J., and J. Clarke. 2017. 'Critical Infrastructure Lifelines and the Politics of Anthropocentric Resilience', *Resilience* 5(3): 161–81.

Coaffee, J., and P. Fussey. 2015a. 'Constructing Resilience through Security and Surveillance: The Politics, Practices and Tensions of Security-Driven Resilience', *Security Dialogue* 46(1): 86–105.

Coaffee, J., and P. Fussey. 2015b. 'Constructing Resilience through Security and Surveillance: The Politics, Practices and Tensions of Security-Driven Resilience', *Security Dialogue* 46(1): 86–105.

Coaffee, J., and P. Rogers. 2008. 'Rebordering the City for New Security Challenges: From Counter-Terrorism to Community Resilience', *Space and Polity* 12(1): 101–18.

Coaffee, J., and D.M. Wood. 2006. 'Security Is Coming Home: Rethinking Scale and Constructing Resilience in the Global Urban Response to Terrorist Risk', *International Relations* 20(4): 503–17.

Coaffee, J. et al. 2011. 'Laminated Security for London 2012: Enhancing Security Infrastructures to Defend Mega Sporting Events', *Urban Studies* 48(15): 3311–27.

Coelho, M.A. 2007. 'From Pickpocket to Bank Robber', *Estudos Avançados* 21(61): 71–5.

Comaroff, J., and J.L. Comaroff. 2006. 'Law and Disorder in the Postcolony: An Introduction', in J. Comaroff and J.L. Comaroff (eds), *Law and Disorder in the Postcolony*. Chicago, IL: University of Chicago Press, pp. 1–56.

Connell, R.W. 2005. *Masculinities*. Berkeley, CA: University of California Press.

Corbeil, L.B. 2014. 'Toronto Documentary Filmmaker Injured during World Cup Clashes. Toronto Star'. Retrieved 28 January 2016 from www.thestar.com/news/gta/2014/07/14/toronto_documentary_filmmaker_injured_during_world_cup_clashes.html.

Cornelissen, S. 2010. 'The Geopolitics of Global Aspiration: Sport Mega-Events and Emerging Powers', *The International Journal of the History of Sport* 27(16–18): 3008–25.

Cornelissen, S. 2011a. 'Mega Event Securitisation in a Third World Setting: Glocal Processes and Ramifications during the 2010 FIFA World Cup', *Urban Studies* 48(15): 3221–40.

Cornelissen, S. 2011b. 'More Than a Sporting Chance? Appraising the Sport for Development Legacy of the 2010 FIFA World Cup', *Third World Quarterly* 32(3): 503–29.

Cornelissen, S. 2011c. 'Towards Redefining the Concept of Legacy in Relation to Sport Mega-Events: Insights from the 2010 FIFA World Cup', *Development Southern Africa* 28(3): 307–18.

Cottee, S. 2011. 'Fear, Boredom, and Joy: Sebastian Junger's Piercing Phenomenology of War', *Studies in Conflict & Terrorism* 34(5): 439–59.

Cottee, S. 2017. '"What ISIS Really Wants" Revisited: Religion Matters in *Jihadist* Violence, but How?', *Studies in Conflict & Terrorism* 40(6): 439–54.

Cottle, E. 2011. *South Africa's World Cup: A Legacy for Whom?* Scottsville: University of KwaZulu-Natal Press.

CPI das Milícias. 2008. *Relatório Final da Comissão Parlamentar de Inquérito Destinada a Investigar a Ação de Milícias no Âmbito do Estado do Rio de Janeiro.* Rio de Janeiro: CPI das Milícias.

da Cunha, C.V. 2014. 'O Medo do Retorno do Medo: Um Ponto de Inflexão no Programa das UPPs', *Dilemas: Revista de Estudos de Conflito e Controle Social* 1: 41–62.

Curi, M. et al. 2011. 'The Pan American Games in Rio de Janeiro 2007: Consequences of a Sport Mega-Event on a BRIC Country', *International Review for the Sociology of Sport* 46(2): 140–56.

Dal Santo, L.P. 2022. 'Killing and Letting Die: Depicting the Brazilian Conundrum Between Police Killings and Private Lethal Practices', in W.C. Wallace (ed.), *Guns, Gun Violence and Gun Homicides: Perspectives from the Caribbean, Global South and Beyond*, Palgrave Studies in Risk, Crime and Society. Cham: Springer International Publishing, pp. 329–48. URL (consulted December 2021): https://doi.org/10.1007/978-3-030-84518-6_15.

Davis, M. 1990. *City of Quartz: Excavating the Future in Los Angeles*. London: Verso.

Davis, M. 2007. *Planet of Slums*. London: Verso.

Debord, G. 1992. *Society of the Spectacle*. London: Rebel Press.

Deleuze, G. 1992. 'Postscript on the Societies of Control', *October* 59: 3–7.

Denyer Willis, G.D. 2014. 'Antagonistic Authorities and the Civil Police in São Paulo, Brazil', *Latin American Research Review* 49(1): 3–22.

Denyer Willis, G. 2015. *The Killing Consensus: Police, Organized Crime and Death in Urban Brazil*. Oakland, CA: University of California Press.

Donald, J. 1992. 'Metropolis: The City as Text', in R. Bocock and K. Thompson (eds), *Social and Cultural Forms of Modernity. Understanding Modern Societies: An Introduction*. Cambridge: Polity Press, pp. 418–61.
Duneier, M. 2001. *Sidewalk* (O. Carter, ed.) (1st paperback ed.). New York: Farrar, Straus and Giroux.
Eick, V. 2011a. 'Lack of Legacy? Shadows of Surveillance after the 2006 FIFA World Cup in Germany', *Urban Studies* 48(15): 3329–45.
Eisenhauer, S. et al. 2013. 'Fifa-Isation: Security, Brand Protection and Media Management at the 2010 World Cup in South Africa', *Surveillance & Society* 11(4): 377–91.
Enloe, C.H. 1980. *Police, Military and Ethnicity: Foundations of State Power*. New Brunswick, NJ: Transaction Books.
Fassin, D. 2013a. *Enforcing Order: An Ethnography of Urban Policing*. Cambridge: Polity Press.
Fassin, D. 2013b. 'Die Moralische Arbeit der Polizei', *WestEnd. Neue Zeitschrift für Sozialforschung* 1: 102–10.
Fassin, D. 2013c. 'Why Ethnography Matters: On Anthropology and Its Publics', *Cultural Anthropology* 28(4): 621–46.
Fassin, D. 2015. 'The Public Afterlife of Ethnography', *American Ethnologist* 42(4): 592–609.
Fausto, B. 2002. *História Concisa do Brasil*. São Paulo: Edusp.
FBSP. 2014. *Anuário Brasileiro de Segurança Pública 2014* (No. 8). São Paulo: Forum Brasileiro de Seguranca Pública, pp. 1–156.
FBSP. 2015. *Anuário Brasileiro de Segurança Pública 2015*. São Paulo: Forum Brasileiro de Seguranca Pública.
FBSP. 2016. *Anuário Brasileiro de Segurança Pública 2016*. São Paulo: Forum Brasileiro de Seguranca Pública.
FBSP. 2020. *Anuário Brasileiro de Segurança Pública 2020*. São Paulo: Fórum Brasileiro de Segurança Pública.
FBSP. 2021. *Anuário Brasileiro de Segurança Pública 2021*. São Paulo: Fórum Brasileiro de Segurança Pública.
FBSP. 2023. *Anuário Brasileiro de Segurança Pública 2023*. São Paulo: Fórum Brasileiro de Segurança Pública.
Feffermann, M. 2006. *Vidas Arriscadas: O Cotidiano dos Jovens Trabalhadores do Tráfico*. Petrópolis: Editora Vozes.
Feltran, G. 2018. *Irmãos: Uma História do PCC*. São Paulo: Companhia das Letras.
Ferrell, J. 1998. 'Criminological Verstehen: Inside the Immediacy of Crime', in J. Ferrell and M.S. Hamm (eds), *Ethnography at the Edge: Crime, Deviance, and Field Research*. Boston, MA: Northeastern University Press, pp. 20–42.
Ferrell, J. 2005. 'The Only Possible Adventure: Edgework and Anarchy', in S. Lyng (ed.), *Edgework: The Sociology of Risk-Taking*. London: Routledge, pp. 75–88.
Ferrell, J. 2013. 'Cultural Criminology and the Politics of Meaning', *Critical Criminology* 21(3): 257–71.
Ferrell, J. et al. 2008. *Cultural Criminology: An Invitation*. London: Sage.
Ferrell, J. et al. 2015. *Cultural Criminology: An Invitation* (2nd ed.). London: Sage.

Fielding, N. 2006. 'Fieldwork and Policework', in D. Hobbs and R. Wright (eds), *The Sage Handbook of Fieldwork*. London: Sage, pp. 277–91.

Fischer, B. 2008. *A Poverty of Rights: Citizenship and Inequality in Twentieth-Century Rio de Janeiro*. Stanford, CA: Stanford University Press.

Floridis, G. 2004. 'Security for the 2004 Athens Olympic Games', *Mediterranean Quarterly* 15(2): 1–5.

Fonio, C., and G. Pisapia. 2015. 'Security, Surveillance and Geographical Patterns at the 2010 FIFA World Cup in Johannesburg', *The Geographical Journal* 181(3): 242–8.

Foucault, M. 1977. *Discipline and Punish: The Birth of the Prison*. London: Allen Lane.

Foucault, M. 1982. 'The Subject and Power', *Critical Inquiry* 8(4): 777–95.

Foucault, M. 2007. *Security, Territory, Population: Lectures at the Collège de France 1977–1978*. Basingstoke: Palgrave Macmillan.

Franzén, M. 2001. 'Urban Order and the Preventive Restructuring of Space: The Operation of Border Controls in Micro Space', *The Sociological Review* 49(2): 202–18.

Franzen, N. 2021, 7 May. 'Anti-Drogen-Einsatz in Brasilien: Blutbad in der Favela', *Die Tageszeitung: taz*. Retrieved 10 May 2021 from https://taz.de/Anti-Drogen-Einsatz-in-Brasilien/!5770604/.

Franzen, N. 2022. *Brasilien über alles: Bolsonaro und die Rechte Revolte*. Hamburg: Assoziation A.

Freeman, J. 2014. 'Raising the Flag over Rio de Janeiro's Favelas: Citizenship and Social Control in the Olympic City', *Journal of Latin American Geography* 13(1): 7–38.

Fussey, P. 2011. 'Surveillance and the Olympic Spectacle', in A. Richards et al. (eds), *Terrorism and the Olympics: Major Event Security and Lessons for the Future*. London: Routledge, pp. 91–117.

Fussey, P. 2012. 'The Regeneration Games: Purity and Security in the Olympic City', *The British Journal of Sociology* 63(2): 260–84.

Fussey, P. 2013. 'Contested Topologies of UK Counterterrorist Surveillance: The Rise and Fall of Project Champion', *Critical Studies on Terrorism* 6(3): 351–70.

Fussey, P. 2015. 'Command, Control and Contestation: Negotiating Security at the London 2012 Olympics', *The Geographical Journal* 181(3): 212–23.

Fussey, P., and J. Coaffee. 2011. 'Olympic Rings of Steel Constructing Security for 2012 and Beyond', in C.J. Bennett and K.D. Haggerty (eds), *Security Games: Surveillance and Control at Mega-Events*. New York: Routledge, pp. 36–54.

Fussey, P., and J. Coaffee. 2012. 'Balancing Local and Global Security Leitmotifs: Counter-Terrorism and the Spectacle of Sporting Mega-Events', *International Review for the Sociology of Sport* 47(3): 268–85.

Fussey, P., and F.R. Klauser. 2015. 'Securitisation and the Mega-Event: An Editorial Introduction', *The Geographical Journal* 181(3): 194–8.

Fussey, P. et al. 2011. *Securing and Sustaining the Olympic City: Reconfiguring London for 2012 and Beyond*. Burlington, VT: Ashgate.

Fyfe, N.R. 1991. 'The Police, Space and Society: The Geography of Policing', *Progress in Human Geography* 15(3): 249–67.

Fyfe, N.R. 1992. 'Space, Time, and Policing: Towards a Contextual Understanding of Police Work', *Environment and Planning D: Society and Space* 10(4): 469–81.

Fyfe, N.R. 1995. 'Policing the City', *Urban Studies* 32(4/5): 759–78.

Gaffney, C. 2010. 'Mega-Events and Socio-Spatial Dynamics in Rio de Janeiro, 1919–2016', *Journal of Latin American Geography* 9(1): 7–29.

Gaffney, C. 2015a. 'Gentrifications in Pre-Olympic Rio de Janeiro', *Urban Geography* 37(8):1–22.

Gaffney, C. 2015b. 'Segurança Pública e os Megaeventos no Brasil', in O. Alves dos Santos Junior et al. (eds), *Brasil: Os Impactos Da Copa Do Mundo 2014 e Das Olimpíadas 2016*. Rio de Janeiro: E-papers, pp. 165–84.

Gaffney, C. 2016. 'What Kind of New World for Whom?' Retrieved 18 October 2016 from http://geostadia.blogspot.com/2016/08/what-kind-of-new-world-for-whom.html.

Gaffney, C., and C. Robertson. 2016. 'Smarter Than Smart: Rio de Janeiro's Flawed Emergence as a Smart City', *Journal of Urban Technology* 1–18.

Ganem Misse, D. 2014. 'Cinco Anos de UPP: Um Breve Balanço', *Dilemas: Revista de Estudos de Conflito e Controle Social* 7(3): 675–700.

Garland, D. 2001. *The Culture of Control: Crime and Social Order in Contemporary Society*. Oxford: Oxford University Press.

Garmany, J. 2014. 'Space for the State? Police, Violence, and Urban Poverty in Brazil', *Annals of the Association of American Geographers* 104(6): 1239–55.

Garmany, J., and A.W. Pereira. 2019. *Understanding Contemporary Brazil*. Abingdon: Routledge.

Garriott, W. (ed.). 2013. *Policing and Contemporary Governance: The Anthropology of Policing in Practice*. New York: Palgrave Macmillan.

Giulianotti, R., and F.R. Klauser. 2009. 'Security Governance and Sport Mega-Events: Toward an Interdisciplinary Research Agenda', *Journal of Sport & Social Issues* 34(1): 49–61.

Giulianotti, R., and F.R. Klauser. 2011. 'Introduction: Security and Surveillance at Sport Mega Events', *Urban Studies* 48(15): 3157–68.

Giulianotti, R., and F.R. Klauser. 2012. 'Sport Mega-Events and "Terrorism": A Critical Analysis', *International Review for the Sociology of Sport* 47(3): 307–23.

Glück, Z., and S. Low. 2017. 'A Sociospatial Framework for the Anthropology of Security', *Anthropological Theory* 17(3): 281–96.

Goffman, A. 2014. *On the Run: Fugitive Life in an American City*, Fieldwork Encounters and Discoveries. Chicago, IL: University of Chicago Press.

Goffman, E. 1959. *The Presentation of Self in Everyday Life*. Garden City, NY: Doubleday.

Gold, J.R., and M.M. Gold. 2017. 'Introduction', in J.R. Gold and M.M. Gold (eds), *Olympic Cities: City Agendas, Planning, and the World's Games, 1896–2020*, Planning, History and Environment Series (3rd ed.). London: Routledge, pp. 1–17.

Goldstein, D.M. 2004. *The Spectacular City: Violence and Performance in Urban Bolivia*. Durham, NC: Duke University Press.

Goldstein, D.M. 2012. *Outlawed: Between Security and Rights in a Bolivian City*, A John Hope Franklin Center Book. The Cultures and Practice of Violence Series. Durham, NC: Duke University Press.

Gonzalez, L. 1988. 'A Categoría Político-Cultural de Amefricandade', *Tempo Brasileiro* 92/93: 69–82.

Graham, S. 2009. 'Cities as Battlespace: The New Military Urbanism', *City* 13(4): 383–402.

Graham, S. 2010. *Cities under Siege: The New Military Urbanism*. London: Verso.

Gray, J.G. 1998. *The Warriors: Reflections on Men in Battle*. Lincoln, NE: University of Nebraska Press.

Grillo, C.C. 2013. *Coisas da Vida no Crime: Tráfico e Roubo em Favelas Cariocas*. PhD Thesis. Rio de Janeiro, RJ: Universidade Federal do rio de Janeiro. Retrieved 10 November 2023 from http://www.neip.info/upd_blob/0001/1540.pdf.

Hagemann, A. 2010. 'From the Stadium to the Fan Zone: Host Cities in a State of Emergency', *Soccer & Society* 11(6): 723–36.

Haggerty, K.D., and R.V. Ericson. 2000. 'The Surveillant Assemblage', *The British Journal of Sociology* 51(4): 605–22.

Hamm, M.S. 2005. 'Doing Terrorism Research in the Dark Ages: Confessions of a Bottom Dog', in S. Lyng (ed.), *Edgework: The Sociology of Risk-Taking*. London: Routledge, pp. 273–91.

Harig, C. 2020. 'Soldiers in Police Roles', *Policing and Society* 30(9): 1097–114.

Hassan, D. 2014. 'Securing the Olympics: At What Price?', *Sport in Society* 17(5): 628–39.

Hayward, K. 2007. 'Situational Crime Prevention and Its Discontents: Rational Choice Theory versus the "Culture of Now"', *Social Policy & Administration* 41(3): 232–50.

Hayward, K.J. 2004. *City Limits: Crime, Consumer Culture and the Urban Experience*. Portland, OR: Glass House Press.

Hayward, K.J. 2008. 'Cultural Criminology', in B. Goldson (ed.), *Dictionary of Youth Justice*. Portland, OR: Willan, pp. 119–20.

Hecht, G. (ed.). 2011. *Entangled Geographies: Empire and Technopolitics in the Global Cold War*. Cambridge, MA: MIT Press.

Hedges, C. 2002. *War Is a Force That Gives Us Meaning*. Oxford: PublicAffairs.

Hentschel, C. 2015. *Security in the Bubble: Navigating Crime in Urban South Africa*. Minneapolis, MN: University of Minnesota Press.

Herbert, S. 1996. 'The Normative Ordering of Police Territoriality: Making and Marking Space with the Los Angeles Police Department', *Annals of the Association of American Geographers* 86(3): 567–82.

Herbert, S. 2000. *Policing Space: Territoriality and the Los Angeles Police Department* (3rd printing). Minneapolis, MN: University of Minnesota Press.

Hill, E. et al. 2020, 31 May . 'How George Floyd Was Killed in Police Custody', *The New York Times*. Retrieved 10 November 2023 from https://www.nytimes.com/2020/05/31/us/george-floyd-investigation.html.

Hinojosa, R. 2010. 'Doing Hegemony: Military, Men, and Constructing a Hegemonic Masculinity', *The Journal of Men's Studies* 18(2): 179–94.

Hobbs, D. et al. 2014. 'Policing, Newham and the 2012 Olympic Games: A Working Paper', University of Western Sydney, 1–21.

Holloway, T.H. 1993. *Policing Rio de Janeiro: Repression and Resistance in a 19th-Century City*. Stanford, CA: Stanford University Press.

Hollway, W., and T. Jefferson. 2013. *Doing Qualitative Research Differently: A Psychosocial Approach* (2nd ed.). Thousand Oaks, CA: Sage.

Huggins, M.K. et al. 2002. *Violence Workers: Police Torturers and Murderers Reconstruct Brazilian Atrocities*. Berkeley, CA: University of California Press.

Husain, S. 2007. *In War, Those Who Die Are Not Innocent ('Na Guerra, Quem Morre Não é Innocente'): Human Rights Implementation, Policing and Public Security Reform in Rio de Janeiro, Brazil*. Amsterdam: Rozenberg Publishers.

Ilan, J. 2016. 'Scumbags! An Ethnography of the Interactions between Street-Based Youth and Police Officers', *Policing and Society* 28(6): 684–96.

International Olympic Committee. 2016. 'IOC President Hails Rio 2016 as "iconic Games"'. Consulted 10 August 2023 https://olympics.com/ioc/news/ioc-president-hails-rio-2016-as-iconic-games.

ISP. 2015. *Série Histórico da Letalidade Violenta*. Rio de Janeiro: Instituto de Seguranca Pública.

ISP. 2016. *Rio de Janeiro: A Segurança Pública em Números. Evolução dos Principais Indicadores de Criminalidade e Atividade Policial no Estado do Rio de Janeiro—2003 a 2015*. Rio de Janeiro: Instituto de Seguranca Pública.

Jauregui, B. 2013. 'Dirty Anthropology: Epistemologies of Violence and Ethical Entanglements in Police Ethnography', in W. Garriot (ed.), *Policing and Contemporary Governance: The Anthropology of Policing in Practice*. New York: Palgrave Macmillan, pp. 125–43.

Jones, T., and T. Newburn. 2006. *Plural Policing: A Comparative Perspective*. London: Routledge.

Jornal Hoje. 2009. *Helicóptero da PM é Derrubado por Traficantes* (consulted October 2016): www.youtube.com/watch?v=QuP-PMjLZzU.

Junger, S. 2011. *War*. London: Fourth Estate.

Jusionyte, I. 2015a. 'States of Camouflage', *Cultural Anthropology* 30(1): 113–38.

Jusionyte, I. 2015b. *Savage Frontier: Making News and Security on the Argentine Border*. Oakland, CA: University of California Press.

Jusionyte, I., and D.M. Goldstein. 2016. 'In/Visible—In/Secure: Optics of Regulation and Control', *Focaal* 2016(75): 3–13.

Kafka, F. 2014. *Das Schloß*. Hamburg: Fabula Verlag Hamburg.

Kant de Lima, R. 1995. *A Policia da Cidade do Rio de Janeiro. Seus Dilemas e Paradoxos*. Rio de Janeiro: Editora Forense.

Kappeler, V.E., and P.B. Kraska. 2015. 'Normalising Police Militarisation, Living in Denial', *Policing and Society* 25(3): 268–75.

Karpiak, K., and W. Garriott (eds). 2018. *The Anthropology of Police*. Routledge Frontiers of Criminal Justice. New York: Routledge.

Kassens-Noor, E. et al. 2016. 'Olympic Transport Legacies: Rio de Janeiro's Bus Rapid Transit System', *Journal of Planning Education and Research* 38(1): 13–24.

Katz, J. 1988. *Seductions of Crime: Moral and Sensual Attractions in Doing Evil*. New York: Basic Books.

Katz, J. 1999. *How Emotions Work*. Chicago, IL: University of Chicago Press.

Kinsella, D. 2013. 'The Global Arms Trade and the Diffusion of Militarism', in A. Stavrianakis and J. Selby (eds), *Militarism and International Relations: Political Economy, Security, Theory*. London: Routledge, pp. 104–16.

Klauser, F.R. 2008. 'Spatial Articulations of Surveillance at the FIFA World Cup 2006TM in Germany', in K.F. Aas et al. (eds), *Technologies of Insecurity: The Surveillance of Everyday Life*. London: Routledge, pp. 61–80.

Klauser, F.R. 2010. 'Splintering Spheres of Security: Peter Sloterdijk and the Contemporary Fortress City', *Environment and Planning D: Society and Space* 28(2): 326–40.

Klauser, F.R. 2011a. 'Commonalities and Specificities in Mega-Event Securitization: The Example of Euro 2008 in Austria and Switzerland', in *Security Games: Surveillance and Control at Mega-Events*. New York: Routledge, pp. 120–36.

Klauser, F.R. 2011b. 'The Exemplification of "Fan Zones": Mediating Mechanisms in the Reproduction of Best Practices for Security and Branding at Euro 2008', *Urban Studies* 48(15): 3203–19.

Klauser, F.R. 2012a. 'Thinking through Territoriality: Introducing Claude Raffestin to Anglophone Sociospatial Theory', *Environment and Planning D: Society and Space* 30(1): 106–20.

Klauser, F.R. 2012b. 'Interpretative Flexibility of the Event-City: Security, Branding and Urban Entrepreneurialism at the European Football Championships 2008', *International Journal of Urban and Regional Research* 36(5): 1039–52.

Klauser, F.R. 2013. 'Spatialities of Security and Surveillance: Managing Spaces, Separations and Circulations at Sport Mega Events', *Geoforum* 49: 289–98.

Klauser, F.R. 2015. 'Interacting Forms of Expertise and Authority in Mega-Event Security: The Example of the 2010 Vancouver Olympic Games', *The Geographical Journal* 181(3): 224–34.

Klauser, F.R. 2017. *Surveillance and Space*, Society and Space Series. London: Sage.

Klauser, F.R., and S. Pedrozo. 2015. 'Power and Space in the Drone Age: A Literature Review and Politico-Geographical Research Agenda', *Geographica Helvetica* 70(4): 285–93.

Koonings, K. 1999. 'Shadows of Violence and Political Transition in Brazil: From Military Rule to Democratic Governance', in K. Koonings and D. Kruijt (eds), *Societies of Fear: The Legacy of Civil War, Violence and Terror in Latin America*. London: Zed Books, pp. 197–234.

Kraska, P.B. 1998. 'Enjoying Militarism: Political/Personal Dilemmas in Studying US Police Paramilitary Units', in J. Ferrell and M.S. Hamm (eds), *Ethnography at the Edge: Crime, Deviance, and Field Research*. Boston, MA: Northeastern University Press, pp. 88–110.

Kraska, P.B. 2007. 'Militarization and Policing: Its Relevance to 21st Century Police', *Policing* 1(4): 501–13.

Kraska, P.B., and V.E. Kappeler. 1997. 'Militarizing American Police: The Rise and Normalization of Paramilitary Units', *Social Problems* 44(1): 1–18.

Krasmann, S., and C. Hentschel. 2019. '"Situational Awareness": Rethinking Security in Times of Urban Terrorism', *Security Dialogue* 50(2): 181–97.

Künkel, J. 2017. 'Gentrification and the Flexibilisation of Spatial Control: Policing Sex Work in Germany', *Urban Studies* 54(3): 730–46.

Larkins, E.R. 2013. 'Performances of Police Legitimacy in Rio's Hyper Favela', *Law & Social Inquiry* 38(3): 553–75.

Larkins, E.R. 2015. *The Spectacular Favela: Violence in Modern Brazil*. Oakland, CA: University of California Press.

Larkins, E.R. 2023. *The Sensation of Security: Private Guards and Social Order in Brazil*. Ithaca, NY: Cornell University Press.

Leal, A.B. et al. (eds). 2010. *Sonho de uma Polícia Cidadã: Coronel Carlos Magno Nazareth Cerqueira*. Rio de Janeiro: NIBRAHC.

Lefebvre, H. 1991. *The Production of Space*. Oxford: Basil Blackwell.

Leite, M.P. 2012. 'Da "metáfora da guerra" ao projeto de "pacificação": favelas e políticas de segurança pública no Rio de Janeiro', *Revista Brasileira de Segurança Pública* 6(2): 347–89.

Lemke, T. 2015. 'New Materialisms: Foucault and the "Government of Things"', *Theory, Culture & Society* 32(4): 3–25.

Lemke, T. 2021. *The Government of Things: Foucault and the New Materialism*. New York: New York University Press.

Lenskyj, H.J. 2000. *Inside the Olympic Industry: Power, Politics, and Activism*, SUNY Series on Sport, Culture, and Social Relations. Albany, NY: State University of New York Press.

Lessing, B. 2012. *The Logic of Violence in Criminal War: Cartel-State Conflict in Mexico, Colombia, and Brazil*. PhD Thesis. Berkely: University of California Berkeley. Retrieved 10 November 2023 from https://escholarship.org/uc/item/03m9r44h.

Lessing, B. 2017. *Making Peace in Drug Wars: Crackdowns and Cartels in Latin America*. Cambridge: Cambridge University Press.

Lewis-Kraus, G. 2016, 12 January. 'The Trials of Alice Goffman', *The New York Times*. Retreived 13 January 2016 from https://www.nytimes.com/2016/01/17/magazine/the-trials-of-alice-goffman.html.

Lima, T. 2020. 'Following Data Blackout, Rio City Government's "Updated" Covid-19 Dashboard Excludes 40% of Deaths. RioOnWatch'. Retrieved 28 May 2020 from www.rioonwatch.org/?p=59883.

Lindsay, I. 2013. 'London 2012: Securing Urban Olympic Delivery', *Sport in Society* 16(2): 223–38.

Lint, W. de et al. 2007. 'The Simulation of Crime Control: A Shift in Policing?', *American Behavioral Scientist* 50(12): 1631–47.

Loader, I. 2000. 'Plural Policing and Democratic Governance', *Social & Legal Studies* 9(3): 323–45.

Londoño, E., and M. Andreoni. 2019, 28 May. '"They Came to Kill": Almost 5 Die Daily at Hands of Rio Police', *The New York Times*.

Low, S.M. 1997. 'Urban Fear: Building the Fortress City', *City & Society* 9(1): 53–71.

Lubet, S. 2015a, 3 June. 'Alice Goffman's Denial of Murder Conspiracy Raises Even More Questions', *New Republic*. Retrieved 30 November 2016 from https://newrepublic.com/article/121958/sociologist-alice-goffman-denies-murder-conspiracy-run.

Lubet, S. 2015b. 'Ethics on the Run', *New Rambler Review*. Retrieved 21 July 2015 from http://newramblerreview.com/book-reviews/law/ethics-on-the-run.

Ludvigsen, J.A.L. 2020. *Sport Mega-Events, Security and COVID-19: Securing the Football World*. New York: Routledge.

Luque-Ayala, A., and S. Marvin. 2016. 'The Maintenance of Urban Circulation: An Operational Logic of Infrastructural Control', *Environment and Planning D: Society and Space* 34(2): 191–208.

Lyng, S. 1990. 'Edgework: A Social Psychological Analysis of Voluntary Risk Taking', *The American Journal of Sociology* 95(5): 851–86.

Lyng, S. 1998. 'Dangerous Methods: Risk Taking and the Research Process', in J. Ferrell and M.S. Hamm (eds), *Ethnography at the Edge: Crime, Deviance, and Field Research*. Boston, MA: Northeastern University Press, pp. 221–51.

Lyng, S. 2005a. 'Sociology at the Edge: Social Theory and Voluntary Risk Taking', in S. Lyng (ed.), *Edgework: The Sociology of Risk-Taking*. New York: Routledge, pp. 17–49.

Lyng, S. 2005b. 'Edgework and the Risk-Taking Experience', in S. Lyng (ed.), *Edgework: The Sociology of Risk-Taking*. New York: Routledge, pp. 3–14.

Lyng, S. (ed.). 2005c. *Edgework: The Sociology of Risk-Taking*. New York: Routledge.

Lyon, D. 2001. *Surveillance Society: Monitoring Everyday Life*, Issues in Society. Buckingham: Open University Press.

Lyon, D. 2007. 'Surveillance, Security and Social Sorting Emerging Research Priorities', *International Criminal Justice Review* 17(3): 161–70.

Lyra, D. 2010. *A República dos Meninos: Valores Éticos e Morais dos Garotos Armados do Morro*. PhD Thesis.

Machado da Silva, L.A. 2015. 'A Experiência das UPPs: Uma Tomada de Posição', *Dilemas: Revista de Estudos de Conflito e Controle Social* 8(1): 7–24.

Maclean, K. 2007. 'Translation in Cross-Cultural Research: An Example from Bolivia', *Development in Practice* 17: 784–90.

Manning, P.K. 2008. *The Technology of Policing: Crime Mapping, Information, Technology, and the Rationality of Crime Control*. New York: New York University Press.

May, T. 2011. *Social Research: Issues, Methods and Process* (4th ed.). Maidenhead: Open University Press.

Mbembe, A. 2003. 'Necropolitics', *Public Culture* 15(1): 11–40.

McCann, B. 2014. *Hard Times in the Marvelous City: From Dictatorship to Democracy in the Favelas of Rio de Janeiro*. Durham, NC: Duke University Press.

McGreal, C. 2010, 5 April. 'Wikileaks Reveals Video Showing US Air Crew Shooting Down Iraqi Civilians', *The Guardian*. Retrieved 21 February 2018 from www.theguardian.com/world/2010/apr/05/wikileaks-us-army-iraq-attack.

McMichael, C. 2013. '"Clearly Blown Away by the End of the Morning's Drama": Spectacle, Pacification and the 2010 World Cup, South Africa', *Socialist Studies / Études Socialistes* 9(2): 111–29.

McRoskey, S. 2010. 'Security and the Olympic Games: Making Rio an Example', *Yale Journal of International Affairs* 5(2): 91–105. Retrieved 2 May 2016 from www.yalejournal.org/publications/security-and-the-olympic-games-making-rio-an-example.

Medeiros, F. 2018. *Linhas de Investigação: Uma Etnografia das Técnicas e Moralidades numa Divisão de Homicídios da Polícia Civil do Rio de Janeiro*. Rio de Janeiro: Editora Autografia.

Medeiros, F. dos S. 2019. 'O morto no lugar dos mortos: classificações, sistemas de controle e necropolítica no Rio de Janeiro', *Revista M. Estudos sobre a morte, os mortos e o morrer* 3(5): 72–91.

MEPCT/RJ. 2014. *Relatório Temático: Megaeventos, Repressão e Privação de Liberdade no Rio de Janeiro*. Rio de Janeiro: Mecanismo Estadual de Prevencao e Combate à Tortura, pp. 1–123.

Mesquita Neto, P. de. 2011. *Ensaios sobre segurança cidadã*. São Paulo: Quartier Latin.

Mingardi, G. 1992. *Tiras, Gansos e Trutas: Cotidiano e Reforma na Policia Civil em São Paulo (1983–1990)*. São Paulo: Editora Corag.

Ministério da Defesa. 2014. 'O Ministério da Defesa na Copa do Mundo FIFA 2014'. Brochure.

Ministério da Justica. 2014. 'Major Events Security Actions'. Brochure.

Misse, M. 1999. *Malandros, Marginais e Vagabundos e a Acumulação Social da Violência no Rio de Janeiro*. PhD Thesis. Rio de Janeiro, RJ: Instituto Universitário de Pesquisas do Rio de Janeiro. Retrieved 10 November 2023 from https://www.researchgate.net/publication/35957970_Malandros_marginais_e_vagabundos_a_acumulacao_social_da_violencia_no_Rio_de_Janeiro.

Misse, M. 2006. *Crime e Violência no Brasil Contemporâneo: Estudos de Sociologia do Crime e da Violência Urbana*, Coleção Conflitos, Direitos e Culturas. Rio de Janeiro: Editora Lumen Juris.

Misse, M. 2007. 'Illegal Markets, Protection Rackets and Organized Crime in Rio de Janeiro', *Estudos Avancados* 21(61): 139–57.

Misse, M. et al. 2010. *O Inquerito Policial no Brasil: Uma Pesquisa Empírica*. Rio de Janeiro: NECVU/IFCS/UFRJ; Booklink.

Misse, M. et al. 2013. *Quando a Polícia Mata: Homicídios por 'Autos de Resistência' no Rio de Janeiro (2001–2011)*. Rio de Janeiro: NECVU; Booklink.

Molnar, A. 2015. 'The Geo-Historical Legacies of Urban Security Governance and the Vancouver 2010 Olympics', *The Geographical Journal* 181(3): 235–41.

Molnar, A., and L. Snider. 2011. 'Mega-Events and Mega-Profits Unravelling the Vancouver 2010 Security-Development Nexus', in K.D. Haggarty and C.J. Bennett (eds), *Security Games: Surveillance and Control at Mega-Events*. New York: Routledge, pp. 150–68.

Mossrion, W. 2004. 'Lombroso and the Birth of Criminological Positivism: Scientific Mastery of Cultural Artifice?', in J. Ferrell et al. (eds), *Cultural Criminology Unleashed*. London: Glass House Press, pp. 67–80.

Moutinho, L. 2006. 'Negociando com a adversidade: reflexões sobre "raça", (homos) sexualidade e desigualdade social no Rio de Janeiro', *Revista Estudos Feministas* 14(1): 103–16.

Müller, F., and M. Richmond. 2023. 'The Technopolitics of Security: Agency, Temporality, Sovereignty', *Security Dialogue* 54(1): 3–20.

Müller, M. 2015. 'What Makes an Event a Mega-Event? Definitions and Sizes', *Leisure Studies* 34(6): 627–42.

Müller, M. et al. 2021. 'An Evaluation of the Sustainability of the Olympic Games', *Nature Sustainability* 4(4): 340–8.

Muñoz Acebes, C. 2016. *'Good Cops Are Afraid': The Toll of Unchecked Police Violence in Rio de Janeiro*. Rio de Janeiro: Human Rights Watch, pp. 1–117.

Murphy, A.B. 2012. 'Entente Territorial: Sack and Raffestin on Territoriality', *Environment and Planning D: Society and Space* 30(1): 159–72.

Mutsaers, P. et al. 2015. 'The Anthropology of Police as Public Anthropology', *American Anthropologist* 117(4): 786–9.

Naegler, L., and S. Salman. 2016. 'Cultural Criminology and Gender Consciousness: Moving Feminist Theory from Margin to Center', *Feminist Criminology* 11(4): 354–74.

Nascimento, A.D. 1989. *Brazil: Mixture or Massacre? Essays in the Genocide of a Black People* (E.L. Nascimento, trans.) (2nd revised ed.). Dover, MA: Majority Press.

Neocleous, M. 2008. *Critique of Security*. Edinburgh: Edinburgh University Press Ltd.

Neri, N.E. 2009. 'Tirando a Cadeia Dimenor': A Experiência da Internação e as Narrativas de Jovens em Conflito com a Lei no Rio de Janeiro. Unpublished Master's Thesis, Federal State University of Rio de Janeiro.

Nielsen, M. 2017. 'Urban Times: Temporal Topographies and Non-Scalable Cities', *Ethnos* 82(3): 393–405.

Norris, C. 1993. 'Some Ethical Considerations on Field-Work with the Police', in D. Hobbs and T. May (eds), *Interpreting the Field: Accounts of Ethnography*. Oxford: Oxford University Press, pp. 123–43.

Online Oxford English Dictionary. 2017. 'Fortress, n. Definition of Fortress in English by Oxford Dictionaroies', *OED Online*. Retrieved 8 May 2019 from https://www.oed.com/dictionary/fortress_n?tab=factsheet#3842371.

Oxford Dictionaries. 2019a. 'Camouflage. Definition of Camouflage in English by Oxford Dictionaries', *Oxford Dictionaries, English*. Retrieved 8 May 2019 from https://en.oxforddictionaries.com/definition/camouflage.

Oxford Dictionaries. 2019b. 'Edge. Definition of Edge in English by Oxford Dictionaries', *Oxford Dictionaries, English*. Retrieved 24 February 2019 from https://en.oxforddictionaries.com/definition/edge.

Paasche, T.F. et al. 2014. 'Territorial Tactics: The Socio-Spatial Significance of Private Policing Strategies in Cape Town', *Urban Studies* 51(8): 1559–75.

Padilha, J. 2002. *Ônibus 174*. Brazil: Zazen Produções.

Paes, V.F. 2006. A Polica Civil do Estado do Rio de Janeiro: Análise de uma (Re) Forma de Governo na Polícia Judiciária. Unpublished Master's Thesis, Federal University of Rio de Janeiro.

Paes Manso, B. 2020. *A República das Milícias: Dos Esquadrões da Morte à Era Bolsonaro*. São Paulo: todavia.

Paes Manso, B., and C. Nunes Dias. 2018. *A Guerra: A Ascensão do PCC e o Mundo do Crime no Brasil*. São Paulo: todavia.

Pauschinger, D. 2019. 'Working at the Edge: Police, Emotions and Space in Rio de Janeiro', *Environment and Planning D: Society and Space* 38(3): 510–27.

Pauschinger, D. 2020. 'The Permeable Olympic Fortress: Mega-Event Security as Camouflage in Rio de Janeiro', *Conflict and Society: Advances in Research* 6(1): 108–27.

Pauschinger, D. 2023. 'The Triangle of Security Governance: Sovereignty, Discipline and the "Government of Things" in Olympic Rio de Janeiro', *Security Dialogue* 54(1): 94–111.

Pauschinger, D., and F. Klauser. 2020. 'Aerial Politics of Visibility: Actors, Spaces, and Drivers of Professional Drone Usage in Switzerland', *Surveillance & Society* 18(4): 443–66.

Penglase, B. 2007. 'Barbarians on the Beach: Media Narratives of Violence in Rio de Janeiro, Brazil', *Crime, Media, Culture* 3(3): 305–25.

Pereira, A.W. 2008. 'Public Security, Private Interest, and Police Reform in Brazil', in P.R. Kingstone and T.J. Power (eds), *Democratic Brazil Revisited*. Pittsburgh, PA: University of Pittsburgh Press, pp. 185–208.

Peres, M.F.T., and P. dos Santos. 2005. 'Mortalidade por Homicídios no Brasil na Década de 90: O Papel das Armas de Fogo', *Revista Saúde Pública* 39(1): 58–66.

Pfeil, G., and M. Wulzinger. 2016. 'Eine Große Lebensschule: Die neue Generalsekretärin Fatma Samoura über ihre schwere Mission, Die Fifa zu reformieren', *Der Spiegel* 69(46): 110–13.

Phillips, T. 2021, 11 May. '"They Came to Kill": Rio's Deadliest Favela Police Raid Sparks Calls for Change', *The Guardian*. Retrieved 12 May 2021 from https://www.theguardian.com/world/2021/may/11/rio-deadliest-police-raid-favela-drugs-protest.

Pinheiro, S. 1990. 'Notas Sobre o Futuro da Violência na Cidade Democrática', *Revista USP* 5(Dossiê Cidades): 43–6.

Pinheiro Ramos, F., and H. Aparecida Nova. 2003. 'Mídia, Violência e Alteridade: Um Estudo de Caso', *Estudos de Psicologia* 8(3): 491–7.

Polsky, N. 1967. *Hustlers, Beats, and Others*. Chicago, IL: Aldine Publishing Company.

Preuss, H. 2017. 'Olympic Finance', in J.R. Gold and M.M. Gold (eds), *Olympic Cities: City Agendas, Planning, and the World's Games, 1896–2020*, Planning, History and Environment Series (3rd ed.). London: Routledge, pp. 139–60.

Prouse, C. 2012. 'Framing the World CUPP: Competing Discourses of Favela Pacification as a Mega-Event Legacy in Brazil', *Recreation and Society in Africa, Asia and Latin America* 3(2): 1–17.

Queiroz Ribeiro, L.C., and O.A. dos Santos Junior. 2017. 'Neoliberalization and Mega-Events: The Transition of Rio de Janeiro's Hybrid Urban Order', *Journal of Urban Affairs* 39(7): 909–23.

Raban, J. 1974. *Soft City*. London: Hamish Hamilton.

Raco, M. 2003. 'Remaking Place and Securitising Space: Urban Regeneration and the Strategies, Tactics and Practices of Policing in the UK', *Urban Studies* 40(9): 1869–87.

Raffestin, C. 2012. 'Space, Territory, and Territoriality', *Environment and Planning D: Society and Space* 30(1): 121–41.

Reeves, M. 2011. 'Fixing the Border: On the Affective Life of the State in Southern Kyrgyzstan', *Environment and Planning D: Society and Space* 29(5): 905–23.

Reith, G. 2005. 'On the Edge: Drugs and the Consumption of Risk in Late Modernity', in S. Lyng (ed.), *Edgework: The Sociology of Risk-Taking*. London: Routledge, pp. 227–45.

Riccio, V., and W.G. Skogan (eds). 2018. *Police and Society in Brazil*. Abingdon: Routledge.

Richmond, M.A. 2015. *Favela, Network and Identity in a Complex City: A Comparative Neighbourhood Study in Rio de Janeiro*. PhD Thesis. London: King's College. Retrieved 10 November 2016 from https://kclpure.kcl.ac.uk/portal/en/studentTheses/favela-network-and-identity-in-a-complex-city.

Richmond, M.A. 2019. '"Hostages to Both Sides": Favela Pacification as Dual Security Assemblage', *Geoforum* 104: 71–80.

Rio 2016. 2009. *Candidate File for Rio de Janeiro to Host the 2016 Olympic and Paralympic Games* (No. 1). Rio de Janeiro: Rio 2016.

Rodrigues, A. et al. (eds). 2012. *Unidades de Policia Pacificadora: Debates e Reflexoes*, Comunicacao Do ISER (Vol. 31). Rio de Janeiro: FAPERJ.

Rolim, M.F. 2007. 'A Segurança como um Desafio Moderno aos Direitos Humanos', *Análise e Propostas* 34(6): 1–20.

Roth-Gordon, J. 2017. *Race and the Brazilian Body*. Oakland, CA: University of California Press. URL (consulted May 2020): www.ucpress.edu/book.php?isbn=9780520293809.

Ruge, E. 2019. 'Rio Mourns Death of 8-Year-Old Ágatha, Protests State's Bloody Security Policy. RioOnWatch'. Retrieved 25 September 2019 from www.rioonwatch.org/?p=55830.

Ruge, E. 2020. 'As Rio Becomes Covid-19 Epicenter, Police Violence Soars to New High. RioOnWatch'. Retrieved 28 May 2020 from www.rioonwatch.org/?p=59799.

de Sa e Silva, F. 2020. 'From Car Wash to Bolsonaro: Law and Lawyers in Brazil's Illiberal Turn (2014–2018)', *Journal of Law and Society* 47(S1): 90–110.

Saad-Filho, A., and M. Boffo. 2021. 'The Corruption of Democracy: Corruption Scandals, Class Alliances, And Political Authoritarianism in Brazil', *Geoforum* 127(August): 300–9.

Saborio, S. 2014. 'The New Military Urbanism Police Repression and Conflict in Rio de Janeiro', *Etnografia e Ricerca Qualitativa* 3(2014): 401–22.

Sack, R.D. 1986. *Human Territoriality: Its Theory and History*, Cambridge Studies in Historical Geography. Cambridge: Cambridge University Press.

Sage, D. et al. 2015. 'Securing and Scaling Resilient Futures: Neoliberalization, Infrastructure, and Topologies of Power', *Environment and Planning D: Society and Space* 33(3): 494–511.

Salem, T., and E.R. Larkins. 2021. 'Violent Masculinities', *American Ethnologist* 48(1): 65–79.

Salla, F. 2003. 'Os Impasses da Democracia Brasileira: O Balanço de uma Década de Políticas para as Prisoes no Brasil', in C. Goirand (ed), *Lusotopie: Violences et Contrôle de La Violence Au Brésil, En Afrique et à Goa*. Bourdeaux: Éditions Karthala, pp. 419–35.

Salzman, P.C. 2002. 'On Reflexivity', *American Anthropologist* 104(3): 805–13.

Samatas, M. 2007. 'Security and Surveillance in the Athens 2004 Olympics: Some Lessons from a Troubled Story', *International Criminal Justice Review* 17(3): 220–38.

Samatas, M. 2011a. 'Surveillance in Athens 2004 and Beijing 2008: A Comparison of the Olympic Surveillance Modalities and Legacies in Two Different Olympic Host Regimes', *Urban Studies* 48(15): 3347–66.

Samatas, M. 2011b. 'Surveilling the 2004 Athens Olympics in the Aftermath of 9/11: International Pressure and Domestic Implications', in C.J. Bennett and K.D. Haggarty (eds), *Security Games: Surveillance and Control at Mega-Events*. New York: Routledge, pp. 55–71.

Samatas, M. 2014. *The 'Super-Panopticon' Scandal of the Athens 2004 Olympics and Its Legacy*. New York: Pella.

Savell, S. 2016. 'Performing Humanitarian Militarism: Public Security and the Military in Brazil', *Focaal* 75(2016): 59–72.

Scheper-Hughes, N. 1993. *Death without Weeping: The Violence of Everyday Life in Brazil* (1st paperback print). Berkeley, CA: University of California Press.

Scheper-Hughes, N. 2006. 'Death Squads and Democracy in Northeast Brazil', in J. Comaroff and J.L. Comaroff (eds), *Law and Disorder in the Postcolony*. Chicago, IL: The University of Chicago Press, pp. 150–87.

Schuilenburg, M. 2015. *The Securitization of Society: Crime, Risk, and Social Order*, Alternative Criminology Series. New York: New York University Press.

Schwarcz, L.M., and H.M. Starling. 2015. *Brasil: Uma Biografia*. São Paulo: Companhia das Letras.

SENASP. 2010. *GTCOPA Brasil: Relatório*. Brasília: Ministério da Justica/Secretaria Nacional de Seguranca Pública.

SESGE. 2012. *Planejamento Estratégico de Segurança para a Copa do Mundo FIFA Brasil 2014*. Brasília: Ministério da Justica/Secretaria Extraordinária de Seguranca para Grandes Eventos.

Shearing, C.D. 1986. 'Policing South Africa: Reflections on Botha's Reforms', *Canadian Journal of Sociology* 11(3, Summer): 293–307.

Silva Filho, J.V. da. 2006. 'A Lição da Crise Paulista da Segurança', *Cadernos Adenauer: Brasil: O Que Resta Fazer?* 2(3): 119–37.

Silvestre, G., and N.G. de Oliveira. 2012. 'The Revanchist Logic of Mega-Events: Community Displacement in Rio de Janeiro's West End', *Visual Studies* 27(2): 204–10.

Sloterdijk, P. 2001. *Globen* (2nd ed.). Frankfurt am Main: Suhrkamp.

Sloterdijk, P. 2003. *Blasen* (1st ed.). Frankfurt am Main: Suhrkamp.

Sloterdijk, P. 2004. *Schäume* (1st ed.). Frankfurt am Main: Suhrkamp.

Smith, C.W. 2005. 'Financial Edgework: Trading in Market Currents', in S. Lyng (ed), *Edgework: The Sociology of Risk-Taking*. London; New York, NY: Routledge, pp. 187–200.

Soares, L.E. 2000. *Meu Casaco de General: Quinhentos Dias no Front da Segurança Pública do Rio de Janeiro*. Rio de Janeiro: Companhia das Letras.

Soares, L.E., and J.T. Sento Sé. 2000. 'Estado e Segurança Pública no Rio de Janeiro: Dilemas de um Aprendizado Difícil', in L. Musumeci (ed), *Segurança pública no Rio de Janeiro: Políticas, instituições e inovações*. Rio de Janeiro: Instituto de Economia Rio, pp. 1–32.

Söderström, O. et al. 2014. 'Smart Cities as Corporate Storytelling', *City* 18(3): 307–20.

Souza, L.A.F. de, and T. Battibugli. 2014. 'O Difícil Caminho Da Reforma: A Polícia e Os Limites Do Processo de Reforma Pós-Redemocratização', *Dilemas: Revista de Estudos de Conflito e Controle Social* 7(2): 293–319.

Spaaij, R. 2016. 'Terrorism and Security at the Olympics: Empirical Trends and Evolving Research Agendas', *The International Journal of the History of Sport* 33(4): 451–68.

Stavrianakis, A., and J. Selby. 2013. 'Militarism and International Relations in the Twenty-First Century', in A. Stavrianakis and J. Selby (eds), *Militarism and International Relations: Political Economy, Security, Theory*. London: Routledge, pp. 3–18.

Steinbrink, M. 2014. 'Festifavelisation: Mega-Events, Slums and Strategic City-Staging—The Example of Rio de Janeiro', *DIE ERDE—Journal of the Geographical Society of Berlin* 144(2): 129–45.

Steinbrink, M. et al. 2011. 'Festivalisation and Urban Renewal in the Global South: Socio-Spatial Consequences of the 2010 FIFA World Cup', *South African Geographical Journal* 93(1): 15–28.

Stuart, F. 2014. 'From "Rabble Management" to "Recovery Management": Policing Homelessness in Marginal Urban Space', *Urban Studies* 51(9): 1909–25.

Taylor, T., and K. Toohey. 2011. 'Ensuring Safety at Australian Sport Event Precincts: Creating Securitised, Sanitised and Stifling Spaces?', *Urban Studies* 48(15): 3259–75.

Teixeira Pinheiro, C. 2015. 'O "Policial Social": Algumas Observações sobre o Engajamento de Policiais Militares em Projetos Sociais no Contexto de Favelas Ocupadas por UPPs', *Dilemas: Revista de Estudos de Conflito e Controle Social* 8(1): 77–96.

Terre des Hommes. 2016. *Breaking Records: Child Rights Violations during the Rio 2016 Olympics*. Cologne: Terre des Hommes.

The World Bank. 2012. *Bringing the State Back into the Favelas of Rio de Janeiro: Understanding Changes in Community Life after the UPP Pacification Process*. Washington, DC: The World Bank Sustainable Development Sector Management Unit Latin American and the Caribbean Region.

Tomlinson, A. 2014. *FIFA: The Men, the Myths and the Money*. London: Routledge.

Toohey, K., and T. Taylor. 2012. 'Surveillance and Securitization: A Forgotten Sydney Olympic Legacy', *International Review for the Sociology of Sport* 47(3): 324–37.

Traverso, E. 2019. *The New Faces of Fascism: Populism and the Far Right* (Translation). London: Verso.

Van Maanen, J. 2011. *Tales of the Field: On Writing Ethnography*, Chicago Guides to Writing, Editing, and Publishing (2nd ed.). Chicago, IL: University of Chicago Press.

Vargas, J.H.C. 2012. 'Gendered Antiblackness and the Impossible Brazilian Project: Emerging Critical Black Brazilian Studies', *Cultural Dynamics* 24(1): 3–11.

Vargas, J.H.C. 2016. 'Black Disidentification: The 2013 Protests, Rolezinhos, and Racial Antagonism in Post-Lula Brazil', *Critical Sociology* 42(4–5): 551–65.

Viana, N. 2021. *Dano Colateral: A Intervenção Dos Militares Na Segurança Pública*. Rio de Janeiro: Editora Objetiva.

Wacquant, L. 2008. 'The Militarization of Urban Marginality: Lessons from the Brazilian Metropolis', *International Political Sociology* 2(1): 56–74.

Wacquant, L.J.D. 2009. *Punishing the Poor: The Neoliberal Government of Social Insecurity*, Politics, History, and Culture. Durham, NC: Duke University Press.

Waever, O. 1996. 'European Security Identities', *Journal of Common Market Studies* 34(1): 103–32.

Wahlström, M. 2010. 'Producing Spaces for Representation: Racist Marches, Counterdemonstrations, and Public-Order Policing', *Environment and Planning D: Society and Space* 28(5): 811–27.

Waiselfisz, J.J. 2014. 'Mapa Da Violência 2014: Homicídios e Juventude No Brasil'. Retrieved 20 May 2016 from https://biblioteca.flacso.org.br/files/2020/03/Mapa2014_JovensBrasil.pdf.

Ward, S.V. 2007. 'Promoting the Olympic City', in J.R. Gold and M.M. Gold (eds), *Olympic Cities: City Agendas, Planning, and the World's Games, 1869–2012*. New York, NY: Routledge, pp. 120–37.

Weber, M. 1949. *The Methodology of the Social Science*. New York: Free Press.

Weber, M. 1978. *Economy and Society*. Berkeley, CA: University of California Press.

Welsh, M. 2014. 'Resilience and Responsibility: Governing Uncertainty in a Complex World', *The Geographical Journal* 180(1): 15–26.

Willis, K.S., and A. Aurigi. 2019. *Digital and Smart Cities*. London: Routledge.

Wolfe, S.D. 2016. 'A Silver Medal Project: The Partial Success of Russia's Soft Power in Sochi 2014', *Annals of Leisure Research* 19(4): 481–96.

Wolfe, S.D. 2022. 'Potemkin Neoliberalism: Developing Volgograd through the 2018 Men's World Cup in Russia', *Sport in Society* 25(10): 2088–106.

World Cup and Olympics Popular Committee of Rio de Janeiro. 2015. *Rio 2016 Olympics: The Exclusion Games. Mega-Events and Human Rights Violations in Rio de Janeiro*. Rio de Janeiro: World Cup and Olympics Popular Committee of Rio de Janeiro.

World Cup and Olympics Popular Committee of Rio de Janeiro. 2016, 1 August. 'Rio de Janeiro of the Exclusion Games', *RIO2016 JOGOS DA EXCLUSÃO*. Retrieved 22 January 2017 from https://medium.com/@jogosdaexclusao/rio-de-janeiro-of-the-exclusion-games-628243a52770.

Yarwood, R. 2007. 'The Geographies of Policing', *Progress in Human Geography* 31(4): 447–65.

Young, J. 2011. *The Criminological Imagination*. Cambridge: Polity Press.

Ystanes, M., and T. Salem. 2020. 'Introduction: Exceptionalism and Necropolitical Security Dynamics in Olympic Rio de Janeiro', *Conflict and Society: Advances in Research* 6(1): 52–67.

Yu, Y. et al. 2009. 'Governing Security at the 2008 Beijing Olympics', *The International Journal of the History of Sport* 26(3): 390–405.

Zaluar, A. 1985. *A Máquina e a Revolta: As Organizações Populares e o Significado da Pobreza*. São Paulo: Editora Brasiliense.

Zaluar, A. 1996. *Condomínio do Diabo*. Rio de Janeiro: UERJ.

Zaluar, A. 2004. *Integração Perversa: Pobreza e Tráfico de Drogas*. Rio de Janeiro: Editora FGV.

Zaluar, A. 2007. 'Unfinished Democratization: The Failure of Public Safety', *Estudos Avançados* 21(61): 31–49.

Zaverucha, J. 2000. 'Fragile Democracy and the Militarization of Public Safety in Brazil', *Latin American Perspectives* 27(3): 8–31.

Zaverucha, J. 2010a. 'Relacoes Civil-Militares: O Legado Autoritário da Constituição Brasileira de 1988', in E. Teles and V. Safatle (eds), *O Que Resta da Ditadura: A Exceção Brasileira*. São Paulo: Boitempo, pp. 41–76.

Zaverucha, J. 2010b. 'A Doutrina da Garantia da Lei e da Ordem e o Crescente Envolvimento das Forcas Armadas em Atividaes de Segurança Pública', in R. Kant de Lima et al. (eds), *Conflitos, Direitos e Moralidades em Perspectiva Comparada. Volume II*. Rio de Janeiro: Editora Garamond Ltda., pp. 11–49.

Index

For the benefit of digital users, indexed terms that span two pages (e.g., 52–53) may, on occasion, appear on only one of those pages.

Tables are indicated by *t* following the page number